ArtScroll Judaica Classics®

Inspiration

Translated and arranged by
Rabbi Shimon Finkelman

from the Hebrew "Yirah VeDa'as"
which was compiled by
Rabbi Yosef Weiss

יראה ודעת

and Insight

DISCOURSES ON THE WEEKLY PARASHAH
BY THE MANCHESTER ROSH YESHIVAH,
RABBI YEHUDAH ZEV SEGAL, SHLITA

Published by
Mesorah Publications, ltd

FIRST EDITION
First Impression . . . June 1990
Second Impression . . . January 2002

Distributed in Europe by
LEHMANNS
Unit E, Viking Industrial Park
Rolling Mill Road
Jarrow, Tyne & Wear NE32 3DP
England

Distributed in Australia & New Zealand by
GOLDS WORLD OF JUDAICA
3-13 William Street
Balaclava, Melbourne 3183
Victoria Australia

Distributed in Israel by
SIFRIATI / A. GITLER — BOOKS
6 Hayarkon Street
Bnei Brak 51127

Distributed in South Africa by
KOLLEL BOOKSHOP
Shop 8A Norwood Hypermarket
Norwood 2196, Johannesburg, South Africa

ARTSCROLL JUDAICA CLASSICS ®
Inspiration and Insight
© Copyright 1990, by MESORAH PUBLICATIONS, Ltd.
4401 Second Avenue / Brooklyn, N.Y. 11232 / (718) 921-9000 / www.artscroll.com

---

ISBN:
0-89906-946-0 (hard cover)
0-89906-947-9 (paperback)

Typography by CompuScribe at ArtScroll Studios, Ltd.
4401 Second Avenue / Brooklyn, N.Y. 11232 / (718) 921-9000

Printed in the United States of America by Noble Book Press Corp.
Bound by Sefercraft Inc., Quality Bookbinders, Brooklyn, N.Y.

We dedicate this *sefer*
in grateful appreciation to the Rosh Yeshiva

הרב יהודה זאב סג"ל שליט"א

Who has been for us a source of Torah, wisdom,
counsel, inspiration and solace.
He has enriched our lives beyond words.

In memory of
our beloved daughter

לעילוי נשמת הילדה

זיסל דינה ע"ה

בת ר' משה שלום הי"ו
נפטרה ו' חשון תשל"ה

תנצב"ה

Moshe Sholom and Gittle Devorah Grussgott

Rabbi J. W. SEGAL

40 BROOM LANE, SALFORD, M7 0FJ

Telephone: 061-792 2543

Principal
Manchester Talmudical College

"Saul Rosenberg House", Seymour Road
Manchester, M8 6BQ.   Telephone: 061-740 0214

יהודא זאב סג"ל

ראש הישיבה, מנשסתר

[handwritten text]

ב"ה יום כח אדר תשמ"ח

לתלמידי היקר והחביב ר' יוסף יונה וייס שליט"א

ע"ד שאמרת לי שאנשים חשובים אמרו שיהי' לתועלת רב אם יתורגם
הספר "יראה ודעת" לשפת אנגלית ובקשת הסכמתי, הנני מסכים לזה וד'
יתן חלקנו בין מצדיקי הרבים.

יהודא זאב סגל

✑§Table of Contents

~§ Publishers' Preface

Few people in our generation can be called living legends. One such person is Rabbi Yehudah Zev Segal, the venerable *Rosh Yeshivah* of the Manchester Yeshivah. Especially during this past decade, Rabbi Segal's influence as a Torah sage has spread far beyond the borders of his native England, to Jewish communities all across the world.

The Hebrew *Yirah VeDa'as*, a two-volume collection of Rabbi Segal's discourses, has already been acclaimed a classic. This English volume, translated and arranged according to the weekly *parashah* by Rabbi Shimon Finkelman, is a worthy companion work.

An eminent Torah scholar and revered *tzaddik*, Rabbi Segal has been a primary force in the world-awakening toward study of the Chofetz Chaim's classic code on the laws of *shemiras halashon* (forbidden speech). On a personal level, his counsel, blessings and prayers are avidly sought wherever he goes. His warmth, concern, and genuine love for every Jew imbue his petitioners wih a feeling that mere words cannot convey.

It is against this backdrop that Rabbi Segal's *shmuessen* (ethical discourses) have had so great an impact on listeners everywhere. His words are down-to-earth, powerful and uplifting; his topics are wide ranging and practical. Among them are faith, love of one's fellow Jew, honesty in business, and the Torah's definition of kindness. He weaves together fundamental concepts from classic Talmudic and Rabbinic literature, his own illuminating insights into the words of our Sages, and illustrative anecdotes. The total is a priceless word portrait of the Jewish ethical world.

Credit for this volume goes to Rabbi Yosef Weiss, a student and disciple of the *Rosh Yeshivah*, who compiled the Hebrew edition and coordinated this English rendition. Rabbi Weiss is a rebbi at Mesivta Keser Torah of Central Jersey and a member of the Kollel Beth Medrash Govoha of Lakewood, N.J.

We are confident that this volume will be a powerful force toward the eternal goals to which Rabbi Segal has devoted his life.

᷇ Foreword

by Rabbi Yosef Weiss

With deep gratitude to *Hashem Yisbarach*, we present to the English-speaking Torah public a selection of *shmuessen* (discourses) of the *gaon* and *tzaddik*, HARAV YEHUDAH ZEV HALEVI SEGAL, שליט״א, *Rosh Yeshivah* of the Yeshivah of Manchester, England. The material is drawn from סֵפֶר יִרְאָה וְדַעַת* — the two-volume Hebrew collection of *shmuessen* delivered by the *Rosh Yeshivah*.

I thank Hashem for having granted me the *zechus* of drinking from the wellsprings of the *Rosh Yeshivah's* wisdom and awesome *yiras shamayim* during my years as a *talmid* at the Manchester Yeshivah. During that time, I was privileged to hear his addresses, delivered with the fire and fervor that flames within him, and with the *ahavas Yisrael* that his words reflect. Indeed, the *Rosh Yeshivah* embodies the sublime levels of *midos* and service of Hashem that his *shmuessen* describe.

The *Rosh Yeshivah* was born in Manchester, where his revered father headed the Yeshivah after having studied in Novaradok under Rabbi Yosef Yoizel Horowitz, זצ״ל. The *Rosh Yeshivah* studied in the famed Mirrer Yeshivah, after which he married in Gateshead,

---

* The *sefer's* title is based on the words of *Mishlei* (2:4-5): אִם תְּבַקְשֶׁנָּה כַכָּסֶף, וְכַמַּטְמוֹנִים תְּחַפְּשֶׂנָּה — אָז תָּבִין יִרְאַת ה׳, וְדַעַת אֱלֹקִים תִּמְצָא, "If you seek it out as you seek silver and search for it as you search for buried treasures — then will you comprehend the fear of Hashem and knowledge of God will you find." Additionally, it is traditional that a *sefer's* title contain an allusion to the author's name; יראה ודעת is the numerical equivalent (*gematria*) of the *Rosh Yeshivah's* full Hebrew name: יהודה זאב בן משה יצחק הלוי.

England, where he was one of the first members of the Kollel that has become one of Europe's primary Torah centers. Later, HaRav Segal succeeded his father as *Rosh Yeshivah* of Manchester.

Not only his knowledge and lectures, but his majestic personal conduct make him an inspirational teacher and example. His every moment is precious; memories of his intensity in Torah study, of the inspirational quality of his *tefillah*, of his reviewing his studies as he walks in the street are indelibly engraved in the hearts of students and onlookers. Whatever he does — Torah study, *tefillah*, or interpersonal relationships — is done with all his heart and mind.

The *Rosh Yeshivah's mussar* discourses are practical, above all, and are intended primarily as vehicles for self-improvement. Those who read and study this volume will see clearly that the *Rosh Yeshivah* speaks from the heart and he speaks to **us**.

It should be pointed out that when the *Rosh Yeshivah* was consulted regarding the idea of producing an English work, he made clear that the *shmuessen* need not be translated literally; rather, they should be adapted in a manner that would be of optimum benefit to the English-reading public. In the Hebrew volumes, where the discourses are arranged by topic only, discourses are virtually unchanged from the *Rosh Yeshivah's* original Yiddish presentation. In the present volume, however, which is arranged according to the weekly *parashah*, it was often necessary to rearrange the order of the subject matter. Also, in many instances, concepts have been expanded upon for the sake of clarity, though without altering the *Rosh Yeshivah's* message. Unless otherwise indicated, the footnotes contain supplementary material added by the translator and are not found in the original Hebrew.

I would like to express my heartfelt thanks to my dear *chaver*, RABBI SHIMON FINKELMAN, for his fine English rendition of the *Rosh Yeshivah's* thoughts. While effecting numerous changes in language and style, Rabbi Finkelman was careful to insure that his presentation remained accurate and faithful to the *Rosh Yeshivah's* intent. May *HaKadosh Baruch Hu* bless him and his family with כל טוב, and may he continue to be מרביץ תורה for many years to come.

My appreciation to RABBI NOSSON SCHERMAN and RABBI MEIR ZLOTOWITZ, as well as the entire staff of ArtScroll/Mesorah Publications, for their superb production of this volume. A particular note of thanks is due ZVI SHAPIRO for his excellent editorial work.

RABBI AVIE GOLD read and made valuable comments. The graphics artistry of REB SHEAH BRANDER is evident throughout.

R' MOSHE SHOLOM GRUSSGOTT and R' DOVID ZVI NEUMANN, of Vienna, have been instrumental in making the publication of this work possible. In addition, they always concern themselves with the *Rosh Yeshivah's* well-being and strive to insure that he can carry on his great service of Hashem and His people amid tranquility. May they be rewarded from Above for all their efforts לשם שמים.

In both the Hebrew and English editions of this work, I benefited from the guidance of HARAV YISROEL ZVI BRODY, שליט"א, *Rav* of Beis Medrash Shaarei Orah in Brooklyn and formerly *Dayan* in Manchester. May he continue to guide me and others בדרך ה' for many years to come.

❧ ❧ ❧

I take this opportunity to thank those who have had a profound influence on my personal growth and development. My parents, MR. AND MRS. ELIEZER WEISS, survived the flames of the Holocaust to dedicate themselves with heart and soul to raising children who would carry on the *mesorah* of their respective families. They spared no effort in my *chinuch* and that of my older brother, REB SHLOMO, who has also guided me along the דרך התורה והיראה.

My in-laws, RABBI AND MRS. CHAIM YAAKOV DAVIS of London, have made their home a true meeting place of *chachamim*. They also epitomize the attribute of *chesed*, as they forever give of themselves for the sake of the community and individuals alike. May they all be granted long life and good health and enjoy much *nachas* from their entire families.

My wife TOVA, תחי', through her goodness of heart and love of Torah, has been a constant source of support to me. May *Hashem Yisbarach* repay her with long life and good health, and may we together merit to raise our children to תורה, חופה, ומעשים טובים.

❧ ❧ ❧

It is impossible for me to thank adequately the many *rabbeim* who have taught me Torah over the years and inspired me to strive for achievement in Torah and *yiras shamayim*. I would, however, like to mention the following *talmidei chachamim*, שליט"א, who head the *yeshivos* in which I have studied since my *mesivta* days began: HARAV YERUCHOM SHAIN, *Rosh Yeshivah* of the Adelphia Yeshivah, and the *Menahel*, HARAV DOVID TRENK; HARAV SIMCHA SCHUSTAL and HARAV MEIR HERSHKOWITZ, *Roshei Yeshivah* of Yeshivah Bais Binyomin, and the *Menahel*, HARAV DOVID HERSH MEYER; the revered *Mashgiach* of Beth Medrash Govoha, HARAV NOSSON WACHTFOGEL; and the *Roshei Yeshivah:* HARAV ARYEH MALKIEL KOTLER, HARAV YERUCHOM OLSHIN, HARAV DOVID SCHUSTAL and HARAV YISRAEL NEUMAN. May they all merit to see their *talmidim* follow in their ways.

I close with an expression of gratitude to the *Rosh Yeshivah*, for having drawn me close to him and given of himself for my benefit since the day that I entered the Manchester Yeshivah.

In the name of the *Rosh Yeshivah's* family, *talmidim*, and the many others who have been inspired by him, I pray that he be granted many more years in good health to spread Torah and *yiras shamayim*. May the *Rosh Yeshivah* lead us all to greet *Mashiach*, speedily and in our days.

Inspiration and Insight

בראשית
Bereishis

Lessons of Kayin

וַיְהִי הֶבֶל רֹעֵה צֹאן, וְקַיִן הָיָה עֹבֵד אֲדָמָה. וַיְהִי מִקֵּץ יָמִים, וַיָּבֵא
קַיִן מִפְּרִי הָאֲדָמָה מִנְחָה לַה'. וְהֶבֶל הֵבִיא גַם הוּא מִבְּכֹרוֹת צֹאנוֹ
וּמֵחֶלְבֵהֶן, וַיִּשַׁע ה' אֶל הֶבֶל וְאֶל מִנְחָתוֹ. וְאֶל קַיִן וְאֶל מִנְחָתוֹ לֹא
שָׁעָה. וַיִּחַר לְקַיִן מְאֹד וַיִּפְּלוּ פָּנָיו.

*Hevel became a shepherd and Kayin became a tiller of
the ground. After a period of time, Kayin brought an
offering to Hashem of the fruit of the ground; and
Hevel, too, brought [an offering] from the firstlings of
his flock and from their choicest. Hashem turned to
Hevel and to his offering, but to Kayin and to his
offering He did not turn. Kayin was exceedingly angry
and his countenance fell (4:2-5).*

✥ The Source of Sin

Kayin's vexation over Hashem's rejection of his offering is readily
understandable. True, he did, as *Chazal* explain, offer fruits of
inferior quality, as opposed to Hevel's "firstlings of his flock and
from their choicest." Still, it was Kayin who had been the first to offer
a *korban* to Hashem. He had originated the concept that man present
a portion of his blessings to the Source whence they flowed. He had
watched as his efforts were ignored while those of his brother, who
had taken a cue from him, were smiled upon. Kayin was distressed by
all this; in the words of *Sforno*, "[He was] jealous of his brother

[whose offering] was accepted." Would we have reacted differently? We must understand that Kayin's spiritual level was awesome. He was the son of Adam and he himself spoke directly to Hashem. In this respect, Kayin was akin to a *navi* (prophet)! Given this understanding, his reaction is, in fact, difficult to fathom. It is not surprising when people like ourselves exhibit jealousy and resentment when faced with situations similar to Kayin's. We do not, however, expect such reactions from the spiritual giants among us. How could the great Kayin harbor jealousy toward his brother?

Chovos HaLevavos (*Sha'ar Yichud HaMa'aseh* 5) writes:

> *Know that your greatest enemy in this world is your evil inclination, which resides within your soul and is blended within your spirit ... While you slumber and are off guard, it remains alert, scheming to cause you harm. You become oblivious to it, but it does not become oblivious to you ...*
>
> *It is told that a chasid (exceptionally pious person) once chanced upon a contingent of soldiers returning triumphantly from fierce battle with their booty in tow. Said the chasid, "You have returned with booty from the small war; now prepare yourselves for the great war!"*
>
> *"And what is the great war?" queried the soldiers.*
>
> *"The war against the yetzer hara (evil inclination) and his legions," responded the chasid. "... For [in any other battle], the enemy will cease to attack you after he has been defeated once or twice. He will have become convinced that your might is superior to his own and he will despair of ever gaining victory over you.*
>
> *"The yetzer hara, however, is different. Whether he has been the victor or the loser a hundred times, he will never cease to do battle ..."*

The only way to escape the incitements of one's *yetzer hara* is to do battle against it. One must be a spiritual warrior, ready to fend off every advancement of his evil inclination. A determined effort on one's part will earn him the Heavenly assistance needed to prevail. This is expressed, homiletically, in the Torah itself. "When you will go to war against your enemy, and Hashem your God will deliver him into your hand . . ." (*Devarim* 21:10). When one actively works at overcoming his negative desires and traits, then he is assured of the *siyata dishmaya*, Heavenly assistance, necessary to succeed.

However, when one fails to do battle, then his *yetzer hara* will get the better of him, even if he is as great a soul as Kayin.

Failure, though, should not be cause for despair. This, too, we can learn from Kayin.

⸙ The Cure

וַיֹּאמֶר ה' אֶל קַיִן, לָמָּה חָרָה לָךְ וְלָמָּה נָפְלוּ פָנֶיךָ? הֲלוֹא אִם תֵּיטִיב שְׂאֵת וְאִם לֹא תֵיטִיב לַפֶּתַח חַטָּאת רֹבֵץ, וְאֵלֶיךָ תְּשׁוּקָתוֹ וְאַתָּה תִּמְשָׁל בּוֹ.

And Hashem said to Kayin, "Why are you angry, and why has your countenance fallen? Surely, if you improve yourself, you will be forgiven, but if you do not improve yourself, sin rests at the door. Its desire is toward you, yet you can conquer it" (4:6-7).

Hashem's question regarding Kayin's fallen countenance requires explanation. Was not the rejection of his offering sufficient reason for Kayin to feel dejected?

Sforno explains, "[Why has your countenance fallen?] When a fault can be remedied, it is not proper to grieve over what has passed, but rather to try to amend and improve (matters) for the future."

One who strives to overcome his *yetzer hara* does so because he desires to fulfill the will of Hashem. He possesses *yiras shamayim*, awe of Heaven. If he does not seem to be succeeding in his struggle, he should in no way despair. Eventually, with Hashem's help, he will succeed. He must, however, be certain that his battle plan is the correct one.

Man's primary spiritual struggle is to refine his *midos ra'os*, his negative character traits. One must ponder how things could be if his *midos* were as they truly should be. Think of the difference this would make in one's dealings with others! In one's honoring of his father and mother! In truth, it is difficult to fathom the degree of honor and respect which the *mitzvah* of *kibud av va'eim* demands; even greater are the obligations of a *talmid* to his *rebbi*, who by teaching his students Torah gains them entrance into the World to Come. Refined *midos* are a prerequisite for fulfillment of these and other prime obligations.

There is only one method by which one can rid himself of *midos ra'os:* the study of *mussar* (works on Torah ethics).

Someone who is physically ill does not dare allow his illness to run its natural course; rather, he seeks out a physician who can provide the necessary cure for his malady. *Midos ra'os* are spiritual maladies; one who is concerned for the health of his soul *must* seek the necessary cure, which is the study of *mussar.*

◆§ R' Akiva's Observation

There are times when one studies *mussar* seriously and regularly, yet feels that he is none the better for it. Similarly, there are *bnei Torah* who take their Torah study seriously and work diligently to succeed, yet come away feeling little or no spiritual uplift from their studies. In a letter,[1] R' Yisrael Salanter addresses such situations:

> One should not be discouraged when he studies mussar and is apparently unaffected, when his soul apparently remains unimpressed toward change. Know well that if one's physical eyes cannot perceive any change, his spiritual eyes can; with the passage of time, as his studies increase, the imperceptible impressions will join together and he will become transformed into a different person. Certain passions will become harnessed while others will disappear entirely. Experience can easily bear witness that the student of mussar . . . is superior to his peers both in his thinking and conduct.

To illustrate this point, R' Yisrael cites the well-known story of R' Akiva (*Avos D'R' Nosson 6*):

> What was R' Akiva's beginning? By age forty, he had still not studied Torah. Then one day, as he stood by the mouth of a well, he asked, "Who hollowed out this

---

1. *Ohr Yisrael*, §10; see *Sefer HaMichtavim* (Bnei Brak 1978).

stone?" They told him, "The water which falls steadily upon the stone day after day."

R' Akiva immediately reflected, "If water can hollow out solid rock, then surely the Torah, whose words are as strong as iron, can make an impression on my heart of flesh and blood!" He set out at once to study Torah.

R' Yisrael takes the approach that R' Akiva *had* studied Torah in his younger years and that his innate intellectual capabilities were more than adequate for him to succeed.[2] However, he had failed to perceive the spiritual uplift that Torah study should bring with it. He grew despondent, telling himself, "It is impossible for me to change."

R' Akiva's desire for Torah had not waned, and Hashem therefore presented him with an opportunity to realize the truth. He chanced upon the stone and was informed that its appearance was the product of dripping water. R' Akiva then observed: When water drips upon a stone drop after drop, one cannot perceive that the stone is undergoing any change. It seems that the water is accomplishing nothing, but in fact, this is not so. Each drop *does* in some way affect the stone, in a manner that the human eye cannot perceive. Only after the impression in the stone becomes apparent does one recognize the accomplishment of every drop. R' Akiva applied this observation to himself. The Torah study of his first forty years seemed to have done nothing to uplift his soul — but, in fact, this could not be. The power of Torah *had* to have affected his heart of flesh and blood in some imperceptible way — and was sure to uplift his soul ever higher, if only he would give it the chance.

Every word of *Gemara* that is studied diligently, every word of *mussar* that one examines with a sincere desire for self-improvement, must bring accomplishment. Spiritual achievement is within everyone's reach. Torah itself is *Kodesh Kadashim*, the holiest of holies. One who approaches his Talmudic or *mussar* studies with a sense of responsibility has no reason for despair.

---

2. *Binyan Yehoshua* to *Avos D'Rav Nosson* interprets *"By age forty, he had still not studied Torah"* as referring to the study of *Mishnah* and *Gemara*, but he had already studied Scripture. Support for this opinion is found in the phraseology of the passage.

◆§ Happenings and Reflections

There is another vital lesson to be learned from the story of R'
Akiva. The following is offered by way of introduction:

It is related that a man once observed a pot-cover being lifted from
the pressure of the steam inside the heated pot. Noting the power
which the bottled-up steam produced, the man began to research the
matter. His investigations culminated with the invention of the steam
locomotive.

The man had seen nothing new. Millions of his contemporaries
observed the same scene daily. But only this man thought into this
everyday phenomenon until he arrived at a monumental finding.

So it was in the case of R' Akiva. This stone that he noted had been
there well before he made his observation. Countless others had seen
what he had seen, but how many of them had thought into the
matter enough for it to change their entire lives?! Had R' Akiva not
reflected and applied his observation to his own life, he might have
remained an ignorant shepherd. Instead, he rose to become the leader
of his generation, the man regarding whom Moshe *Rabbeinu* asked
Hashem (*Menachos* 29b), "There will exist such a man and You are
giving the Torah through me?!" He is the R' Akiva about whom the
aged R' Dosa ben Hurkanos exclaimed, "Are you the R' Akiva whose
name is spread from one end of the world to the other? Be seated, my
son, be seated! May there be many like you in Israel!" (*Yevamos* 16a).
Chazal did not employ such praises indiscriminately. R' Akiva stood
out among his peers, the great *Tannaim* of his generation. He was
deserving of such distinction, for it was he who pondered and
reflected upon what others simply passed by.

When one studies a *pasuk* of *Chumash* or a teaching of *Chazal*, he
must stop and ask himself, "What have I just learned? What lesson
can I glean from this?" One must also learn to reflect upon the
happenings around him in order to apply what lessons they have to
offer to his daily life. Finally, one must learn to reflect upon his own
desires and aspirations, to ponder them well and ascertain which stem
from his *yetzer tov*, positive inclination, and which are rooted in the
opposite.

Such is the way to true greatness.

Ascending the Mountain

וַיֹּאמֶר אֱלֹקִים לְנֹחַ, קֵץ כָּל בָּשָׂר בָּא לְפָנַי, כִּי מָלְאָה הָאָרֶץ חָמָס מִפְּנֵיהֶם – לֹא נֶחְתַּם גְּזַר דִּינָם אֶלָּא עַל הַגָּזֵל.

Hashem said to Noach, "The end of all flesh has come before Me, for the earth is filled with robbery . . ." [6:13]. *The decree of punishment was sealed only on account of robbery* (*Rashi from Sanhedrin* 108a).

מִי יַעֲלֶה בְהַר ה', וּמִי יָקוּם בִּמְקוֹם קָדְשׁוֹ. נְקִי כַפַּיִם וּבַר לֵבָב . . .

Who may ascend the mountain of Hashem and who may stand in the place of His sanctity? One with clean hands and pure heart . . . (*Tehillim* 24:3-4).

❧ For Seven Cents

In the early years of the Volozhiner Yeshivah, one of its outstanding students suddenly fell seriously ill. The yeshivah administration decided that it was in the *bachur's* best interests that he be sent home, where his family would care for him and render decisions regarding medical treatments. The yeshivah assigned another student to accompany the *bachur* on his journey.

On the way, the two students spent the night at an inn. In the morning as they prepared to leave, the innkeeper presented them with the bill. They were seven cents short. The innkeeper told the ill *bachur*, who accepted responsibility for the bill, that he fully trusted the *bachur* to pay the balance at some future time. The two students continued on their way.

When they reached their destination, it was time to part. The ill *bachur* gave his friend the seven cents and asked that he pay the debt to the innkeeper on his journey back to Volozhin. The friend wished his ill companion well and promised to fulfill his mission. That was the last time the two friends saw each other, for the ill *bachur* succumbed to his sickness shortly thereafter. A brilliant future in the world of Torah had been predicted for him; news of his death shook the very foundations of the yeshivah.

R' Chaim Volozhiner could often be seen strolling through the halls of his yeshivah after midnight, keeping watch over those students who studied during the late night hours.[1] On one particular night, R' Chaim was walking alone, when suddenly he found himself face to face with the deceased *bachur!* Maintaining his composure, R' Chaim spoke to this soul which had returned from the Upper World, and asked how it had fared before the Heavenly tribunal. The *bachur* replied as follows:

It had been decided that he be granted immediate entrance to *Gan Eden*, as his sins had been expiated by the sufferings of his illness. However, as he approached the gates to *Gan Eden*, Satan stood blocking his way. "This soul is guilty of robbery!" Satan declared. It was then revealed that the *bachur* had left this world still having failed to pay his debt of seven cents to the innkeeper. His companion had forgotten about the payment he was to have made on his way back to Volozhin.

The Heavenly tribunal was in a quandary. The deceased *bachur* had done all that he could have done to pay the debt; he was certainly not to blame for his friend's memory lapse. Still, he had come to the World of Truth owing another person seven cents. How could he be admitted into *Gan Eden* with this blemish on his soul?

It was decided that since the *bachur* was blameless, he would be permitted to return to this world and request of his teacher that he have the matter rectified.

R' Chaim promised to tend to the matter at once. Just as suddenly

---

1. When R' Chaim founded his famed yeshivah, he instituted that Torah be studied within its walls twenty-four hours every day. The world's continued existence was predicated on the Jews' acceptance of the Torah at Mount Sinai; R' Chaim taught that as a corollary of this axiom, were even a moment to pass without Torah being studied somewhere on this earth, the world would cease to exist (*Nefesh HaChaim* 4:25). Thus, at every moment of day and night, *talmidim* of the Volozhiner Yeshivah were ensuring the world's existence, literally.

as he had appeared, the *bachur* disappeared. R' Chaim summoned the other student, who was left trembling by his *rebbi's* words; he readily admitted his guilt. Shortly thereafter, he set out for the inn and paid the debt, bringing eternal rest to the soul of his departed friend.[2]

If such is the judgment against one who *innocently* failed to repay a debt, then one shudders to think of how the Heavenly court views a man who intentionally or even negligently possesses that which is not rightfully his own.

ᵛᶳ Keeping One's Hands Clean

The Chofetz Chaim (*S'fas Tamim* ch. 3) writes:

> *"Who may ascend the mountain of Hashem ... one with clean hands ..." From here we learn that one who has been guilty of gezel (robbery) is distant from Hashem and His sanctity. In fact, our Sages have taught, "Anyone who is in possession of gezel is not permitted to dwell in the province of Hashem's Presence."*

Yesod V'Shoresh Ha'Avodah (11:11) writes that the sin of *gezel* causes one's *tefillos* to be rejected above.

Of course, the term *gezel* encompasses far more than outright robbery. Any unlawful withholding of someone's else's money or possessions falls under the category of *gezel*. Moreover, there are instances where the *halachah* exonerates one from paying for the financial loss he has caused, but he is nevertheless liable to incur Heavenly retribution. *Grama b'nesakin*, indirectly causing damage to another's property or self, is one such example. One who very indirectly causes someone else a loss of profit is guilty of *gezel* and will face judgment for this before the Heavenly court. It is even regarding such indirect forms of robbery that the Talmud states (*Bava Kamma* 119a), "R' Yochanan said: One who robs his friend of

<hr>

2. This story was transmitted by R' Chaim Volozhiner to R' Zundel of Salant, to R' Yisrael Salanter, to the *Alter* of Kelm, to R' Zvi Hirsh Brode to R' Eliyahu Lopian.

even a cent is considered as if he has taken his life." In Heaven, stealing the smallest coin is tantamount to murder![3]

Gezel can assume very subtle forms. The Talmud (*Bava Metzia* 41a) rules that one who borrows without permission is deemed a robber. Unfortunately, there are many who, wittingly or not, are guilty of this form of *gezel*. Certain general monetary laws are commonly known, but the nuances of these laws are not well known. The following is a case in point: A worker has been hired without any agreement on wages. After the job has been completed, the worker approaches his employer and names a sum equal to or above the accepted rate. A discussion ensues, with the employer succeeding in bringing the figure below the accepted rate. The worker's acceptance of this amount might possibly be due to his fear of arousing his employer's ire. The Chofetz Chaim (*S'fas Tamim* Ch. 5) rules that if the worker is in fact dissatisfied with the payment, then the employer is guilty of withholding wages, a form of *gezel*. To avoid such a situation, the Chofetz Chaim advises that wages always be fixed before the employee begins his work.

⋖§ Unique Among Mitzvos

In truth, while the prohibition against *gezel* is one of the seven Noachide laws and its concept is readily understood and accepted by virtually every sort of society, the application of this prohibition in Torah law is unique, as we shall explain.

A basic principle in Talmudic law regarding monetary litigations is הַמּוֹצִיא מֵחֲבֵרוֹ עָלָיו הָרְאָיָה, "the burden of proof lies on the one who seeks to exact something from the other." That is, if one person is in possession of something and another claims that it is his, the latter must bring witnesses or other substantial evidence in order to prove his claim.

In *Masechta Kesubos* (12a; see *Tosafos*), we find the following application of this principle: A man approaches his friend and demands payment for a loan. The friend responds, "I don't know," meaning that he is unsure as to whether he did in fact borrow the

---

3. *Maharal* (*Chiddushei Agados*) explains that this is because people depend on their livelihood for their needs and, ultimately, their survival.

money. The claimant, on the other hand, *is* sure of his claim. According to one opinion, the alleged borrower need not pay; since the other man wishes to exact money, it is for him to prove that his claim is correct.

The *Acharonim* are troubled by this ruling. How can we permit the man in doubt to remain in possession of the contested sum, when if in fact the loan *had* been made he would be guilty of *gezel?*

Kuntreis HaSefeikos (cited in *Sha'arei Yosher* 5:1) resolves this by explaining the uniqueness of the Torah's monetary laws. Other *mitzvos* associated with a specific object are dependent on certain unchangeable facts. A pair of *tefillin*, for example, must conform to specific requirements without which its bearer cannot possibly fulfill the *mitzvah*, regardless of how extenuating the circumstances might be. The commandments governing monetary disputes are different. It is the law *as opposed to the facts* that determine what constitutes *gezel*. In our example, the principle of הַמּוֹצִיא מֵחֲבֵרוֹ עָלָיו הָרְאָיָה determines that the burden of proof *does not* lie on the alleged borrower. As a result, even if in fact that loan had occurred, the man would not be guilty of *gezel* since his claim was sincere and the *halachah* does not require that he pay.

The same holds true of laws governing *hasagas gevul* (encroachment), *sechirus* (hiring), and other money-related areas. If the *halachah* requires one to pay and he does not, then he is a *gazlan* (robber); if the *halachah* rules in his favor, then he is innocent.

It is clear that without a thorough knowledge of *Choshen Mishpat*,[4] it is virtually impossible for a Jew to conduct his business in conformity with the Torah's monetary laws.

A *shochet* cannot be a practicing slaughterer without *kabbalah*, verification that he is skilled and well versed in the pertinent laws. It would be proper if similar verification of expertise in *Choshen Mishpat* would be required of those who enter the business world.[5]

---

4. The section of *Shulchan Aruch* that covers monetary laws.

5. A *shochet* once informed R' Yisrael Salanter that he was giving up his practice, for he found the responsibility of slaughtering properly an unbearable pressure.

"And what will you do instead?" asked R' Yisrael.

"I will open a store," came the reply.

R' Yisrael responded adamantly, "Do you think that entering into business bears no halachic responsibilities? Why, virtually any transaction is governed by laws of stealing, lying, cheating, inaccurate measures and more! These laws are more difficult to observe than the laws of *shechitah*."

◈ Source of Sin

מִי הָאִישׁ הֶחָפֵץ חַיִּים, אֹהֵב יָמִים לִרְאוֹת טוֹב. נְצֹר לְשׁוֹנְךָ מֵרָע,
וּשְׂפָתֶיךָ מִדַּבֵּר מִרְמָה.
Which man desires life, who loves days of seeking
good? Guard your tongue from evil, and your lips from
speaking deceit (Tehillim 34:13-14).

מִרְמָה, deceit, refers to any word that is spoken with the intent of
misleading the listener. Trickery and deceit in money matters are, of
course, prime examples of mirmah. In S'fas Tamim (Ch. 3), the
Chofetz Chaim discusses the causes of such negative behavior:

> The primary causes of this are a general lack of regard
> for the laws prohibiting gezel and sheker (falsehood).
> The natural result is an irresponsibility toward mir-
> mah, which is a combination of gezel and sheker.

Unfortunately, there are those who conduct their business as if
business was outside the parameters of the Shulchan Aruch!
Trickery, denial of a claim, or even outright robbery from a gentile is,
to their minds, permissible. The truth eludes them. Rambam (Hilchos
Gezeilah 1:1) and Shulchan Aruch make perfectly clear that to rob a
gentile is forbidden. Those who err in these matters do so because
such is their desire. As the Chofetz Chaim expressed it, they have
no regard for these laws. Such offenses do not occur with those
who dread falsehood and are terrified of transgressing the laws of
gezel.

The very same people who are negligent with regard to monetary
laws have a very different attitude towards Shabbos observance
and Kashrus. They see these prohibitions as extremely severe,
as opposed to their view regarding the laws of Choshen Mishpat.
Such a discriminating form of observance, to decide that certain
mitzvos are to be approached with utmost gravity while others can be
taken lightly, brings to mind the philosophies of Reform Judaism
which encourage Jews to practice only those mitzvos which they
find to their liking. This is not the way of Torah. Torah must
be observed in its entirety, without compromising on a single
mitzvah.

◆§ Avraham and Moshe

We find that our ancestors remained ever cognizant of their monetary obligations toward their fellow men, even as they were in the midst of attaining awesome levels of spirituality and Divine revelation. In the chapter of the *Akeidah*, after Hashem had sent an angel to prevent Avraham from sacrificing his son, Avraham noticed a ram caught in the thicket which he then offered as a sacrifice. *Sforno* (*Bereishis* 22:13) comments, "Since he did not see a ram there [before the angel intervened] — only immediately afterward — caught in the thicket, he realized that the ram had been sent through the will of Hashem and there was no fear of theft [attached to taking it]."

Ponder this for a moment. Avraham had just withstood the greatest of his ten trials. He had elevated himself to the very Heavens — and yet, his mind was still down on this earth, concerned that he not be guilty of robbing another man![6]

In *Sidrah Shemos*, the Torah relates that as Moshe *Rabbeinu* was about to receive his first prophecy, he was leading his flock toward the desert. *Rashi* (*Shemos* 5:10) explains, "Toward the edge of the desert: To distance himself from robbery, so that the flock should not graze in the fields of others." The very next verse tells of the revelation of the burning bush. This is not coincidental. Moshe was surely engaged in lofty thoughts even in the moments *prior* to his revelation; he had to have been to be in a state of preparedness to communicate with Hashem. Yet, even then, he did not overlook his monetary obligations toward his fellow man. The Torah makes mention of this because it is precisely for this sort of zealousness that Hashem deemed Moshe fit to attain prophecy.

---

6. *Sforno* offers another penetrating insight. To the phrase "And he [i.e., Avraham] offered it [the ram] in place of his son," he comments, "As an exchange for his son, since he had committed himself to offering him as a sacrifice, in keeping with וְדֹבֵר אֱמֶת בִּלְבָבוֹ, 'And speaks truth in his heart' " (*Tehillim* 15:2). Avraham understood that Hashem had sent the ram his way so that he could fulfill his intent of offering a sacrifice.

If a person lives by truth, then Heaven assists him in fulfilling his every utterance and thought.

~§ The Antidote

How does one achieve purity and avoid *gezel, mirmah* and similar sins? The Chofetz Chaim offers the following antidote: "He should reflect regularly on the gravity of the sins and punishments of *gezel* and *sheker;* then he will be saved from them" (*S'fas Tamim,* Ch. 3). Note the term "regularly." Pondering the matter once or twice is not sufficient. Our Sages (*Moed Katan* 27b) tell us that when a person transgresses the same sin twice it becomes to him like something permissible — such is the power of the *yetzer hara,* evil inclination. It follows, then, that the effects of a sin which one has transgressed countless times during his lifetime will not be easily undone. One must ponder the matter again and again until his old attitudes are uprooted and the sin takes on its true look. With regard to monetary matters, one must come to view his friend's money and possessions as he would *hekdesh,* that which has been consecrated for the *Beis HaMikdash.* Just as one would never willfully benefit an iota from that which has been sanctified for Hashem, so must he keep away from that which Hashem has bequeathed to someone else.

Laxity in monetary matters can have the gravest consequences. Death and the judgments of the Next World do not atone for *gezel* if the sinner has not returned the money or an item of comparable value. His soul will have no rest until it returns as a *gilgul,* reincarnation, and makes proper amends. The Chofetz Chaim (*S'fas Tamim,* Ch. 4) cites an incident from the days of the *Rishonim,* where a man was reincarnated as a horse and worked with all his strength to repay a debt to the man who was now his owner. In an earlier chapter, the Chofetz Chaim cites *Sefer Rokeach* that when a man is reincarnated as a person he is unaware of this fact until after his death, but such is not the case when he is reincarnated as an animal.

In portraying the consequences of *gezel,* the Chofetz Chaim offers the following parable:

A man had fallen upon hard times and was unable to support his wife and small children. With no alternative, he set sail for a faraway island on a new business venture, leaving his family behind.

He remained on the island for years, barely earning enough to purchase the most basic needs. He often lamented his bitter plight and that of his loved ones as he struggled on in vain. Then his fortunes suddenly took a turn for the better. His business began to thrive; before long, he had amassed a small fortune. With a happy heart, he sent word to his family that he would soon be sailing for home on a seven-month sea voyage. The news was received at home with wild rejoicing.

The day of departure arrived. As he headed toward the dock, the man was met by an acquaintance, who had some parting advice. Take a few moments, the friend advised, to try and recall if there is someone on this island to whom you might still owe even a few cents. Be sure to clear your debts now, for even a small unpaid amount will interfere with your plans.

The man laughed off his friend's warning and boarded the ship without a worry in his heart. At a stop along the way, he sent word home as to his expected date of arrival.

Dawn broke on the long-awaited day. The man's family headed for the wall that separated their city from the seashore. They waited for hours, until finally they spotted a boat in the distance.The excitement rose with each passing moment as the boat churned closer and closer to the dock. Finally, the ship anchored and the man stepped off the plank. The moment of reunion had arrived — or had it? As the man began his walk from the shore, the gates to the city — which had been open all this time — were suddenly slammed shut. The distraught family listened from their side of the wall to a dialogue on the other side between the man and a government officer. The island had sent word that the man had left without having paid a debt that he had incurred more than ten years earlier. The debt had to be paid in person. The man was to return at once.

The man began to weep; he pleaded with the officer for mercy. His family was only yards away; for more than ten years they had waited for him and he longed to see them. Couldn't his return to the island be delayed for just a year? A month? A week?

His entreaties did him little good. The officer agreed to open the city gates to allow him and his family but a glance at one another. Imagine the family's shock and anguish when, once again, the gates were closed without their loved one walking through.

The man was herded aboard the ship and thus began the trip back to that faraway place.

Said the Chofetz Chaim:

> Man's primary purpose in descending to this world is to accrue Torah and mitzvos, by the merit of which he will bask in the eternal light of the Upper World. Man must therefore see himself as he would a stranger who has come to a distant land for business alone; nothing but his business should concern him. Why should anything else matter when his true dwelling place is elsewhere?
>
> But alas! Already in his youth, man forgets his true purpose in life. He sees himself not as a sojourner on this earth, but as a permanent resident. It is only when he reaches old age that the truth begins to sink in. He attempts to gather in his merchandise — his Torah and mitzvos — and begins the journey home ...
>
> As is stated in the holy Zohar, man must endure seven judgments before coming to his eternal rest ... If after all the judgments have passed one is found to have been guilty of gezel in any of its various forms, the angels who guard the entrance to Gan Eden will not permit him to make his way to the place that has been designated as his. At most, if he has some great source of merit, they will permit him to view his portion from a distance.
>
> He will weep bitterly over his being forced to return to this lowly world, again to be born, again to die, again to endure judgment ...

The first question posed by the Heavenly tribunal after a man's death is whether or not he has conducted his monetary affairs in good faith (Shabbos 31a). May we merit that when our time comes, we will be counted among those of clean hands and pure hearts.

The Enemy Within

◆§ Avraham's Oath

A major portion of this *parashah* tells of the battle between the kingdoms, in which Lot was captured and subsequently freed after Avraham joined the battle and achieved a miraculous victory on behalf of Sodom and its four allies.

In tribute to Avraham's valiant efforts on his and his allies' behalf, the king of Sodom offered Avraham all his previously captured possessions, which Avraham had retrieved during his conquest. Avraham replied:

הֲרִמֹתִי יָדִי אֶל ה׳ אֵ-ל עֶלְיוֹן קוֹנֵה שָׁמַיִם וָאָרֶץ. אִם מִחוּט וְעַד שְׂרוֹךְ נַעַל וְאִם אֶקַּח מִכָּל אֲשֶׁר לָךְ וְלֹא תֹאמַר אֲנִי הֶעֱשַׁרְתִּי אֶת אַבְרָם.

I lift up my hands to Hashem, God Most High, Maker of heaven and earth, if so much as a thread to a shoestrap, nor shall I take from anything of yours! So you shall not say, 'It is I who made Avram rich' (14:22-23).

As *Rashi* (ibid.) explains, the language used by Avraham is that of an oath. One may wonder why an oath was necessary. Would not a simple declaration have been sufficient?

In truth, it would have been foolhardy for the king of Sodom to have gone about proclaiming that he had made the great Avraham rich. To have done so would have inevitably reminded everyone of the embarrassing truth: Avraham had actually saved the king of Sodom from death after the latter had fallen into a well (see *Ramban* to 14:10). Nevertheless, Avraham was concerned that there not exist even a remote possibility of *chilul Hashem*, desecration of Hashem's Name. Among the blessings which Hashem had conferred upon Avraham at the opening of *Lech Lecha* was that of wealth. Were Avraham to have accepted Sodom's possessions as tribute for his war effort, people might have seen this not as a fulfillment of Hashem's blessing, but as a reward decided upon by the king of Sodom.[1] Avraham, whose life was totally dedicated to spreading Hashem's truths, would never allow such a misconception to occur. It was thus that he firmly refused the offer made by Sodom's king.

While the above interpretation is certainly plausible, one might be inclined to view this incident from a different angle. Would not Avraham's acceptance of the reward have resulted in a great *kiddush Hashem?* His acquisition of additional wealth would possibly have enhanced his stature and would have surely drawn attention to his miraculous military victory. Avraham, though, understood that this sort of reasoning still did not justify his acceptance of the tribute. Since such an act might have caused doubt regarding the fulfillment of Hashem's blessing to him, it had to be avoided. To insure that he not be swayed by any sort of rationalization, Avraham invoked an oath, for, as is stated in *Sifri*,[2] a *tzaddik* adjures his *yetzer hara* so as to avoid any possibility of sin.

We may liken this to a person who has been informed that there is a remote possibility that a certain beverage contains poison. Surely no one in his right mind would consider partaking of the beverage. In the words of *Mesilas Yesharim*, sin is poison for the *neshamah*. Unfortunately, we are not as sensitive toward sin. *Tzaddikim*, however, dread sin like poison, for they perceive clearly the destructiveness caused by transgressing Hashem's will. It is thus that they undertake seemingly unnecessary oaths when a remote possibility for sin exists.

The same idea is illustrated in *Parashas Chayei Sarah* through the words and deeds of Avraham's righteous servant, Eliezer.

---

1. A distinction must be drawn between Avraham's rejection of the king of Sodom's possessions and his acceptance of gifts from Pharaoh earlier in the *parashah*. See *Sifsei Chachamim* to 12:13; *HaKesav VeHaKabbalah* to 12:16; and *Gur Aryeh* to 14:23.

2. Cited by *Ramban* to 14:22.

✄§ Eliezer's Oath

Parashas *Chayei Sarah* relates how Avraham entrusted Eliezer with the mission of finding a wife for Yitzchak, and Eliezer's subsequent fulfillment of this charge. Avraham required Eliezer to undertake a sacred oath that he would not arrange a match with a daughter of the cursed tribes of Canaan. After making the oath, Eliezer immediately set out on the journey which resulted in the wedding of Yitzchak and Rivkah.

Ostensibly, it seems difficult to understand why an oath was necessary. Eliezer was no simple servant. The Torah refers to him as זְקַן בֵּיתוֹ הַמּשֵׁל בְּכָל אֲשֶׁר לוֹ, the senior servant of Avraham's household, the executor of his master's every command and in whose trust Avraham left all that he possessed. Indeed, he was much more, as is clear from *Chazal*.

The words הַמּשֵׁל בְּכָל אֲשֶׁר לוֹ — which taken literally mean that Eliezer controlled all that was Avraham's — *Chazal* interpret homiletically to mean that Eliezer was in control of *himself*, meaning his passions and desires. Also, Eliezer absorbed his master's lofty teachings and transmitted them to others. Where Avraham refers to his servant as דַּמֶּשֶׂק אֱלִיעֶזֶר, "Eliezer of Damascus" (15:2), the *Gemara* (*Yoma* 28b) comments:

> דַּמֶּשֶׂק אֱלִיעֶזֶר, שֶׁדּוֹלֶה וּמַשְׁקֶה מִתּוֹרַת רַבּוֹ לַאֲחֵרִים.
> *Eliezer of Damascus, who drew and gave others to drink of his master's Torah.*[3]

Moreover, Avraham's own spirituality surely filtered down to his most trusted servant. The *Gemara* relates that the donkey of R' Pinchas ben Yair would not eat from barley that had not been tithed (*Chullin* 7a). *Chazal* derive from here that a Divine protection against spiritual mishap is provided *tzaddikim* and extends even to their livestock. This is accomplished by the spiritual aura which flows from a *tzaddik's* being and comes to rest upon all that he owns. R' Pinchas ben Yair's donkey would not eat untithed produce because its master's spirituality prevented this from happening. We may say

---

3. This is based on a homiletic understanding of דַּמֶּשֶׂק as a contraction of דּוֹלֶה, *he draws*, and מַשְׁקֶה, *he gives to drink*.

with certainty, then, that aside from Eliezer's own merits, his spiritual level was enhanced by his being the servant of Avraham *Avinu*.

Without a doubt, Eliezer understood the cosmic nature of his mission. He was not going to arrange just any match. From this *shidduch* would come Avraham's descendants, Hashem's Chosen People — *Klal Yisrael!* Surely, Eliezer approached this calling with the greatest sense of responsibility.

Why, then, did Avraham find it necessary to have Eliezer swear that he would properly fulfill his mission? Why was a mere assurance not enough? Could there have been any doubt in Avraham's mind as to whether Eliezer would obey him by not approaching the Canaanite tribes?

To resolve this question, we must say that while Avraham was well aware of Eliezer's spiritual qualities, he was equally well aware of the *yetzer hara's* power of persuasion. Avraham knew that without an oath, Eliezer might have at some point come across a Caananite woman whom he would deem most suited for Yitzchak. Eliezer could then have reasoned that the exceptional qualities of this woman *obligated* him to waive the assurance he had given his master — for Avraham's sake!

In fact, Eliezer did entertain such thoughts. As the *Midrash* (*Bereishis Rabbah* 59:9) relates, Eliezer — who was himself a Canaanite — actually considered his own daughter for Yitzchak:

כְּנַעַן בְּיָדוֹ מֹאזְנֵי מִרְמָה: זֶה אֱלִיעֶזֶר שֶׁהָיָה יוֹשֵׁב וּמַשְׁקִיל אִם בִּתּוֹ רְאוּיָה הִיא אוֹ אֵינָה רְאוּיָה לְיִצְחָק.

"The Canaanite — in his hands are scales of deception" (Hoshea 12:8): this is Eliezer who sat and considered whether or not his daughter was worthy of Yitzchak.

Avraham rejected this proposal, telling Eliezer, "My son is blessed and you are cursed (see 9:25); the accursed cannot unite with the blessed."[4]

It was a keen awareness of the *yetzer hara's* skill in presenting wrongful actions on a platter of seeming righteousness that impelled Avraham to extract a solemn oath from his loyal, God-fearing servant.

---

4. The *Midrash* further states that in the end Eliezer, by way of his faithful service of Avraham, freed himself of the curse of Canaan. He erred, though, in thinking that he had already changed his status before his mission was completed.

ও‌§ Eliezer's Prayer

Upon reaching Padan Aram, home to the family of Rivkah, Eliezer prayed that his mission be successful. "Hashem, God of my master Avraham, may You so arrange it for me this day that You do kindness [*chessed*] with my master Avraham" (24:12). It seems strange that a prayer of this sort was necessary. Avraham epitomized the attribute of *chessed*. In the words of the *Midrash* (*Bereishis Rabbah* 60:2), it is to Avraham's credit that the attribute of *chessed* is to be found among mankind. We know that Heaven conducts itself toward each individual in the manner that he conducts himself toward others. Surely there could be no one more deserving of Divine *chessed* than the paragon of *chessed* on this earth, Avraham *Avinu*! Why, then, did Eliezer feel a need to pray that his master merit *chessed* from Hashem?

Our above explanation of Eliezer's oath resolves this question. Eliezer realized why Avraham had required him to swear. He also understood why Avraham had himself undertaken an oath during his encounter with the king of Sodom. As Eliezer started out on his mission, he reflected upon his own inner feelings and he realized that personal considerations were nagging at him. In the depths of his heart, he wanted Yitzchak for his own daughter. He knew that this desire could impede him from fulfilling his charge properly; thus, he prayed. He begged Hashem to help him overcome his inclination, that he not be the cause of his mission's ruination. This was the *chessed* that he sought from Hashem.

ও‌§ Conversations of Servants

In *Bereishis Rabbah* (60:8), R' Acha declared:

יָפָה שִׂיחָתָן שֶׁל עַבְדֵי בָּתֵּי אָבוֹת לִפְנֵי אָבוֹת מִתּוֹרָתָן שֶׁל בְּנֵיהֶם, שֶׁהֲרֵי פָּרָשָׁה שֶׁל אֱלִיעֶזֶר כְּפוּלָה בַּתּוֹרָה וְהַרְבֵּה גוּפֵי תוֹרָה לֹא נִתְּנוּ אֶלָּא בִּרְמִיזָה.

The conversation of the servants of the Patriarchs' homes is more beautiful before the Omnipresent than the teaching of [their] descendants: for the chapter of Eliezer is repeated in the Torah while many essentials in the Torah were given only by allusion.

The Torah repeats this episode a second time when it relates Eliezer's own recounting of his mission to Rivkah's family. It is possible that Eliezer's primary purpose in relating everything in such detail was not to convince the scheming Lavan and Besuel to accept his offer. Rather, Eliezer was speaking to himself. His opening words were, עֶבֶד אַבְרָהָם אָנֹכִי, "I am a servant of Avraham." Again and again he refers to Avraham as אֲדֹנִי, "my master"; not once does he mention his own name. Eliezer was reminding himself that in carrying out his task, he had no personal identity. He was nothing more than a servant who was doing his master's bidding. His telling of Avraham's instructions to him, of his own prayer that he succeed and of the events which followed strengthened his resolve to see his mission through to completion.[5]

The "beauty" inherent in Eliezer's words is his active effort at subjugating his *yetzer hara*. He undertook an oath, prayed for Divine assistance and retold the story of his mission at length in order to negate the self-interest that lay beneath the surface. That he did so is a great lesson to us and it is for this reason that the Torah recounts the narrative at length a second time.

---

5. In commenting on one of the subtle differences between Eliezer's account and the original narrative, *Rashi* (24:39, citing *Midrash*) points out that Eliezer was alluding to his earlier self-interest in Yitzchak marrying his own daughter.

Tangible Faith[1]

✎§ Sarah's Laughter

וַיֹּאמְרוּ אֵלָיו, אַיֵּה שָׂרָה אִשְׁתֶּךָ? וַיֹּאמֶר, הִנֵּה בָאֹהֶל. וַיֹּאמֶר שׁוֹב
אָשׁוּב אֵלֶיךָ כָּעֵת חַיָּה וְהִנֵּה בֵן לְשָׂרָה אִשְׁתֶּךָ. וְשָׂרָה שֹׁמַעַת פֶּתַח
הָאֹהֶל וְהוּא אַחֲרָיו. וְאַבְרָהָם וְשָׂרָה זְקֵנִים, בָּאִים בַּיָּמִים; חָדַל
לִהְיוֹת לְשָׂרָה אֹרַח כַּנָּשִׁים. וַתִּצְחַק שָׂרָה בְּקִרְבָּהּ לֵאמֹר, אַחֲרֵי
בְלֹתִי הָיְתָה לִי עֶדְנָה? וַאדֹנִי זָקֵן! וַיֹּאמֶר ה׳ אֶל אַבְרָהָם, לָמָּה זֶּה
צָחֲקָה שָׂרָה לֵאמֹר, הַאַף אֻמְנָם אֵלֵד, וַאֲנִי זָקַנְתִּי. הֲיִפָּלֵא מֵה׳
דָּבָר? לַמּוֹעֵד אָשׁוּב אֵלֶיךָ כָּעֵת חַיָּה וּלְשָׂרָה בֵן.
They said to him, "Where is Sarah, your wife?" He replied, "In the tent." And he [i.e., the guest] said, "I will return to you this time next year, and behold Sarah your wife will have a son." Sarah was listening at the entrance of the tent which was behind him.

Now Avraham and Sarah were old, well on in years; the manner of women had ceased to be with Sarah.

Sarah laughed to herself, saying, "After I have withered will I again be youthful? And my husband is old!"

Hashem said to Avraham, "Why is it that Sarah laughed, saying: 'Shall I in truth bear a child after I have aged?' — Is anything beyond Hashem?! At the appointed time I will return to you next year and Sarah will have a son" (18:9-14).

---

1. Delivered on the 50th *yahrzeit* of the Chofetz Chaim (24 Elul 5743).

Upon hearing her guest's amazing pronouncement, Sarah reflected upon her own withered physical condition and wondered incredulously how she could possibly bear a child. *Ramban* comments that Sarah was unaware of the true identity of her three guests. As far as she knew, they were idol-worshiping wayfarers.

Let us imagine that a stranger, a gentile, has suddenly appeared at our door and pronounced a blessing upon us which contradicts the laws of nature. Who among us would not laugh off the entire scenario? Why, then, was Sarah faulted for laughing?

Ramban (v. 15) explains that she should not have considered the prediction an impossibility. "It would have been proper for her to believe [in its possibility] or to have said, 'Amen, may Hashem do so.' "

This sort of faith is not expected only from the Sarahs among us. Although more than five thousand years have passed since Creation, *HaKadosh Baruch Hu* is still involved in the day-to-day running of the world today just as He was then. All of us affirm our faith in this truth when we declare each morning that Hashem "in His goodness renews daily, perpetually, the work of creation." A related concept is that of *hashgachah pratis*, the unceasing Providential involvement in all aspects of this world, including the private affairs of every individual. One whose belief in *hashgachah pratis* is complete knows with certainty that nothing, absolutely nothing, is impossible.

Yiddishkeit is rooted in *emunah*, faith. We Jews are *ma'aminim bnei ma'aminim*, believers who are descendants of believers. We are all firm believers in the Divine origin of Torah, in reward and punishment with regard to *mitzvah* observance and in *hashgachah pratis*. However, not all of us understand clearly the meanings of *emunah* and *hashgachah pratis*.

◄§ Emunah and Bitachon

In *Sha'arei Teshuvah* (3:§31-32), *Rabbeinu Yonah* states:

> It is written (*Devarim* 7:17-18), "If you will say in your heart, 'These nations are more numerous than ours. How will I be able to drive them out?' — Do not fear them ..." It is also written (ibid. 20:1), "If you will go

*out to war against your enemy and see horses, riders
and multitudes more numerous than your own, do not
fear them . . ." In these verses we are cautioned that
when travail appears to be near, [the belief] in salvation
from Above should be present in one's heart and he
should trust in it . . .*

Rabbeinu Yonah's intent is that the above verses are not directed
solely toward those engaged in war; rather, they apply to every
person all the days of his life.

In his commentary to *Mishlei* (3:26), *Rabbeinu Yonah* further
states:

*The meaning of bitachon (trust in Hashem) is that one
knows in his heart that all is through the hand of
Heaven and that it is in His power to deviate from the
ways of nature . . . Even when someone is so deathly ill
that according to the natural way of things there is
no chance that he will live, one should believe and
trust that Hashem can save him. He [i.e., Hashem]
can change the fortunes of man and no one can stop
Him. Though travail is near — salvation can be near as
well.*

This is proper *emunah*. Were one to possess such faith, he would
merit the fulfillment of, "And a *tzaddik* lives by his faith,"
(*Chavakuk* 2:4) both in this world and in the next. Every person
experiences trying situations through the course of his lifetime. When
someone lacking in proper *emunah* encounters such a situation,
he becomes broken and sinks into despair. However, one who
lives by his faith will not be overwhelmed or daunted by such
happenings.

David *HaMelech* said, בִּטְחוּ בוֹ בְכָל עֵת, "Trust in Him at every
moment" (*Tehillim* 62:9). At any moment, a situation that is most
grave can suddenly be turned around for the good. Such belief is
required of us; it was Sarah's apparent lack of faith that prompted
Hashem's criticism of her.

ᴥ§ The Chofetz Chaim

When discussing these concepts, it is fitting to speak of the Chofetz Chaim, of blessed memory. Far be it for us to even attempt to say the praises of a man whose greatness is beyond our grasp. We can, however, examine how we can emulate him in some small way.

When pondering how the Chofetz Chaim attained so lofty a spiritual level, we must conclude that it was primarily through the strength of his powerful *emunah*. His faith in Hashem was almost tangible. Whatever is stated in the Torah or by *Chazal* was to him a reality.[2]

While studying in Mir, I was told the following anecdote: A non-religious physician once called on the Chofetz Chaim. The Chofetz Chaim asked the doctor, "How do you know that the sun will rise tomorrow?" The doctor replied, "Does not the sun rise every morning? Why should tomorrow be different?" The Chofetz Chaim disagreed. "Not because of this do we know the sun will rise, but because the Torah states, '. . . and day and night shall not cease' " (*Bereishis* 8:22).

It is related that once when studying the chapter regarding the plague of boils upon the Egyptians (*Shemos* ch. 9), the Chofetz Chaim burst into laughter. In his mind, he vividly envisioned Pharaoh and his servants covered with boils from head to toe. It was a reality.

As a young man, the Chofetz Chaim took seriously ill and could not study from a *sefer* for an entire year. The Chofetz Chaim himself related that during that period he suffered heart failure, to the point where he could actually hear the pounding of his heart. Yet, by some accounts, he lived past one hundred.[3]

In what merit?

מִי הָאִישׁ הֶחָפֵץ חַיִּים, אֹהֵב יָמִים לִרְאוֹת טוֹב? נְצֹר לְשׁוֹנְךָ מֵרָע,
וּשְׂפָתֶיךָ מִדַּבֵּר מִרְמָה. סוּר מֵרָע וַעֲשֵׂה טוֹב, בַּקֵּשׁ שָׁלוֹם וְרָדְפֵהוּ.

---

2. An elderly native of Radin who knew the Chofetz Chaim as a friend and neighbor put it this way: "The Chofetz Chaim believed in *Olam Habba* (the World to Come) and you and I believe in *Olam Habba*. But to us, *Olam Habba* is an abstract matter of faith. To the Chofetz Chaim, *Olam Habba* was as real as the room next door."
3. The Chofetz Chaim is generally believed to have lived to age ninety-five. HaRav Segal was told by a Jew who knew the Chofetz Chaim personally that he actually lived past one hundred. There are others who corroborate this.

Which man desires life, who loves days of seeking good? Guard your tongue from evil, and your lips from speaking deceit. Turn from evil and do good, seek peace and pursue it (Tehillim 34:13-15).

The message of these verses was a fact of life to the Chofetz Chaim. He lived by this message and merited the longevity it assures. Tangible *emunah!*

⊸§ R' Yochanan's Faith

This sort of *emunah* was common to the sages of old. The *Gemara* (Gittin 56a) relates that after Jerusalem fell under siege shortly before the destruction of the Second *Beis HaMikdash*, R' Yochanan ben Zakkai managed to leave the city in order to speak with the Roman general Vespasian. When the two met, R' Yochanan said, "Greetings, Your Majesty." Vespasian responded that R' Yochanan was deserving of death on two accounts. Firstly, he had slighted the emperor and also mocked his general by referring to Vespasian as "Your Majesty." Secondly, if Vespasian was indeed king then why had R' Yochanan waited so long to visit him?

R' Yochanan replied, "With regard to your statement that you are not a king — but indeed, you are a king! For if not, Jerusalem would not be given over into your hands, for it is written (Yeshayahu 10:34), וְהַלְּבָנוֹן בְּאַדִּיר יִפּוֹל, 'And Lebanon shall fall by a mighty one.' 'A mighty one' refers to a king ... and 'Lebanon' refers to the *Beis HaMikdash* ...'' [4] Let us examine this incident. As related in the *Gemara*, R' Yochanan risked death in trying to leave Jerusalem to meet Vespasian. It was necessary for R' Yochanan to leave the city in a coffin borne by his disciples who claimed to be transporting their deceased teacher to his final resting place. That R' Yochanan safely reached the Roman camp was in itself a miracle. Why, after having gone through so much, did R' Yochanan address Vespasian in a manner that was sure to arouse his ire or worse? It is certain that had R' Yochanan felt the slightest doubt with regard to the interpretation of the terms לְבָנוֹן and אַדִּיר in the verse he cited, he would have found

---

4. With regard to Vespasian's second indictment, R' Yochanan replied that a militant group known as the Biryonim had prevented him from coming until then.

some other form of greeting rather than risk death! Only a clear and absolute *emunah* in the Written and Oral Torah could have impelled him to speak as he did. To R' Yochanan, the verse, along with the interpretation transmitted by his teachers, was real. When studying it he saw before him a king leading his armies to take Jerusalem and destroy the *Beis HaMikdash*.

When one comes face to face with reality there can be no doubts. This is the epitome of *emunah*.

⊷§ Strengthening One's Faith

It is incumbent upon us to make a conscious effort to strengthen our *emunah*. As *Ramban* writes (*Shemos* 13:16), the Redemption from Egypt occupies so central a place among the *mitzvos* because it serves as a fundamental of faith for all generations. In discussing the admonition that we not forget the awesome scene when the Torah was given at Sinai (*Devarim* 4:9), *Ramban* further writes that our *emunah* is based upon the accepted principle that a father does not bequeath teachings to his child which he knows to be false. Our belief in the Divine origin of both the Oral and Written Law is based upon the fact that more than one million of our ancestors stood together at Sinai and heard the voice of Hashem as He spoke the first two of the *Aseres HaDibros* (Ten Commandments). For more than three thousand years, our *mesorah* (tradition) has been transmitted by giants of Torah whose belief in these teachings was rock-firm. Our surest path to proper *emunah* is not by analyzing or philosophizing. It is through *emunah p'shutah*, unquestioning faith in that which the sages of yesteryear imparted to our fathers and grandfathers. It is precisely because of the need for *emunah p'shutah* that *HaKadosh Baruch Hu* implanted in us a natural acceptance of the teachings of our parents. Thus, acquiring pure and proper *emunah* is within everyone's grasp.

There exists a small *sefer* entitled *Mitzvas HaBitachon*[5] which every Jew should own. It is a marvelous collection of quotations from the *Gemara*, *Midrash*, *Rishonim* and *Acharonim* regarding *emunah* and *bitachon*. The work's introduction cites the words of *Maharal*

---

5. By R' Shmuel Hominer, Jerusalem 5736.

that a Jew should recite Scriptural verses relating to *emunah* and *bitachon* as a method of infusing himself with proper faith and trust. ".. . For this is the basis of Jewish belief and one must strengthen himself exceedingly in this regard. After reciting such verses, one should pray that Hashem grant him the merit to be exceedingly strong in matters of *emunah* as is His desire" (*Mitzvas HaBitachon*, p. 3).

One should take the advice of *Maharal* to heart and pray that he merit proper *emunah*. How different would our introspection be during the month of Elul were we to possess the *emunah* of the Chofetz Chaim! How different would our *Rosh Hashanah* be . . . our *Aseres Yimei Teshuvah* . . . *Yom Kippur!*

Among the better-known *tefillos* recited during that time of year is the '*U'nesaneh Tokef*' piece:

> *Let us now relate the power of this day's holiness, for it is awesome and frightening . . . On Rosh Hashanah will be inscribed and on Yom Kippur will be sealed how many will pass from the earth and how many will be created; who will live and who will die; who will die at his predestined time and who before his time; . . . who will rest and who will wander, who will live in harmony and who will be harried, who will enjoy tranquility and who will suffer . . .*

All of us want only health and happiness for ourselves and our loved ones. Were our *emunah* in the above words — as well as in the teaching "Repentance and good deeds are like a shield against retribution" (*Avos* 4:13) — of a tangible sort, our Days of Awe would be of a very different nature.

⁍ Striving for Greatness

It is for us to strive to emulate the Chofetz Chaim and attain his awesome levels of *emunah* and *bitachon*. We should seek to emulate his other sublime attributes as well. How we develop spiritually is entirely up to us. As *Rambam* writes (*Hilchos Teshuvah* 5:1), every Jew has within himself the ability to attain the highest spiritual levels or the opposite, God forbid.

How does one begin to develop an attachment to the Chofetz Chaim and his ways? This can only be accomplished by studying his works. When one studies his *sefarim*, is committed to following the daily study schedule in *Sefer Chofetz Chaim*,[6] and makes a sincere effort to improve his observance of *mitzvos* between fellow men, then he has attached himself to the Chofetz Chaim.

The Chofetz Chaim was and is a symbol of spiritual perfection.

מִי הָאִישׁ? — Who was a person deserving of the title אִישׁ, *man*, who abstained all his life from every form of forbidden speech and did only good for his fellow man? — הֶחָפֵץ חַיִּים, the Chofetz Chaim! His works are wellsprings of *kedushah*, the holiest of holies.

Let us accept upon ourselves to study each day two *halachos* in *Sefer Chofetz Chaim* and one page of *Sefer Shemiras HaLashon*. This study is not for men alone. A husband should learn these works with his wife and children. A Jewish home should be a place where *everyone* exercises caution with regard to forbidden speech. Also, children should be reared to be *gomlei chessed*, to seek to do kindness to others and to abstain from all forms of *ona'as devarim*, hurt caused to others through the spoken word. Such is the way of a proper Jewish home.

May the One Above assist us in developing a desire to emulate the Chofetz Chaim and may we merit to follow in his ways.

---

6. I.e., a schedule consisting of the daily study of two *halachos* in *Sefer Chofetz Chaim* and one page of *Sefer Shemiras HaLashon*. A yearly calendar for this study system is published annually in England and can be obtained in Torah communities around the world.

Rivkah's Test

⋖ৡ Fundamentals

R' Chaim Vital, in his *Sha'arei Kedushah* (1:2), writes:

> ... *Midos (character traits) are not included in the 613 mitzvos; rather, they are basic determinants in the fulfillment or disregard of the mitzvos ... Therefore, midos ra'os (negative traits) are much worse than transgressions themselves.*
>
> *Understandably, then, the Sages say (Zohar Chadash 1:27) that one who becomes angry is considered as if he has worshiped idols — a sin which is comparable to [the transgression of] all other mitzvos combined. They have also taught (Sotah 5a) that one who is arrogant is as if he has denied the primary principle [of God's existence], is fit to be uprooted like a tree of idolatry, and will not awaken at the time of techias hameisim (resurrection of the dead).*
>
> *Thus, one can also understand the astounding words of the Sages concerning midos, that modesty and humility lead one to Ruach HaKodesh (Divine Inspiration) and the Shechinah rests upon him ... and many such statements. They speak not of the performance of the mitzvos but of midos tovos (positive traits)!*
>
> *... Therefore, one must beware of midos ra'os even more than he is zealous with regard to mitzvos, for by being a virtuous person, he will readily perform the mitzvos.*

Be ever cognizant of this fact, and you will succeed in your endeavors without a doubt.

When Eliezer was dispatched to find a suitable mate for Yitzchak, his priority was the girl's character. Beseeching Hashem to make his mission successful, Eliezer set up a test. Standing before the community well, he would ask the maidens who had come to water their flocks to give him a drink. The maiden who would offer water not only for him, but for his camels as well, would be the one designated by Hashem to be Yitzchak's wife. Before Eliezer had completed his prayer, Rivkah was already coming toward him to pass the test.

Rivkah was the daughter of a wicked man, the sister of a wicked man, and was from a place whose general population was wicked (see *Rashi* 25:20). She was reared and enveloped in an atmosphere of idolatry. Yet, Eliezer made no attempt to ascertain her degree of religious purity, to try and discover whether she did, in fact, possess even a minimal awareness of the true God. He was concerned with uncovering one important fact — how well developed was her attribute of *chesed*. A person *is* what his *midos* are, for it is *midos*, more than anything else, which determine how dedicated one will be to Hashem and His *mitzvos*. Rivkah, with her magnanimous efforts on a stranger's behalf, demonstrated the quality of her *midos*. Additionally, she responded to Eliezer's request with *zerizus*, alacrity, an attribute which *Chazal* associate with the ways of *tzaddikim* (see *Mesilas Yesharim*, ch.7). To Eliezer, there was no doubt that this young girl was a fitting receptacle for the lofty teachings of Avraham and Yitzchak. If her lowly upbringing had deprived her of the opportunity to attain *yiras shamayim*, awe of Heaven, she certainly had the potential for it. Attaining *yiras Hashem* is a minor accomplishment in comparison to developing superlative *midos*, which Rivkah had done.

◄§ Afflictions and Cures

In *Mesilas Yesharim* (ch. 11), R' Moshe Chaim Luzzato writes:

We will now discuss the primary negative traits at great length and analysis, because of the relative frequency with which they are used. They are: arrogance, anger, jealousy and lust. The destructiveness inherent in these traits is obvious; they are all inherently bad as are their products . . . Each one is in itself sufficient to cause a person to transgress the most serious sins.

Let us discuss each trait individually. The matter of arrogance is as follows: One thinks highly of himself and in his heart imagines himself worthy of being lauded. Now, this sort of feeling can be the result of many and varied reasonings. One person may consider himself to be of superior intellect, another may see himself as handsome, a third views himself as honorable, a fourth considers himself a leader, while yet another thinks himself to be knowledgeable. In short, when a person sees himself as being endowed with anything that is considered good in this world, he is immediately in danger of stumbling into the abyss that is arrogance.

We have already cited some of the forceful statements of *Chazal* regarding arrogance. We now add to this the powerful words of *Mesilas Yesharim* which relate how easy it is to be ensnared by this despicable trait and that this and other *midos ra'os* can bring one to transgress the most serious sins.

How can one sleep at night after hearing such words?! Were a person to be apprised by a physician that he was, God forbid, afflicted — or even *possibly* afflicted — with a serious illness, would he then immediately retire for the night? Or would he first seek a remedy for his malady?

Every person is born with *midos ra'os* such as those we have mentioned. It is incumbent upon us to seek ways to rid ourselves of them. This can only be achieved through a proper study of *mussar*, meaning a form of *mussar* study that focuses on absorbing the subject matter rather than seeking to propound original insights.

In *Sefer HaYirah*, *Rabbeinu Yonah* writes: "Words of *yiras shamayim* should forever be on your lips ... then you will not stumble." R' Simchah Zissel of Kelm explains this with a parable:

A yeshivah student was preparing to travel home for a visit. On the day that he was to depart, he was approached by another student from his home town. "I hear you are leaving for home today," the second student began. "Please do me a favor and deliver a very important letter to my parents." The first student was happy to oblige and packed the letter among his belongings.

Fifteen minutes later, the departing student was again approached by his friend. "I just want to remind you again about my letter. Please don't forget to deliver it. It's really very important."

And so the day went. Every fifteen minutes the second student would reappear to sound another reminder about his letter, until the first student finally started on his way.

Turmoil greeted the student as he arrived in his home town. The town had been ravaged by fire. The damage was extensive and people were desperately trying to salvage whatever possible. The student's immediate reaction was to dash to his own house and lend a hand ... but then he remembered his friend's incessant reminders. "It's really very important that my parents get this letter ..."

The student delivered the letter; only then did he head for home.

Said R' Simchah Zissel: When one's passion is aroused to sin and the fire of the *yetzer hara* burns within him, he can easily become swept away by the turmoil of the moment and completely forget any thoughts of *yiras shamayim* that he might have reflected upon in more tranquil times. It is therefore necessary that one ponder and review such thoughts until they become deeply embedded in his soul.

We cited above the Talmudic teaching: כָּל הַמִּתְגָּאֶה אֵין עֲפָרוֹ נִנְעָר לִתְחִיַּת הַמֵּתִים, "The dust of an arrogant person will not stir for *techias hameisim*." When one comes upon this or other important ethical teachings, he should repeat the dictum to himself many times until it becomes ingrained in his mind and heart.

In the second blessing of *Shemoneh Esrei*, mention of *techias hameisim* is made no less than five times. When reciting this blessing, a student of *mussar* should take to heart that he must rid himself of arrogance if he is to be among those who will arise from the dead in the End of Days. Surely, he will then seek means by which to perfect himself in this regard.

◄§ Glorifying God

While on the subject of character refinement, another daily prayer comes to mind. *Baruch She'amar*, the lofty prayer which introduces the morning *Pesukei D'Zimrah*, concludes with a blessing:

בָּרוּךְ אַתָּה ה' אֱלֹקֵינוּ מֶלֶךְ הָעוֹלָם, הָאֵל הָאָב הָרַחֲמָן הַמְהֻלָּל בְּפֶה עַמּוֹ, מְשֻׁבָּח וּמְפֹאָר בִּלְשׁוֹן חֲסִידָיו וַעֲבָדָיו ...

Blessed are You, Hashem, our God, King of the universe, the God, the merciful Father, Who is lauded by the mouth of His people, praised and glorified by the tongue of His devout ones and His servants ...

Who are חֲסִידָיו, *His devout ones*, and what is it about the praise which emanates from their לָשׁוֹן, *tongue[s]*, which sets it apart from that of the פֶה, *mouth[s]*, of other Jews?

Chazal state:

וְאָהַבְתָּ אֵת ה' אֱלֹקֶיךָ — שֶׁיְהֵא שֵׁם שָׁמַיִם מִתְאַהֵב עַל יָדְךָ.

You shall love Hashem your God (Devarim 6:5) — that the Name of Hashem should become beloved through you.

A Jew should study Scripture and Mishnah, serve Torah scholars, deal honestly in business, and speak pleasantly to others. Then, his fellows will say of him, "Praiseworthy is his father who taught him Torah! Praiseworthy is his teacher who taught him Torah! Woe to those who do not study Torah! He who studies Torah — how pleasant is his behavior, how proper are his deeds! To him may the verse be applied (Yeshayahu 49:3): And He said to me: 'You are My servant Israel, in whom I will be glorified' " (Yoma 86a).

In his famous letter to his son, *Ramban* wrote: "Forever be accustomed to speaking in a pleasant manner, to any person on any occasion." Thus is Hashem מְשֻׁבָּח וּמְפֹאָר, "praised and glorified," through לְשׁוֹן חֲסִידָיו, "the tongue of His devout ones." חֲסִידָיו, "chasidav," are the true "chassidim" (i.e., followers) of God, for it is their לְשׁוֹן, meaning their refined manner of speech, which, along with their upright deeds, cause others to love Hashem and His Torah. It behooves us to exercise proper caution with regard to matters of speech so that we, too, will be counted among those who bring praise and glory to Hashem.

Tefillah

◈ The View from Two Worlds

There is much to be learned from the contrasts between Yaakov and Eisav, whether in deed, speech or general approach to life. One contrast that bears particular mention is that of their varying views of Eisav's sale of the birthright to Yaakov, views that were expressed years after the sale took place. Let us begin by examining Eisav's reaction after he learned that Yaakov, having successfully posed as his brother, had been granted the coveted blessings by their father Yitzchak:

"He [Eisav] said, 'Is it because he was named Yaakov[1] that he should outwit me these two times? He took away my birthright and, see, now he took away my blessings!' " (27:36).

In Eisav's view, Yaakov had taken advantage of his brother in initiating the sale of the birthright at a time when Eisav was famished and desperate for the stew which Yaakov was cooking (25:29-34). As Eisav saw it, were it not for his unfortunate circumstances, the birthright would still be his.

Yaakov, however, had an entirely different view of things, as he made clear shortly before his own death. At that time, Yaakov conferred the birthright upon Rachel's elder son, Yosef, giving Yosef's two sons the status of *shevatim* (Tribal ancestors). Later, Yaakov (according to one interpretation) again made reference to the birthright. He told Yosef: "And as for me, I have given you one

---

1. The name יַעֲקֹב, Yaakov, connotes both *heel* (see 25:26) and *deceive* (*Radak*) or *outwit* (*Rashi*), which is the intent here in Eisav's play on words.

portion more than your brothers, which I took from the hand of the Emorite with my sword and my bow" (48:22). *Targum Onkelos*[2] (see also *Bava Basra* 123a) understands חַרְבִּי, *my sword*, as a reference to prayer and קַשְׁתִּי, *my bow*, as an allusion to supplication. Yaakov was informing his son that he had acquired the birthright through the power of his *tefillos*. That Eisav came in famished from the field at precisely the time when Yaakov had a stew cooking was merely Providence's way of bequeathing to Yaakov that which he had earned by way of his prayers.

What impelled Yaakov to make this point to Yosef at that time? Earlier, Yosef, at his father's behest, had undertaken an oath to accompany Yaakov's body out of Egypt after his death and insure its interment in the Cave of Machpelah in Hebron. This was no simple undertaking, for, as Yaakov knew well, Pharaoh would steadfastly oppose both Yosef's temporary departure from the land and the removal of Yaakov's body from Egyptian soil (see *Rashi* to 50:6). Yaakov used his conferring of the birthright upon Yosef as a vehicle for a lesson in *hashgachah*, Providence. Even that which seems unattainable can be accomplished through *tefillah*. To wrest the birthright from Eisav seemed impossible; yet, Hashem had arranged the circumstances by which it could occur. With help from Above — merited through *tefillah* — Yosef would honor his oath.

Yaakov was speaking to us as well. Nothing is beyond the power of *tefillah*. When one prays sincerely, with proper dedication, his prayers are truly potent.

✦§ Only Through Tefillah

In a number of instances in Scripture, it was *tefillah* alone that achieved a desired result. *Midrash Tanchuma* (*Mikeitz* §9) states:

> ... *There is nothing greater than tefillah. As proof: It was decreed against Moshe that he not enter the Land and not even view it, but in the merit of his bountiful prayers it is written: "And Hashem showed him the entire Land" (Devarim 34:1). Similarly, King*

---

2. See *Rashi* for another interpretation.

Chizkiyahu prayed and the decree against him was rescinded. Also, Yaakov prayed for his sons when he sent them down to Egypt, as is written: "And may the Almighty grant you mercy before the man" (Bereishis 43:14).

Moshe *Rabbeinu* had countless sources of merit to his credit. The study of Torah is the greatest *mitzvah* of all and who could claim this merit if not Moshe?! Yet, only through *tefillah* was his yearning to gaze upon *Eretz Yisrael* realized.

King Chizkiyahu, too, possessed the merit of Torah study in abundant measure. His reign generated an unprecedented spread in Torah knowledge, to the point where every young child in the Land was fluent in the most obscure Talmudic laws (*Sanhedrin* 94b). Yet, when Chizkiyahu fell deathly ill it was necessary for him to pray that his life be spared — and his *tefillos* were answered (*Berachos* 10b).

Yaakov, in the verse cited by *Tanchuma*, was sending his sons to Egypt for a second time, after their brother Yosef, whom they knew as the viceroy, had warned them not to return without their brother Binyamin. The brothers were about to set out on an apparently dangerous mission, together with Binyamin and an assortment of gifts for Yosef, who had imprisoned their brother Shimon as a guarantee that they would return. As *Rashi* (ibid.) explains, Yaakov told his sons, "Now, you lack nothing except prayer; therefore, I pray for you."

When one is in need of Divine assistance, he dare not rely on what he perceives as his merits, even that of Torah study. *Tefillah* is a must. Those desires for which an individual yearns most, desires which mean so much but which often seem out of reach, can be acquired through *tefillah*.[3]

---

3. This does not contradict *Chazal's* statement that Torah study is the paramount *mitzvah* (*Shabbos* 127a). *Tefillah* is unique in its potency for awakening the Divine attribute of mercy. *Ramban* (*Sh'mos* 2:25) writes that the Redemption process in Egypt was set in motion in the merit of the Jews' *tefillos*, though they were not fit to be redeemed at that time. This is *Tanchuma's* intent when it states, "There is nothing greater than *tefillah.*"

~§ Preconditions

The *Gemara* (*Berachos* 6b; see *Rashi*) refers to *tefillah* as something which stands בְּרוּמוֹ שֶׁל עוֹלָם, *at the pinnacle of the universe*, but which people do not accord proper respect. As commonly understood, בְּרוּמוֹ שֶׁל עוֹלָם refers to the exalted status of *tefillah*. *Nefesh HaChaim* (2:§10) offers a different interpretation, based on the following *Zohar* (*Va'eschanan* 260b):

> At the time when one is praying, all the words which one utters during his prayer ascend Above. They pierce the firmament and Heavens until they arrive at their destination, where they are made into an adornment for the King.

Thus, says *Nefesh HaChaim*, words of *tefillah* literally stand at the pinnacle of the universe. However, this status is conditional. As mentioned above, Yaakov referred to *tefillah* as his bow. Actually, the words of prayer are likened to arrows; it is the mouth which is the bow, propelling the words to their destination. Now, a bow when used properly can propel an arrow quite some distance with amazing accuracy. A defective bow, though, can accomplish little. For a *tefillah* to be potent, it must be uttered by a mouth which is holy and pure, unsullied by forbidden speech.

Midrash Tanchuma (*Mikeitz* §9) states: "One must rise early to pray, for there is nothing greater than *tefillah*." *Tanchuma* is exhorting us to ready ourselves properly before we *daven*. This can be accomplished through focusing our minds on the fact that we are about to address the King of kings and through studying Torah prior to *davening*. Of what value, however, can a *tefillah* have when it is preceded by idle chatter — or worse, by *lashon hara*?!

At the opening of *Pesukei D'Zimrah* we say: הֲרֵינִי מְזַמֵּן אֶת פִּי לְהוֹדוֹת וּלְהַלֵּל וּלְשַׁבֵּחַ אֶת בּוֹרְאִי, "I now prepare my mouth to thank, laud and praise my Creator." Before beginning to *daven* one should first ask himself, "Have I really prepared my mouth? With what have I prepared my mouth? With a glass of tea or cup of coffee?!" If one has engaged in idle chatter or worse and then begins to *daven*, dare he add yet another sin to his account by uttering a falsehood in declaring that his mouth is "readied" to laud his Creator? Only a person who is careful with regard to *shemiras halashon* (guarding one's tongue) can claim to live up to this declaration.[4]

Thus, the guarding of one's tongue is the first precondition for *tefillah* to be effective.

The second condition is that the words be enunciated clearly and distinctly.[5] Finally, a *tefillah* can be potent only when it is said with proper *kavanah*, concentration. It is not for us to pray with the Kabbalistic intents revealed by the *Arizal*. Simple concentration on *peirush hamilos* (the plain meaning of the text) is both required and sufficient. The words of *Nefesh HaChaim* (2:13) in this regard are noteworthy:

> As the Maggid told the Beis Yosef in the second admonition found at the opening of Maggid Meisharim[6]: "Be careful not to think any thought during tefillah — even with regard to Torah and mitzvos — other than the words of prayer themselves." Note that he did not say "the intent of the words themselves," for in truth, we have no inkling as to the depths of the inner meanings of the tefillos. For even the little which has been revealed to us by our supernal teachers — from the Rishonim of blessed memory, until the holy and awesome man of God, the Arizal . . . — is not even a drop in the sea in comparison to the deep kavanos [intended by] the composers of the tefillah, the Anshei K'nesses HaGedolah (Men of the Great Assembly) — one hundred and twenty elders among whom were many prophets. Any man of perception understands that there is not a soul on this earth [today] who could establish so awesome and wondrous an ordinance of prayer, one which encompasses and conceals within

---

4. HaRav Segal cited the words of R' Elimelech of Lyzhansk in his *Sefer Hanhagas HaAdam* (§9), that one should refrain from all conversation in a *beis haknesses* prior to *tefillah*.

5. See *Orach Chaim* 61:22. HaRav Segal frequently stresses to his *talmidim* that when reciting a *brachah* one should not slur the words מֶלֶךְ הָעוֹלָם so that they form one long meaningless מֶלְבָּעוֹלָם.

6. R' Yosef Karo (1504-1575), author of *Beis Yosef* and *Shulchan Aruch*, was for many years visited regularly by an angel (referred to as a *maggid*; i.e., *revealer*) who revealed to him secrets of the Torah. He recorded these revelations and they were eventually published as a *sefer* entitled *Maggid Meisharim*.

*it the sublimations of all the Upper and Lower Worlds.
Each time that we pray, perfections in the orders of the
Worlds are brought about ..."*

Thus, it is incumbent upon us to understand what we are saying
when we pray and to develop a feeling for the *tefillos*. Take, for
example, the second blessing of the *Shemoneh Esrei*: ... "He sustains
the living with kindness, resuscitates the dead with abundant mercy,
supports the fallen, heals the sick, releases the confined ..." These
declarations are the essence of *emunah*, faith, and reciting them
should infuse us with *emunah*; that is, if we recite them with proper
concentration.

Another case in point is that of *Bircas HaTorah*, the Blessings of
the Torah, that we recite every morning. With these blessings, we
offer thanks to Hashem for having given us the greatest gift all, for
without Torah our lives would be devoid of meaning, our existence
would be no more significant than that of beasts.

Is it proper, then, to recite these blessings while still half asleep,
swallowing the words in haste, with lips moving while one's mind is
elsewhere? One must recite *Bircas HaTorah* with a genuine feeling of
boundless gratitude to Hashem; only then has he discharged his
obligation in the desired manner.

In the *tefillah* of *Ahavah Rabbah (Ahavas Olam)* we ask: "Our
Father, merciful Father, Who acts Mercifully, have mercy upon us,
instill understanding in our hearts, to understand and elucidate,
teach, safeguard, perform and fulfill all the words of Your Torah's
teachings with love ..." One's success in Torah study and fulfillment
of all other *mitzvos* hinges on the proper recitation of this *tefillah*.

A *ben Torah* spends his waking hours totally immersed in Torah.
He struggles and strains to plumb the depths of the words he studies,
to find the solution to an obscure comment of *Rashi* or *Tosafos*.
Whether or not he will succeed may well be determined by how
much importance he attaches to *tefillah*.

ᴈ Yosef's Blessing

The Torah relates that following the death of Yaakov, the brothers grew fearful that Yosef would avenge their abduction and sale of him:

> Yosef's brothers perceived that their father was dead, and they said, "Perhaps Yosef will nurse hatred against us and then he will surely repay us all the evil that we did him." So they instructed that Yosef be told, "Your father gave orders before his death, saying, 'Thus shall you say to Yosef: O please, kindly forgive the spiteful deed of your brothers and their sin for they have done you evil; so now, please forgive the spiteful deed of the servants of your father's God.'" And Yosef wept when they spoke to him (50:15-17).

Da'as Zekeinim wonders why the brothers waited until after their father's death to convey the above to Yosef:

> Why did they not instruct [that Yosef be spoken to] during their father's lifetime? They reasoned, "Why should we awaken the hatred which is already gone and forgotten?" However, as they returned from burying their father, Yosef passed the pit into which they had cast him. He said: "Blessed is the One Who performed a miracle for me at this place." "Hatred is still hidden in his heart!" the brothers said. Immediately, they instructed that Yosef be spoken to.

Da'as Zekeinim's words demand clarification. In reciting a blessing near the pit, Yosef was doing that which is required of one who returns to a site where a miracle was wrought for him.[7] How did this indicate that Yosef bore his brothers ill will?

Let us imagine that someone had been miraculously rescued from bandits who aimed their weapons at him as they were about to take his life. How would an average person recite the required blessing when returning to the site of his rescue? It would probably depend on

---

7. See *Orach Chaim* 218:4.

how much time had elapsed from when the miracle had occurred. Immediately following his rescue when he could still sense the fright of being near death and the subsequent exhilaration of being freed, the man would no doubt offer praise of his Rescuer with fervor and emotion — as it should be. However, were he to pass the spot ten years later, the blessing would probably sound altogether different. Then, with the incident but a distant memory, the fervor and emotion would be gone.

From the time of the sale of Yosef until the death of Yaakov, thirty-nine years elapsed. Thirty-nine years after he had been abducted, Yosef passed the pit into which he had been cast and imagined himself once again at its bottom, surrounded by snakes and scorpions. He relived that episode and experienced again the feeling of boundless joy at being Divinely protected against all harm — and he offered his blessing on High. It was a blessing charged with emotion, *exactly* as it would have been pronounced thirty-nine years earlier. The brothers took note of the emotion with which Yosef recited the blessing. It was obvious that he was reliving what had occurred. They realized that the incident was by no means "gone and forgotten"; thus their fear.

May we merit that our *tefillos* be recited in the correct manner, with concentration and with feeling.

Kiddush Hashem

❧ Rachel's Sacrifice

K*iddush Hashem*, sanctification of Hashem's Name, can take on various forms. A most basic form of *kiddush Hashem* is when one perseveres in following the way of Torah at a time when his inclination is attempting to draw him in the very opposite direction, as is illustrated by two examples found in this *parashah*.

The first involves the famous episode in which the scheming Lavan substituted Leah for Rachel on what should have been Rachel's wedding night to Yaakov. Yaakov, recognizing that Lavan could not be trusted, had given Rachel a prearranged sign to insure that such a substitution would not take place. When Rachel saw that her father was indeed substituting Leah in her stead, she confided the sign to her sister so that Leah would not be put to shame.

In her selflessness, Rachel was giving up much more than an exceedingly righteous husband. She understood full well that Yaakov was heir to the spiritual legacy of Avraham and Yitzchak and that his progeny would be charged with carrying out Hashem's will in this world. In confiding the sign to Leah, unaware that in the end they would both marry Yaakov, Rachel was relinquishing to her sister the privilege of being mother to *Klal Yisrael*.

There is more. *Chazal (Bava Basra* 123a; see *Rashi* 18:17) relate that Leah's eyes were tender from excessive weeping, for people said that since Rivkah had two sons and her brother Lavan had two daughters, the elder daughter (Leah) would marry the elder son (Eisav), while the younger daughter (Rachel) would marry the younger son (Yaakov). By allowing Leah to marry Yaakov, Rachel was leaving open the possibility of her being forced to marry the wicked Eisav. Yet Rachel was not deterred by all this. In making her decision, Rachel saw before her one decisive factor — the tremendous shame that her sister would experience were Lavan's ruse to be revealed. The *Gemara* (*Berachos* 43b) states, "Better that a person let himself be hurled into a furnace rather than shame his friend in public." Rachel could not stand by silently and allow her sister to be shamed, whatever the personal sacrifice. Such behavior is the epitome of *kiddush Hashem*.[1]

⊷§ Reuven's Triumph

Rashi in this *parashah* (29:32) cites an Aggadic comment in which the sublime conduct of Reuven, son of Leah, is contrasted with the dismal behavior of Eisav. In both instances, the matter concerned the birthright. Eisav willingly sold the birthright to Yaakov (ch. 25). Reuven lost the birthright for having "defiled his father's couch" (see 35:22); as a result, the distinction of having his two sons achieve the status of *shevatim*, tribes, was transferred to Rachel's elder son, Yosef. The difference between the two is alluded to in the name רְאוּבֵן, Reuven, which *Chazal* (in one interpretation) see as a contraction of רְאוּ בֵּין, *see between*:

> Leah (prophetically) said: See the difference between my son and the son of my father-in-law [i.e., Yitzchak's son Eisav] who sold his birthright to Yaakov [voluntarily, yet later hated him for his superiority], whereas my son did not [voluntarily] sell his birthright to Yosef, but did not complain concerning his loss. Moreover, he even tried to rescue Yosef from the pit (Rashi based on Berachos 7b).

As the commentators explain, at the time of the sale of Yosef, the righteous sons of Yaakov judged their brother as halachically deserving of death. Even later, when they descended to Egypt to obtain food and their fortunes seemed to be plummeting, they

---

1. Rachel's selfless act is further discussed in the discourse to *Parashas Vayishlach*.

regretted only their callousness in having ignored Yosef's pleas of mercy, not their decision that he deserved to die.[2] Yet it was of Reuven that the Torah writes, "Reuven heard [his brothers' plan] and he rescued him [i.e., Yosef] from their hand. He said, 'We will not strike him mortally! ... Shed no blood! Throw him into the pit in the wilderness, but lay no hand on him!' — intending to rescue him from their hand, to return him to their father" (37:21-22).

Among the brothers, Reuven surely stood to gain the most from Yosef's demise, for with Rachel's first-born dead, the birthright might have reverted back to the eldest son of Leah. At the very least, one could understand if Reuven had felt a tinge of jealousy or hatred towards the one to whom the birthright had been transferred. To better appreciate Reuven's spiritual struggle, it is worthwhile to cite the words of *Mesilas Yesharim* (ch.11):

> It is exceedingly difficult for man's spiteful heart to be entirely free of hate and revenge, for man is extremely sensitive to insult and is deeply pained by it. Revenge is sweeter than honey, for that is the only thing that will put him at ease. [Being entirely free of such feelings] is easy only for ministering angels, in whom such traits do not exist.

Despite the difficulty, it is a Jew's obligation to strive to overcome all feelings of jealousy and hatred, no less than he is obligated to wear *tefillin* and observe the laws of *Kashrus*. Rambam in *Sefer HaMitzvos* (*lo sa'aseh* 317) writes:

> We are warned not to curse any Jew, as is written, "Do not curse the deaf" (Vayikra 19:14) ... For when a soul is aroused to extract vengeance from one who has caused it harm ... it does not cease until having responded with what it considers a reprisal commensurate with the damage that it has suffered ... Sometimes this takes the form of a curse or blasphemy ... other times, when a more grievous offense has been committed, the soul will not rest without having taken vengeance physically ... still other times, the soul will

---

2. See *Sforno* to 37:18.

not be put at ease until it has taken the life of the one that has caused it harm.

There are other times, however, when a soul is aroused in a small way to extract a vengeance that is [relatively] minor. It will put itself at ease with shouts and curses that are uttered when the individual is not present and cannot hear what is being said. It is a well-known fact that people who are bent towards anger calm their spirits in this manner when the grievance committed against them is minor in nature.

Lest we think that we are forbidden to curse a Jew only when he can hear the curse and is pained and wounded by it, but to curse the deaf who cannot hear and thus are not pained by the curse is not a sin, the Torah therefore warns us that this, too, is forbidden. For the Torah is not concerned solely with the one who is the object of the curse; rather, it is concerned also with the soul of he who utters the curse, cautioning him not to be bent toward vengeance or anger.

In *Yad HaChazakah* (*Hilchos Dei'os* 7:8), *Rambam* writes, "The Torah is exacting with regard to bearing a grudge, [requiring] that one erase the matter from his mind completely and not think about it at all."

For Reuven to seek to rescue Yosef at a time when the brothers found him deserving of death and had already decided to kill him (see 37:20), his heart had to have been free of even a tinge of personal animosity or jealousy toward Rachel's son. Thus was he able to think the matter through clearly, analyzing the situation in the light of the Torah that had been taught to him by his father Yaakov. Reuven was convinced that it was the will of Hashem that the brothers not kill Yosef and he acted accordingly. This — Reuven's personal triumph in allowing Torah and not his natural inclination to guide his actions — is another classic example of *kiddush Hashem*.

✍ Beyond the Letter of the Law

Yet another example of *kiddush Hashem*, one which is particularly relevant in our everyday lives, is related in the *Midrash* (*Devarim Rabbah* 3:3):

> It happened once that Shimon ben Shetach[3] bought a donkey from an Ishmaelite. His [i.e., Shimon's] students went and found a precious stone hanging from the donkey's neck. They said to him, "The blessing of Hashem — that is what enriches!" (*Mishlei* 10:22). Shimon ben Shetach replied, "I bought a donkey, I did not buy a stone." He went and returned the stone to the Ishmaelite, who declared, "Blessed is Hashem, the God of Shimon ben Shetach!"

Stealing from a gentile is clearly forbidden by *Halachah* (*Choshen Mishpat* 348:1), but one is not required to return that which was handed him, albeit unwittingly, by someone of another faith. In returning the stone, Shimon ben Shetach went beyond the strict requirements of *Halachah*. It is noteworthy to cite the words of *Be'er HaGolah* (ibid. 348:5) in this regard. He begins by quoting the words of *Shulchan Aruch* (ibid. 266:1), ". . . that if one returns a lost article to a gentile so that the name of Hashem be sanctified and so that they [i.e., the gentiles] will laud the Jewish People and know that they are men of good faith, then he is deemed praiseworthy."

Be'er HaGolah then comments:

> This applies as well to returning that which one received through an error on the part a gentile. I am writing this for all generations, for I have seen many who have become rich and powerful through benefiting by a gentile's error — but in the end they failed, as they lost all their wealth and left nothing behind (as is found in Sefer Chassidim, §1074).[4] And [I have seen] many

---

3. The leading Sage of his generation during the Second Temple era (see *Avos* 1:8).

4. *Sefer Chassidim's* words are: "One should not commit an iniquity [against his fellow], even against a gentile. These are matters which bring a person downward, causing him to see no success in his endeavors. If the moment is fortuitous for him, retribution will be exacted from his descendants."

who glorified Hashem's Name by returning such
money — sizable amounts — and then went on to
achieve success, becoming rich and powerful and
leaving much behind for their progeny.

There is no doubt as to what Shimon ben Shetach would have done with the stone had he kept it. Surely, he would have sold it and used the money to strengthen Torah study, thereby benefiting his entire generation. How noble a purpose! Shimon ben Shetach, however, realized that it was the will of Hashem that he return the stone, thereby bringing glory to Hashem, His Torah, and His people.

For the Ishmaelite would perceive this Jew's behavior to be a result of his internalizing the teachings of God's Torah, which obviously taught a morality of the highest standard. "Blessed is Hashem, the God of Shimon ben Shetach!"

There is another side to Shimon ben Shetach's deed. How was he able to perceive that which his students did not? What convinced him that the benefits in returning the stone outweighed the gains in keeping it? Shimon ben Shetach, leader of his generation, had freed himself of the urgings of his inclination. His heart was dictated solely by the will of Hashem. Such a heart has no difficulty perceiving the truth, for it is guided solely by truth.

Kiddush Hashem.

In the Merit of
Righteous Women[1]

⁓§ 'Restrain Your Voice from Weeping'

וַתָּמָת רָחֵל, וַתִּקָּבֵר בְּדֶרֶךְ אֶפְרָתָה הוּא בֵּית לָחֶם.

Rachel died, and she was buried on the way to Ephrath,
which is Bethlehem (35:19).

In this *parashah*, Rachel dies as Yaakov is returning to his parents' home after a long period of separation. She dies on the road and there she is laid to rest. Many years would pass before Yaakov would explain to Rachel's elder son Yosef why she had to be buried there:

> *Though I am troubling you to take me [after death] to be buried in the land of Canaan, I did not do this for your mother. For she died near Bethlehem and I did not even take her to Bethlehem . . . I realize that in your heart you have [a grievance] against me. You should know that it was through the word of Hashem that I buried her there, so that she will be a help for her children when Nevuzarradan will exile them [during the destruction of the first Beis HaMikdash] and they will pass by there. Rachel will come out above her grave and weep, begging for compassion for them, as is written, "A voice was heard on high — wailing, bitter weeping — Rachel*

---

1. This discourse is drawn from an address by HaRav Segal at a gathering for the benefit of the Bais Rochel girls school in Monsey, New York.

weeps for her children; she refuses to be consoled ...''
(Yirmiyahu 31:14). HaKadosh Baruch Hu will respond
to her (ibid. v. 15), "Restrain your voice from weeping
and your eyes from tears; for there is reward for your
accomplishment — the words of Hashem — and they
shall return from the enemy's land" (Rashi to Bereishis
48:7).

In its introduction to *Megillas Eichah, Midrash Rabbah* (§24) recounts Rachel's poignant plea before Hashem during the time of the Destruction. Her words were preceded by those of Avraham, Yitzchak and Yaakov who had been aroused by Moshe *Rabbeinu* to come with him to plea before Hashem on behalf of their descendants. Each one of them mentioned a personal source of merit as a way of arousing Heavenly compassion. Avraham cited his readiness to offer his son unto Hashem at the *Akeidah* (*Bereishis* ch. 22), while Yitzchak spoke of the joy with which he was prepared to die at that time. Yaakov recounted how he had reared his twelve righteous sons amid tribulation and suffering. Moshe, too, mentioned his own merit as the faithful shepherd of his people. All of this did not prove sufficient.

At that moment, our Matriarch Rachel came suddenly
before Hashem and said, "Ribono shel Olam: It is
plainly revealed before You that Your servant Yaakov
felt an exceptional love for me. He therefore worked for
my father seven years [for the right to marry me].
When those years were complete and the time for my
marriage arrived, my father schemed to exchange me
for my sister. The ruse became known to me and I
found it extremely upsetting. I therefore apprised my
designated husband of this and gave him a sign[2]
whereby he could distinguish between myself and my
sister so that my father would not be able to exchange
me.

"However, I later reconsidered my plan. I restrained
my desire [to marry Yaakov] and took pity on my
sister, lest she be shamed. In the evening, they

---

2. According to the *Gemara* (*Megillah* 13b), it was Yaakov who gave the signs to Rachel.

exchanged my sister for me. I gave over all the signs to her . . . I was not jealous of her. I did not permit her to be shamed.

"Now, if I, who was but flesh and blood, dust and ashes, was not jealous of my 'competitor' and did not bring about her shame and derision, then You, Who are living, eternal and compassionate — why have You taken vengeance over idol worshiping, which is of no substance, and exiled my children, allowing them to be killed by sword and permitting their enemies to do with them as they please?'

Hakadosh Baruch Hu's mercy was immediately aroused. He said, "Because of you, Rachel, I will return Bnei Yisrael to their Land." Thus it is written, "A voice was heard on high — wailing, bitter weeping — Rachel weeps for her children . . ."

How incredible! One single selfless act to save someone else from being shamed had the power to ensure the Jewish nation's eventual return from exile. "Better that a person let himself be hurled into a furnace rather than shame his friend in public" (*Berachos* 43b). One should take these words to heart and develop a proper sensitivity for the honor of his fellow. Concurrently, we must also instill in our children a desire to emulate our mother Rachel. The effect of such efforts cannot be underestimated, for as we have seen, it was this *midah tovah*, positive trait, more than anything else which aroused the Divine attribute of mercy at the time of the Destruction.

◈§ Proper Chinuch

Of course, proper *chinuch*, rearing, of our children encompasses far more than one *midah* alone. Above all, children must be infused with *yiras shamayim*, Heavenly fear. Understanding the gravity of sin, appreciating the value of a *mitzvah*, learning the importance of *mitzvos* between man and his fellow and the destructiveness of improper behavior towards others — all this comes under the heading of *yiras shamayim*.

It is a serious mistake to postpone imparting these lessons to one's children. As the Chofetz Chaim writes (*Shemiras HaLashon* 9:5), a parent is commanded to reprimand even his young children when they speak *lashon hara*.[3] Similarly, they should be taught the severity of lying, of taking the possessions of another, of anger, etc.

How vital it is for parents to ensure that their children study in a school where even secular studies are transmitted within a framework that is predicated on *yiras shamayim*. *Baruch Hashem*, our generation is blessed with thousands of religious young children, may they continue to multiply. The future of our nation hinges on their being given a proper *chinuch*.

◄§ The Daughters of Israel

When we speak of *chinuch*, we are referring also to the education of Jewish daughters. Proper *chinuch* of our daughters is crucial: for themselves, for the men whom they will one day marry, and for the homes that they will one day build. How beloved to Hashem is the one who instills *yiras shamayim* into the hearts of young Jewish girls!

I am a stranger here in America, but I am an old Jew, so therefore permit me to express something which I find particularly upsetting. During the past decade, it has become common practice for young

---

3. It is noteworthy to cite the Chofetz Chaim's footnote to that *halachah*:

"How much must a father strive to consistently guide his children from their youth in matters of *shemiras halashon* (as well as with regard to other forbidden speech such as lying and causing strife). As the *Gra* [*Gaon* R' Eliyahu of Vilna] writes, [proper] speech and *midos* require an abundance of reinforcement, for habit prevails in any given matter.

"In truth, when one ponders the matter well, he will discover that the cause for the breach in the grave sin of *lashon hara* is that people are accustomed from their youth to speaking whatever they please without any sort of reproof; it does not even enter their mind that they are doing something sinful. Therefore, when they are later made aware that this is, in fact, forbidden, they find it exceedingly difficult to avoid that to which they are already accustomed.

"Such would not be the case were a father to admonish his children in their youth, and train them not to speak *lashon hara* ..."

women here to embark on a career in the field of computers, though they are well suited to serve as teachers of *limudei kodesh*, Hebrew studies, to girls. Their intentions are praiseworthy. Teaching is not a well-paying profession, while computer programming is. These young women aspire to marry *bnei Torah* who they hope will be able to study in *kollel* for many years, supported by their earnings. Thus, a well-paying profession seems the obvious choice.

However, though their intentions are honorable, their thinking is misguided, for they are placing themselves in spiritual danger. I cannot understand how fathers can permit their daughters to work in offices other than those run by God-fearing Jews. How, in today's world of immorality, can one send his daughter to work in such places?! Who will they meet there? What will they see there?! They will become exposed to the negative influences that abound in today's society. How can anyone accept upon himself the responsibility of saying, "No harm will come to my daughter"?

As for the monetary considerations, one can never know what will be. Pharaoh intended to slaughter all Jewish boys when the astrologers told him that the redeemer of the Jews would soon be born. What happened in the end? Moshe *Rabbeinu*, the redeemer himself, grew up in the king's palace! "Many designs are in man's heart, but the counsel of Hashem — only it will prevail" (*Mishlei* 19:21).

On the other hand, it is wrong for us to demand of our young women that they expend great effort to educate our children while receiving poor recompense in return. *Mesiras nefesh*, self-sacrifice, is required of us as well. We must raise the salaries of our teachers so that the teaching profession will be financially attractive. Where will the funds come from? With proper resolve and a concerted effort, funds *can* be raised. Our lives are filled with daily miracles. The existence of many a Torah institution can be attributed only to miracles. By the rules of nature, they could never enjoy the enormous success and growth that we are witnessing. With proper resolve and *siyata dishmaya*, Divine assistance, the means for higher salaries will be found as well.

I close with a blessing, that of a simple Jew, that your daughters merit good health and long life, that they grow to become true righteous women, and that they merit to marry *talmidei chachamim* and give birth to children who will be a source of pleasure to the *Ribono shel Olam*.

The Jews were redeemed from Babylon in the merit of Rachel. The Redemption from Egypt occurred in the merit of righteous Jewish women (*Sotah* 11b). In the merit of the homes which the Jewish daughters of today will create, may we witness the arrival of *Mashiach*, speedily and in our days.

Spiritual Growth and the Light of Chanukah

⋙ Intents and Results

Parashas Vayeishev relates the narrative of Yosef, up to and including his languishing in prison after having been falsely accused by the wife of Potiphar, whose enticements to sin Yosef had resisted. The narrative is interrupted with the story of Yehudah and the righteous Tamar, who concealed her identity from Yehudah so that he would unknowingly live with her. Through their union, Peretz, who was the ancestor of David *HaMelech* and ultimately *Mashiach*, was born. *Rashi* (39:1, based on *Midrash Rabbah*) notes the juxtaposition of these two accounts and comments:

> *[They are juxtaposed] to teach that just as this one's [i.e., Tamar's] intent was for the sake of Heaven, so was the other's [i.e., Potiphar's wife's] intent for the sake of Heaven. She [i.e., Potiphar's wife] saw through her astrology that she was destined to establish descendants from Yosef, but she did not know whether it would be from her or from her daughter.*

It seems paradoxical that Potiphar's wife is said here to have acted for the sake of Heaven, when later she is referred to by *Rashi* as אוֹתָהּ אֲרוּרָה, *that accursed one*. In explaining the juxtaposition of the episode of Potiphar's wife and that of the dreams of the two chamberlains, *Rashi* (40:1) states:

Because that accursed one had accustomed everyone to speaking of the tzaddik [i.e. Yosef] and degrading him, HaKadosh Baruch Hu now brought about the offense of these [chamberlains] so that the people's attention should be diverted to them and away from him.

The answer to this apparent paradox lies in the conclusion of the respective episodes of Tamar and Potiphar's wife. In the case of Tamar, the death sentence was pronounced against her when it seemed obvious that she had sinned. Tamar's only hope at that point was to reveal the truth of Yehudah's involvement, but this she refused to do. Tamar was prepared to die in silence rather than humiliate someone else. Potiphar's wife acted in the very opposite manner. *She* was the guilty one, enticing Yosef day after day and finally forcing Yosef to flee from her house when she resorted to coercion. Concerned for her own honor, she slandered Yosef, thus bringing about the imprisonment of an innocent man.

How could someone whose intent was *lesheim shamayim,* for the sake of Heaven, behave this way? It is clear that though Potiphar's wife's original intentions were honorable, her behavior was eventually influenced by passion and self-interest. Her evil inclination misguided her thinking, causing her to resort to ploys that were dishonorable and even treacherous. When one's approach to a matter is influenced by his *yetzer hara,* then his original intentions, however noble, cannot endure. Thus, Potiphar's wife failed. Tamar, on the other hand, maintained her original pure intentions throughout. Her thoughts remained unsullied, totally free of any personal wants. Thus was she able to offer the ultimate sacrifice — her very life — when the situation warranted it. Her motives were purely *lesheim shamayim,* and therefore she succeeded.

The greater an individual's inherent or potential spiritual greatness, the more the *yetzer hara* seeks to destroy that spirituality, ר״ל. One should take special note of this susceptibility as we approach the *yom tov* of Chanukah, a time that is auspicious for spiritual growth, as we shall explain.

◆§ Exceedingly Precious

At the conclusion of *Hilchos Chanukah*, *Rambam* (4:12) writes:

> *The mitzvah of ner Chanukah (the Chanukah light) is exceedingly precious. One should be meticulous with regard to it, in order to make known the miracle and enhance the praise of God and thanksgiving to Him for the miracles that He wrought for us. Even one whose needs are provided from tzedakah should borrow or sell his garment in order to have oil and wicks with which to light.*

Rambam later adds that in case of extreme poverty, *ner chanukah* takes precedence over wine for the Shabbos *kiddush*, "... because it is a remembrance of the miracle." *Maggid Mishneh* (ibid.) writes that the source of *Rambam's* requirement that one must fulfill the *mitzvah* even if he is supported from *tzedakah* is the *mitzvah* of *arba kosos*, the four cups, on the *Seder* night, where an identical requirement is found. The common denominator between these two *mitzvos* is that both accomplish *pirsumei nisa*, the publicizing of the miracle which they respectively represent.

Publicizing a miracle leads to a keener awareness of the greatness of its Performer, which in turn inspires *hallel*, praise of Him, and a strengthening of one's *avodas Hashem*, service of Hashem. There is, however, another aspect of *pirsumei nisa*, as is evident from the *Gemara (Shabbos* 21b) and is implicit in *Rambam's* words. *Ner Chanukah*, *Rambam* writes, leads to הוֹדָיָה לוֹ עַל הַנִּסִּים שֶׁעָשָׂה לָנוּ, *thanksgiving to Him for the miracles that He wrought for us.* Kindling the Chanukah lights inspires one not only לְהַלֵּל, *to praise*, but also לְהוֹדוֹת, *to express thanks*. Chanukah is a time of *hakaras hatov*, recognition of Hashem's goodness. Thus does *Rambam* inform us that the *mitzvah* of *ner Chanukah* is חֲבִיבָה עַד מְאֹד, *exceedingly precious*.

In fact, *hakarah*, recognition, defines the very nature of Chanukah and is at the root of the great miracle which the *yom tov* commemorates.

ᐓᐧ Chanukah and Purim

Tur (*Hilchos Chanukah*, ch. 670), citing *Maharam of Rothenburg*, states: "The customary indulging in feasts on Chanukah is not obligatory, for they [i.e., *Chazal*] established these days as ones of הַלֵּל and הוֹדָאָה, *praise and thanksgiving*, and not מִשְׁתֶּה and שִׂמְחָה, *feasting and joy*."[1]

To this statement of *Tur*, *Bach* writes:

> *This is intrinsically difficult: Why did [Chazal] not establish these days for feasting, as with Purim? The resolution to this seems to be: With regard to Purim, the Heavenly decree [against the Jews] was issued primarily because they partook of his [i.e., Achashveirosh's] feast; therefore, it was decreed to slay and eradicate their bodies which had derived pleasure from forbidden eating, drinking, feasting and joy. When repenting, they afflicted themselves, as is written, "Go, assemble all the Jews to be found in Shushan, and fast for me. Do not eat or drink for three days, night or day . . ." (Esther 4:16). Therefore [Purim] was established for מִשְׁתֶּה and יוֹם טוֹב, feasting and holiday-making, in order to commemorate the essence of the miracle. With regard to Chanukah, however, the Heavenly decree was issued essentially because they became weak in their Divine service. Therefore, it was decreed that their service be abolished. As the braisa relates, Antiochus decreed that the Tamid service cease. In addition, he told [his officers], "There is one mitzvah which they possess, the nature of which is, that if you abolish it, then they are immediately lost." Which [mitzvah] is this? The kindling of the [Temple] menorah, of which it is written: לְהַעֲלוֹת נֵר תָּמִיד, "to bring up [i.e., to kindle] a constant flame" — so long as they kindle it, they constantly remain erect . . .*
>
> *They then went and defiled all the oil. When the Jews*

---

1. See *Orach Chaim* 670:2.

repented and risked their lives for the service, Hashem saved them through the Kohanim, those who performed the service in the House of Hashem.

Therefore, the miracle too was done with the lamps of the menorah, for they had risked their lives for the sake of upholding the service. Thus was the festival established only to offer praise and thanksgiving, a service of the heart.

Chanukah is an entire chain of הַכָּרוֹת, *recognitions*. The *Ribono shel Olam* took note that *Klal Yisrael* had failed in their service of Him. He punished them measure for measure by bringing about the abolishment of the service in the *Beis HaMikdash* and permitting the Syrian-Greeks to forbid the practice of certain *mitzvos*. Recognizing their own iniquities as the real source of their suffering, the Jews responded by risking their lives to observe *mitzvos* that Antiochus had declared capital offenses. Hashem, in turn, brought about their miraculous salvation through the *Kohanim* who performed the Temple service, and He wrought a miracle through the very service which Antiochus understood as being crucial to the survival of the Jewish nation. All this is reflected in the *hallel* and *hoda'ah* that is Chanukah's essence.[2]

⤳ Means of Expression

We now understand that Chanukah is a festival of recognition, and that the requirement of *hoda'ah* during these days demands that we express our gratitude to Hashem for the many miracles He

---

2. In this context, HaRav Segal cited *Rabbeinu Yonah's* comment (*Sha'arei Teshuvah* ch. 2) that when Divine retribution is meted out, it serves both as an atonement and as a means of awakening the person to repentance. That Divine punishment is administered *midah k'neged midah*, measure for measure, is a great kindness of Hashem, since the form of punishment indicates the corresponding sin for which the sinner must repent.

It is in this vein that *Sefer HaIkrim* interprets the verse וּלְךָ ה' חָסֶד כִּי אַתָּה תְשַׁלֵּם לְאִישׁ כְּמַעֲשֵׂהוּ, "And Yours, my Lord, is kindness, for You pay each man in accordance with his deeds." The חֶסֶד, *kindness*, to which the verse refers is Hashem's way of punishing [i.e., "paying"] each person in a manner that corresponds to his negative needs and allows him to recognize his follies.

wrought. How does one express his gratitude to Hashem? Can one even begin to show gratitude to Him?

True *hoda'ah* to Hashem is more than mere verbal thanks. A Jew shows his appreciation to his Creator by applying himself toward observance of His *mitzvos* with renewed zeal and strength. As one grows spiritually, he must be ever mindful that his noble intentions not be corrupted by the *yetzer hara's* own devious schemes. In our approach to service of Hashem, let us emulate the righteous Tamar who never wavered from fulfilling the Divine will. If we succeed, then we will have truly expressed our *hakaras hatov* to the One Above.

Times of Opportunity

הִנֵּה שֶׁבַע שָׁנִים בָּאוֹת, שָׂבָע גָּדוֹל בְּכָל אֶרֶץ מִצְרָיִם. וְקָמוּ שֶׁבַע
שְׁנֵי רָעָב אַחֲרֵיהֶן, וְנִשְׁכַּח כָּל הַשָּׂבָע בְּאֶרֶץ מִצְרָיִם; וְכִלָּה הָרָעָב
אֶת הָאָרֶץ . . .
וְעַתָּה יֵרֶא פַרְעֹה אִישׁ נָבוֹן וְחָכָם, וִישִׁיתֵהוּ עַל אֶרֶץ מִצְרָיִם . . .
וְיִקְבְּצוּ אֶת כָּל אֹכֶל הַשָּׁנִים הַטֹּבוֹת הַבָּאֹת הָאֵלֶּה . . . וְהָיָה הָאֹכֶל
לְפִקָּדוֹן לָאָרֶץ לְשֶׁבַע שְׁנֵי הָרָעָב אֲשֶׁר תִּהְיֶיןָ בְּאֶרֶץ מִצְרָיִם, וְלֹא
תִכָּרֵת הָאָרֶץ בָּרָעָב.

*Behold! seven years are coming — a great abundance
throughout all the land of Egypt. Then seven years of
famine will arise after them, and all the abundance in
the land of Egypt will be forgotten. The famine will
ravage the land . . .*

*Now let Pharaoh seek out a discerning and wise man
and set him over the land of Egypt . . . And let them
gather the food of all those approaching good years . . .
The food will be a reserve for the land against the seven
years of famine which will befall the land of Egypt, so
that the land will not perish in the famine (41:29-36).*

↞§ Yosef's Message

The opening of this *parashah* relates how Hashem, using Pharaoh
and his dreams as vehicles, brought about the ascendancy of
Yosef from prisoner to viceroy of Egypt. Particularly striking is the

manner in which Yosef spoke to Pharaoh upon being brought before the king for the first time to interpret his dreams. No less than five times does Yosef underscore to the heathen king that all is from Hashem:

> Yosef answered Pharaoh, saying, "That is beyond me. It is Elokim Who will respond with Pharaoh's welfare" (41:16). "The dream of Pharaoh is a single one. What Elokim is about to do He has told to Pharaoh" (41:25). "It is the matter that I have spoken to Pharaoh: What Elokim is about to do He has shown to Pharaoh" (41:28). "As for the repetition of the dream to Pharaoh twice, it is because the matter stands ready before Elokim and Elokim is hastening to accomplish it" (41:32).

We would expect that such talk be directed to someone who possessed some degree of Heavenly awe, or who could at least be inclined toward such awe. It would seem, though, that invoking the name of Hashem when speaking to Pharaoh would achieve little, if anything. Egypt was a place steeped in idol worship and immorality; all the greatness that Pharaoh was later to see in Yosef, his father, and brothers would not sway the king from his heathen doctrines.[1] Would it not have sufficed for Yosef to state once that the dream and its interpretation were Divinely ordained? What did Yosef hope to accomplish in speaking of Hashem again and again?

With this precise recounting of Yosef's words to Pharaoh, the Torah is revealing a deeper message in Yosef's interpretation and subsequent advice. It is a message directed not at Pharaoh, but at ourselves. Yosef's frequent mention of אֱלֹקִים, Elokim, as the Source of the dream and what it foretold, conveys the timelessness of his words; for a situation and solution that is Divinely ordained serves as a lesson for all time. Let us understand this lesson.

Yosef informed Pharaoh that his dreams foretold the approach of שְׁנֵי הַשָּׂבָע, the years of abundance, which would be followed by שְׁנֵי

---

1. Pharaoh later revealed his true measure when he attempted to have Yosef break a solemn oath he had made to his father Yaakov that he would ensure his burial in the Cave of Machpelah (see Rashi to 50:6). According to one opinion (Sotah 11a), this was the very same Pharaoh who would later declare (Shemos 5:2): "Who is Hashem that I should listen to His voice?! I do not know Hashem and I also will not send out the Israelites!"

הָרָעָב, *the years of famine*. Yosef advised that the years of abundance be spent gathering and storing food so that the land would survive the time when absolutely nothing would grow. In short, the time of abundant production should be spent preparing for the time of no production.

This lesson can be applied to a person's life in a variety of ways.

◄§ World of Opportunity

In the opening chapter of *Mesilas Yesharim*, R' Moshe Chaim Luzzato writes:

> *Our Sages of blessed memory have taught us that man was created solely to delight in [closeness to] God and to derive pleasure from the splendor of His presence, for this is the quintessential delight, the greatest pleasure that is to be found. The place where this pleasure may be derived is actually the World to Come, which was created with the prerequisites that are needed for this. However, the pathway to reach this place of our desire is this world, as our Sages of blessed memory said (Avos 4:21): "This world is like a corridor to the World to Come."*
>
> *The means which bring man to this goal are the mitzvos regarding which God, Blessed is His Name, has commanded us. The only place where these mitzvos can be performed is this world.*

It is related that shortly before his death, the Vilna *Gaon* grabbed hold of his *tzitzis* and burst into tears, saying, "Through observing the *mitzvah* of *tzitzis*, one can merit to bask in the glory of the *Shechinah* (Divine Presence). In this world, the *mitzvah* of *tzitzis* can be obtained for a little bit of money. In the next world, it cannot be obtained at all." The *Gaon* had countless numbers of good deeds to his credit. Yet he cried, for he understood that is there no end to accumulating *mitzvos*. Every additional *mitzvah* means that much more הֲנָאַת זִיו הַשְּׁכִינָה, *pleasure from the splendor of the Shechinah*, in the Next World.

Thus are our days in this world יְמֵי הַשָּׂבָע, *days of abundance*, when one has unlimited opportunity to gather and store abundant merits for the יְמֵי הָרָעָב, *days of famine*, of the future when this opportunity will be no more. Every Jew should emulate Yosef by being an אִישׁ נָבוֹן וְחָכָם, *a discerning and wise man* (41:33), and make the most of the precious years that he is allotted on this earth.

⊷§ Moments of Opportunity

R ambam, in *Hilchos Berachos* (1:1), writes:

> *It is a positive Torah commandment to recite a blessing after eating a meal ... The Sages decreed that one should recite a blessing over every food and only then partake of it ... They also decreed that one recite a blessing after all eating and drinking ...*
>
> *In the same way that one must recite a blessing when deriving pleasure, so must he recite a blessing before doing any mitzvah, and only then should he perform it. The Sages also established many blessings in the way of praise and thanksgiving and in the manner of supplication, even when not deriving pleasure or performing a mitzvah, so that one be ever cognizant of his Creator.*
>
> *Thus, all blessings can be divided into three categories: blessings of pleasure; blessings of mitzvos; and blessings of ... praise, thanksgiving, and supplication, so that one be ever cognizant of his Creator and be fearful of Him.*

That the blessings established by *Chazal* are actually a means of acquiring *yiras shamayim*, Heavenly fear, is expressed in a Talmudic passage. "R' Meir said: A person is obligated to recite one hundred blessings each day, as is written (*Devarim* 10:12): וְעַתָּה יִשְׂרָאֵל מָה ה' אֱלֹקֶיךָ שֹׁאֵל מֵעִמָּךְ [כִּי אִם לְיִרְאָה אֶת ה' ...], "And now, Israel, what does Hashem your God ask of you? [Only that you fear Hashem ...]" (*Menachos* 43b). *Rashi* (ibid.) understands this teaching as derived from the word מָה, *what*, which is homiletically read as מֵאָה, *one hundred*. The verse would then be saying, "One hundred [blessings] is what Hashem your God asks of you, so that you fear Hashem ..."

Through the course of a day, one often comes upon moments of 'famine,' when his spiritual strength is strained and he is need of chizuk, spiritual support, to overcome the trials of the hour. How one has utilized his moments of 'abundance' will spell the difference between success or failure during rough times, for it is the moments of שָׂבָע that must fuel those of רָעָב. As we have seen, the daily recitation of one hundred blessings is meant to instill in us awe of Hashem, and, as Rambam said, should cause us to be ever cognizant of Him.

The three daily tefillos are prime sources of daily spiritual sustenance. In fact, Kuzari compares the tefillos to the three daily meals; in the same way that each meal provides a person with the necessary nourishment to sustain him until the next meal, each tefillah provides one with the necessary spiritual strength until the time for the next tefillah has arrived. Of course, this is only said for one whose tefillos are recited in the proper manner, particularly with regard to kavanah, concentration.

⋖§ Years of Opportunity

In truth, one's life in this world can be sub-divided into שְׁנֵי הַשָּׂבָע and שְׁנֵי הָרָעָב. It is a minority of bnei Torah who merit dedicating their entire lives to the full-time study and dissemination of Torah; the majority eventually enter various professions. The yeshivah years are the שְׁנֵי הַשָּׂבָע which must sustain one throughout the שְׁנֵי הָרָעָב to follow. A true ben Torah will always remain just that, setting aside time for Torah study each day and making Torah and mitzvos the focus around which his life revolves. However, the degree to which he will dedicate his life in this manner will largely depend on how well his years in yeshivah were spent. It is therefore vital that every ben Torah make the most of his yeshivah years, immersing himself in the full-time pursuit of spiritual achievement to the exclusion of all else. One must study with hasmadah, diligence, and ameilus, intense toil, as he strives to attain a proficiency in learning that will make him deserving of the title talmid chacham.

And he must do more. During his yeshivah years, a ben Torah must expend much effort toward refining his midos and acquiring yiras shamayim. Someone who takes leave of his yeshivah years having attained proficiency in Torah study but lacking in yiras *shamayim* will see his knowledge dissipate with the passage of time. He will surely not succeed in increasing his proficiency in study and he will likewise not have the ability to withstand the trials of life. Without *yiras shamayim*, one cannot possibly hold on to the Torah knowledge that he has acquired — but he may, God forbid, plummet to the level of a low, corrupt person, literally.

A world of opportunity. Moments of opportunity. Years of opportunity. May we be counted among those who make the most of their lives.

Roots of Greatness

וַיֹּאמֶר יוֹסֵף אֶל אֶחָיו אֲנִי יוֹסֵף.
And Yosef said to his brothers, "I am Yosef" (45:3).

Yosef's dramatic revelation to his brothers spelled the end of the long, painful saga that had begun when he was sold twenty-two years earlier. The term "revelation" is particularly appropriate here, for Yosef's decision to make his identity known at that point and the words which followed reveal much about his own lofty spirituality.

❧ For His Brothers' Sake

וְלֹא יָכֹל יוֹסֵף לְהִתְאַפֵּק לְכֹל הַנִּצָּבִים עָלָיו, וַיִּקְרָא: הוֹצִיאוּ כָל
אִישׁ מֵעָלָי; וְלֹא עָמַד אִישׁ אִתּוֹ בְּהִתְוַדַּע יוֹסֵף אֶל אֶחָיו.
Now Yosef could not restrain himself before all those that stood by him, so he called out, "Make everyone withdraw from me!" Thus no one remained with him when Yosef made himself known to his brothers (ibid. v. 1).

The words וְלֹא יָכֹל יוֹסֵף לְהִתְאַפֵּק are explained variously by the commentators. According to one opinion, Yosef is portrayed here as being unable to control his emotions following Yehudah's moving appeal to him. Yehudah had ended his speech by speaking of the untold anguish that his father Yaakov would experience were the brothers to return home without Binyamin, who was then Yaakov's only link to the family of Rachel. "... *If I come to your servant my father, and the youth is not with us — and his soul is so bound up with his soul — ...When he sees the youth is missing he will die...*" Hearing these words, Yosef could no longer restrain himself from revealing his true identity.

As for why Yosef commanded that his attendants leave the room prior to his revelation, *Rashi* explains that he could not bear for the Egyptians to witness his brothers' shame when he made himself known to them. The *Midrash* relates that Yosef risked great danger by remaining alone with his brothers.

Yosef knew full well that upon learning his true identity, the brothers would fear that he intended to avenge their sale of him. His behavior up until that point seemed to point to such a conclusion. He had accused them of being spies, imprisoned Shimon, and planted his prized cup in Binyamin's sack as a pretext for forcing his return to Egypt. These actions had baffled the brothers, for they could not understand why the viceroy bore them any ill will. Once Yosef would reveal himself, his actions until that point could easily be interpreted as motivated by revenge. The brothers might have further reasoned that Yosef planned to kill them, and they might have attempted to kill him in self-defense.

Yosef understood that he might be killed. He realized that the reunion with his father for which he had yearned so long might never occur. Can we begin to imagine the depth of Yosef's yearning to see his father? Yet, to Yosef's mind, all this was not as important as was avoiding a situation that might bring additional shame to his brothers — the same brothers who had initiated his suffering of the last twenty-two years. Yosef therefore told himself, "Better I should die than that my brothers be shamed before the Egyptians" (*Midrash Tanchuma* §5).

That Yosef responded at that awesome moment in the way that he did is proof not only of his exceptional character, but of his powerful *emunah*, faith, as well. Only someone whose *emunah* permeated the very depths of his soul could have acted in such a manner.

✺ Reconciliation

Yosef's words of reconciliation to his brothers are replete with illustrations of his rock-firm *emunah*. Better said, Yosef's speech was uttered in the language of *emunah*:

> And now, be not distressed, nor reproach yourselves for having sold me here, for it was as a source of sustenance that Hashem sent me before you (45:5).

"Do not be distressed, just as I am not distressed. All is from Hashem, all is through *hashgachah pratis*, exacting Divine Providence!"

> Hashem sent me ahead of you to insure your survival in the land and to sustain you for a momentous deliverance (ibid. v. 7).

"True, my rise from rags to royalty came about through my interpretation of the king's dream. I am fully aware, though, that my interpretations were Divinely inspired. I take credit for nothing."

> And now: it was not you who sent me here, but Hashem (ibid. v. 8).

"Now that Hashem's plan has become apparent, it is obvious that it was not you who sent me here but He. You were acting only as His instruments — and accordingly, I harbor absolutely no hatred toward you."

> Hurry — go up to my father and say to him, "So said your son Yosef: 'Hashem has made me master of all Egypt. Come down to me please, do not delay' " (ibid. v. 9).

"Tell my father the following words of consolation: 'During our long separation, Hashem set in motion a chain of events which has brought me to be ruler over Egypt — so that I will be able to provide for you and your family when you will join me here.' "

When the brothers returned to Canaan and informed Yaakov,

"Yosef is still alive" (ibid. v. 26), their father at first did not believe the incredible tidings. "However, when they related to him all the words that Yosef had spoken to them, and he saw the wagons that Yosef had sent to transport him[1], then the spirit of their father Yaakov was revived" (v. 27). We may suggest that the דִּבְרֵי יוֹסֵף, *words of Yosef*, which Yaakov accepted and which revived his mournful spirit, were the words of *emunah* that Yosef had continuously spoken. The brothers informed their father that the viceroy who had treated them in so strange a manner *had* to be his long-lost son, for he spoke with a faith and trust in the One Above that could exist only in someone who had grown up in Yaakov's home.

This last point is of prime significance, as we shall see.

❧ The Source

To fully appreciate the greatness of Yosef *HaTzaddik*, as he is referred to by *Chazal*, one must contemplate the trials that this son of Yaakov endured. At age seventeen, he was separated from his father's house and cast into an atmosphere that was the very opposite of that which he had previously known. First, he served in the house of Potiphar where immorality and idol worship were the order of the day. Then, he was thrown into prison where he languished for twelve years. What could Yosef have seen among the convicts of a land that our Sages say was steeped in immorality? What do murderers, thieves, and other criminals speak of as they serve time together for their crimes against humanity? Do they perhaps study *mussar*?! And what of their overlords? In such circles, the more prominent the position, the greater the degree of moral decadence. For twelve years, Yosef lived amid such debasement. Yet, he remained Yosef *HaTzaddik*, unaffected by the goings-on around him and the tests which confronted him. His *emunah* remained rock-firm, his conversation replete with an unfailing awareness of Divine Providence. His *midos* were still finely tuned, and he maintained an incredible sensitivity towards the feelings of others.[2]

---

1. *Rashi* (47:21) explains the significance of these wagons.

2. HaRav Segal added that Yosef also maintained a refined manner of speech. To his

Whence did Yosef draw such spiritual might? All this was the result of the *chinuch* (upbringing) that he received in his father's home. In the first seventeen years of his life, Yosef drew bountifully from the spiritual light of Yaakov *Avinu*. He became saturated with his father's *emunah*, an *emunah* that enabled Yaakov to overcome the many travails that he himself lived through. Yosef basked in the glory of his father's behavior towards others, in the shine of the scintillating *midos* which were the trademark of the Patriarchs. Only with such an upbringing was Yosef able to withstand the enormous tests that he later faced.

In today's world, a Jew is forever confronted with tests. The forces of evil are powerful, while Torah ideals are openly rejected and even ridiculed. It is crucial that parents infuse their children with *emunah* and *bitachon*, with an outlook on life that is in absolute accordance with Torah, and with the *midos* that are to be expected of a nation of Torah. Then, our children will be prepared to face the tests of life, and triumph — in the way of Yosef *HaTzaddik*.

---

brothers, he said, "... for it was as a source of sustenance that Hashem sent me before you ... to insure your survival ... and to sustain you" (vs. 5-7). However, when instructing his brothers to tell their father to descend to Egypt, Yosef expressed himself more mildly. "And I will provide for you there ... so you do not become impoverished ..." (v. 11) [see *Ramban*].

Light in the Darkness

◄§ And Yaakov Lived

וַיְחִי יַעֲקֹב בְּאֶרֶץ מִצְרַיִם שְׁבַע עֶשְׂרֵה שָׁנָה.

And Yaakov lived in the land of Egypt seventeen years (47:28).

Rashi (citing *Midrash* and *Zohar*) notes that this *parashah* is unique in that it is סְתוּמָה, *closed*, meaning that in a Torah scroll it is separated from the previous *parashah* by only a one-letter space.

S'fas Emes explains this by interpreting the term וַיְחִי, *And he lived*, in a spiritual sense: Yaakov lived a heightened form of living in the land of Egypt, concealing within it a radiance of *kedushah*, holiness, that would allow his progeny to remain holy and upright even in exile. This *kedushah* was סְתוּמָה, closed off and concealed, not readily discernible to someone who was unwilling to shed the external trappings of his *galus* existence and search for a higher form of existence. But it was there for all who sought to uncover it.

To what degree this *kedushah* was manifest during the two-hundred-and-ten-year Egyptian exile can be seen from an incident that occurred during *Bnei Yisrael's* forty-year sojourn in the Wilderness. A man born from a Jewish mother and Egyptian father blasphemed the name of Hashem, ר״ל. The Torah relates: "His mother's name was Shelomis the daughter of Divri, from the tribe of Dan" (*Vayikra* 24:11). *Rashi* comments that in stating this fact, the Torah is telling us the praise of the Jewish Nation, namely, that during the many years of the Egyptian exile no other Jew committed an act of immorality. *Rashi* further states that the woman's name alludes to the habits which led to her sinful act:

> שְׁלוֹמִית, *Shelomis* — *She would prattle, "Peace* (שָׁלָם) *unto you. Peace unto you. Peace unto all of you!"*
> בַּת־דִּבְרִי, *Daughter of Divri* — *She was talkative* (דַבְרָנִית הָיְתָה); *she talked with every man. Therefore she sinned.*

In relating who this woman was, the Torah is informing us that no other woman had even been guilty of breaching the barriers of *tznius*, modesty, by chatting with other men. Only Shelomis, whose name alludes to her wayward behavior, was guilty of such conduct.[1]

This was the level of *kedushah* which the Jews maintained throughout two hundred and ten years of persecution and suffering! The strength for so high a level of sanctity found its source in the seventeen years of 'living' which Yaakov bequeathed to his progeny.[2]

৵§ His Best Years

We may further suggest that וַיְחִי, *And he lived*, indicates that Yaakov *Avinu's* years in Egypt were the best years of his life, better than those spent in the academies of Shem and Ever and better than those spent in the home of his father Yitzchak. Of course, 'best' is to be understood in a spiritual sense. It was in Egypt that Yaakov attained his greatest spiritual heights.[3]

---

1. It should be noted that according to the *Midrash* (see *Rashi* to *Shemos* 2:11), Shelomis sinned unwittingly, as the Egyptian had entered her home in the darkness of night and posed as her husband. However, (as *Rashi* there states) the Egyptian's having "set his eyes upon her" by day precipitated his ruse. Shelomis is faulted for having behaved in a manner that attracted the Egyptian's attention.

2. The *Midrash* states that the Jews' having remained pure of immorality in Egypt was also due to the *kedushah* bequeathed to them by Yosef when he overcame the trials involving the wife of Potiphar (see discourse to *Parashas Vayeishev*).

3. *Tanna d'Vei Eliyahu* writes that these years were for Yaakov מֵעֵין עוֹלָם הַבָּא, *a semblance of the World to Come.*

A number of factors account for this, one being the events that immediately preceded Yaakov's arrival in Egypt. For twenty-two years he had mourned over his precious son Yosef, believing him to be dead. During those years, *Ruach HaKodesh*, the Divine Spirit, which is manifest only upon one who is in a state of joy, did not rest upon Yaakov. Finally, the brothers returned from Egypt with the incredible news: עוֹד יוֹסֵף חַי, "Yosef still lives!" (45:26). The Torah then relates: וַתְּחִי רוּחַ יַעֲקֹב אֲבִיהֶם, "And the spirit of their father Yaakov was revived" (v. 27). Yaakov was once again in a state of joy, and with that joy, his *Ruach HaKodesh* returned.

Human nature is such that when a person comes upon something precious after having been deprived of it for a period of time, he clings to it with a heightened degree of affection. When Yaakov felt his soul becoming bound up once again with the Divine Spirit, after a separation of so many years, his soul became ignited with spiritual desire and he soared to heights that he had never before reached. Thus was he able to attain new levels of spirituality while surrounded by the moral decadence of Egypt.

As we have already seen, Yaakov's achievements made it possible for his offspring to emerge from that bitter exile without having fallen prey to the immorality for which the Egyptians were known. Yaakov knew full well that how he lived his years in Egypt would have a great bearing on the spiritual well-being of his descendants. This awareness spurred him on to ever higher levels of spirituality.

❧ For All Generations

Ramban, in *Parashas Lech Lecha*, states the well-known principle of מַעֲשֵׂה אָבוֹת סִימָן לְבָנִים, "The deeds of the Patriarchs are a portent for their descendants." The deeds of Avraham, Yitzchak and Yaakov were of a cosmic nature, symbolizing and having a bearing on events that would transpire generations later. Yaakov's years in Egypt had an effect not only on that exile, but on the four succeeding exiles as well. *S'fas Emes* writes that the *kedushah* which Yaakov 'concealed' during his years in Egypt is there to this very day, and can be 'revealed' by anyone who seeks to uncover it.

Before beginning his journey to Egypt, Yaakov sent Yehudah ahead of the rest of the family. *Rashi* (46:28 citing *Midrash*) says that Yehudah was sent to establish a house of study from which the teaching of Torah would go forth.[4] Yaakov saw a Torah center as being so vital to his family that it had to already be established and functioning when he would arrive in Egypt. Here, Yaakov was setting an example for all generations. The primary building in any new settlement is a Torah center, for without Torah, we cannot survive as a nation of God.

The book of *Shemos* begins with the enumeration of the twelve sons of Yaakov. *Rashi* (*Shemos* 1:1) notes the fact that the tribes had already been listed in *Parashas Vayigash* when all seventy members of Yaakov's family were enumerated:

> *Even though He counted them by name during their lifetime, He counted them again after their death, to make known His love for them. For they are likened to the stars which He takes out and brings in by number and by name, as is written, "He brings out their hosts by number, He calls them all by name" (Yeshayahu 40:26).*

The likening of the sons of Yaakov — and all Jews, for that matter — to stars can be explained as follows: Just as a star gives off light in the darkness, so does every Jew have within him the ability to bring spiritual light to the darkness of *galus*. This ability, unique to *Bnei Yisrael*, is indicative of the great love that exists between Hashem and His chosen people.

---

4. To quote *Midrash Tanchuma:* [He sent Yehudah ahead] to prepare a study house from which Yaakov would teach Torah, and where the *shevatim* (Tribal ancestors) would study Torah ... for it is known that the Patriarchs studied the Torah before it was given.

שמות
Sh'mos

Kindness — the Torah Way

◄§ The Midwives' Heroism

וַתִּירֶאןָ הַמְיַלְּדֹת אֶת הָאֱלֹקִים וְלֹא עָשׂוּ כַּאֲשֶׁר דִּבֶּר אֲלֵיהֶן מֶלֶךְ מִצְרָיִם; וַתְּחַיֶּיןָ אֶת הַיְלָדִים.

But the midwives feared God and they did not do as the king of Egypt had instructed them; rather, they kept the children alive (1:17).

As the bondage of *Bnei Yisrael* in Egypt intensified, Pharaoh ordered the Jewish midwives to murder every newborn Jewish boy. The midwives, who our Sages tell us were Yocheved the mother of Moshe *Rabbeinu* and his sister Miriam, ignored the king's orders. Not only did they allow the infants to live, they even went so far as to provide them with food and water (see *Rashi* ibid.).

The heroic behavior of Yocheved and Miriam is surely a classic illustration of *mesiras nefesh*, self-sacrifice. The persecution of Israel was by that time severe. "A new king arose ... and said, 'Come, let us deal wisely with them, lest they increase ...' They set over them taskmasters in order to afflict them with their burdens ... They made their lives bitter with mortar and bricks ..." (1:8-14). Then came the decree to murder the infant boys. Ignoring a king's command is a great risk in any situation, let alone amid the climate that then existed. Yocheved and Miriam were equal to the challenge.

In telling of their heroism, the Torah makes a point of relating that which inspired their behavior. "But the midwives feared God." Their self-sacrifice did not stem from an innate compassion which would not allow them to carry out the brutal genocide of infants in order to save their own lives. Rather, their deeds were rooted in pure, lofty *yiras shamayim*, Heavenly awe. Their recognition of Hashem was so deep, their awe of Him so penetrating, that they much preferred to die rather than do that which was obviously the antithesis of His will.

⊷§ Their Reward

Further on, the *parashah* tells of the midwives' Divine reward. The Torah makes clear that their reward was not so much for their deeds as for the *yiras shamayim* which motivated them. "And it came to pass, because the midwives feared God, that He made for them houses" (v. 21). *Rashi* (quoting *Sotah* 11b) writes that these 'houses' were בָּתֵּי כְהֻנָּה וּלְוִיָּה וּמַלְכוּת, *houses of priesthood, of Levites, and of royalty.* From Yocheved descended *Kohanim* and *Levi'im*, while Miriam was mother to the Davidic dynasty.

There is an obvious *midah k'neged midah* (measure for measure) relationship between these rewards and their cause, for the respective roles of *Kohanim*, *Levi'im* and Jewish kings are inextricably bound with *yiras shamayim*. A primary mission of *Kohanim* and *Levi'im* is to spread Torah and fear of Hashem among the masses. In his blessing to the tribe of Levi, Moshe declared, "They will teach Your law to Yaakov and Your Torah to Yisrael" (*Devarim* 33:9). Generations later, the last of the prophets, Malachi, said, "For the lips of the *Kohen* will safeguard knowledge and they will seek Torah from his mouth, for he is an angel of Hashem, the Master of Legions" (*Malachi* 2:7).

A Jewish king is commanded to write a *sefer Torah* which is to accompany him wherever he goes. "And it shall be with him, and he will read from it all the days of his life, so that he will learn to fear Hashem his God, to safeguard all the words of this law and of these statutes, to execute them" (*Devarim* 17:19). The *sefer Torah* is a constant reminder to the king of his role as emissary of the King of kings. He is to be a living embodiment of Torah, uplifted by its statutes and inherent holiness, and he is to use the power of the throne not for personal gain, but to spread fear of Hashem and respect for His word.

⋖ Of a Different Sort

Thus we see that Yocheved and Miriam were repaid for their *yiras shamayim* with descendants who embodied and spread true *yiras shamayim*. In analyzing the magnanimous deeds of these women, we should note that kindness which is motivated by *yiras shamayim* is not the same as that which stems from a natural tendency toward compassion.[1] When one acts according to his natural tendencies, he does only so much as those tendencies dictate, often falling short of assisting his fellow in the best possible way. Not so the person who seeks to help others because such is the will of Hashem.

Beginning with Avraham *Avinu* and until this very day, our history is replete with scores of anecdotes which illustrate what can be called "*chesed shel Torah*," the Torah's brand of kindness. It is a form of kindness which requires a would-be benefactor to imagine himself as being the beneficiary. *Chesed shel Torah* demands that a benefactor ask himself, "Were I to be in need of this kindness, what would I hope to receive from those who sought to help me? What would be my fears and apprehensions, my needs and aspirations?" Only when one endeavors to feel the pain of another can he be inspired to help him in the most desired manner.

Avraham *Avinu's* tent was forever open to any and all wayfarers who chanced by. A great illustration of *chesed*? Yes, but not enough by Avraham's standards, which reflected the standards of his Creator, Whose existence he came to recognize and Whom he sought to emulate. As the *Midrash (Bereishis Rabbah 48:9)* relates, Avraham's tent was open on all four sides, so as to make his tent as

---

1. One may suggest that had their behavior been motivated by natural compassion, Yocheved and Miriam would have not further jeopardized their lives by supplying food and water for the newborns. When confronted by Pharaoh regarding their having ignored his command, the midwives excused themselves by saying that the Jewish women were giving birth without the aid of a midwife. This explanation did not excuse their supplying provisions. That they endangered themselves for this is indicative that their kindness stemmed from their lofty level of *yiras shamayim*.

accessible as possible. Let us ponder this for a moment. A wayfarer is walking down a road and is overjoyed to find a stranger's tent open to him. Do an additional few steps to the entrance side of the tent really make much difference to him? Is not opening one's home to total strangers a sufficient kindness? No, it is not, if one seeks to perform *chesed shel Torah*. Avraham imagined himself as a hot, tired wayfarer trudging down the road and he understood that to save the person a few extra steps was a kindness that could and should be performed.

In a similar vein, the *Gemara (Berachos* 58b) relates that R' Chana bar Chanilai always walked with his hand in his purse so that if he chanced upon a beggar, the man would be spared the few seconds of shame it would have taken for him to reach into his purse for some coins.

Conversely, when one's compassion is not an expression of fulfillment of the Divine will, the result can be destructive. King Shaul was commanded through the prophet Shmuel to lead his armies against Amalek and eradicate the nation completely, including its livestock. However, Shaul reasoned, "If it is a calamity when a single wayfarer dies (see *Devarim* ch. 21), how tragic it would be to slaughter an entire nation! If the people have sinned, have the livestock sinned? If the adults have sinned, have the children sinned?" Shaul did not kill the livestock, nor did he kill Amalek's King Agag — from whom descended the wicked Haman. A Heavenly voice called out to Shaul, אַל תְּהִי צַדִּיק הַרְבֵּה, "Do not be too righteous"! [*Koheles* 7:16] (*Yoma* 22a). Later, when Shaul erroneously ordered the annihilation of the *Kohanim* of Nov, a voice called out, אַל תִּרְשַׁע הַרְבֵּה, "Do not be too wicked" (ibid.). The *Midrash* sums up these two incidents as follows:

אָמַר ר׳ יְהוֹשֻׁעַ בֶּן לֵוִי: כָּל שֶׁהוּא רַחֲמָן עַל אַכְזָרִים, לְסוֹף נַעֲשֶׂה
אַכְזָר עַל הָרַחְמָנִים.

Whoever is merciful to the cruel will in the end be cruel to the merciful (*Yalkut Shimoni, I Shmuel 121*).

Shaul's spiritual stature was awesome, otherwise he would not have been Divinely chosen as Israel's first king. However, he erred in exercising compassion at a time when this was not Hashem's will. From the above statement of *Chazal*, we see a connection between that mistake and Shaul's dreadful error in ordering the slaughter of the *Kohanim* of Nov. When one relies on his own reasoning to decide when compassion is called for, the result may be too much or too little compassion, depending on the situation.

◦§ Erev Yom Kippur Lessons

It is told that R' Yisrael Salanter was seen one *Erev Yom Kippur* extracting nails that were protruding from benches in the women's section of his *shul*. Who but a person whose sole desire was to please his Creator could have such matters on his mind as he prepared himself for the awesome Day of Atonement? When R' Yisrael noticed the protruding nails, he immediately conjured in his mind the sight of an upset woman whose *yom tov* clothing had gotten caught on a nail and torn. He felt her aggravation. He knew that by taking the time to correct the problem, he would be fulfilling the will of Hashem. Given this attitude, it is no wonder that he found time for this on *Erev Yom Kippur*. This is *chesed shel Torah*.

On *Erev Yom Kippur* each year, I relate the following to the students of my yeshivah. It is a classic illustration of kindness motivated by *yiras shamayim*:

It was late afternoon one *Erev Yom Kippur* in Pressburg. The Chasam Sofer summoned his daughter and entrusted her with the following mission: She was to make her way to the home of a certain orphan boy and tell him that after the fast, her father would propose a *shidduch* between the boy and an orphan girl who also resided in Pressburg. Having done that, the Chasam Sofer continued, his daughter was to go to the very opposite end of the city, where the orphan girl lived, and tell her the same good news.

The Chasam Sofer's daughter was ready and willing to do her father's bidding. However, she had one question. "It will soon be time to leave for *shul* to begin *Kol Nidrei*. Could this not wait one more day?"

The Chasam Sofer replied, "My daughter, I must take this *mitzvah* along with me to *shul*. It cannot wait."

Chesed shel Torah.

Reliving the Redemption

◆§ The Obligation

וְהוֹצֵאתִי אֶתְכֶם מִתַּחַת סִבְלֹת מִצְרַיִם, וְהִצַּלְתִּי אֶתְכֶם מֵעֲבֹדָתָם.
וְגָאַלְתִּי אֶתְכֶם בִּזְרוֹעַ נְטוּיָה וּבִשְׁפָטִים גְּדֹלִים. וְלָקַחְתִּי אֶתְכֶם לִי
לְעָם, וְהָיִיתִי לָכֶם לֵאלֹקִים.

*I will take you out from beneath the burdens of Egypt,
and I will save you from their servitude. I will redeem
you with an outstretched arm and great judgments;
and I will take you for Me for a people, and I will be
God to you (6:6-7).*

The above verses occupy a central place in the Pesach *seder*, as
they represent the various stages of deliverance from the
Egyptian exile. Each of the *arba kosos*, four cups, that we drink on
that night correspond to one of these stages. This *mitzvah*, like the
many others of the *seder* night, is related to the well-known
statement found in the *Mishnah* (*Pesachim* 10:5) and quoted in the
Haggadah:

בְּכָל דּוֹר וָדוֹר, חַיָּב אָדָם לִרְאוֹת אֶת עַצְמוֹ כְּאִלּוּ הוּא יָצָא
מִמִּצְרָיִם.

*In every generation, one is obligated to regard himself
as though he himself had actually gone out from Egypt.*

The term חַיָּב, *[one is] obligated*, as opposed to צָרִיךְ, *[one] needs to*,
implies that one must strain himself to his very limits in reliving the
Redemption. One must actually see himself suffering under the

burden of slavery; he must feel the exhilaration which Israel surely experienced with the arrival of each of the Ten Plagues; and finally, he must sense the ecstasy of leaving that land of persecution and impurity as a nation of Hashem heading toward Sinai to receive the Torah. One who fulfills this obligation has surely accomplished a most lofty spiritual achievement.

In truth, the fulfillment of this obligation seems quite difficult to attain. It is not easy for someone living more than three thousand years after an event has occurred to experience the emotions of those who actually lived through those events. Why indeed is such a requirement demanded of us?

For a better understanding, let us delve into the workings of man's intellect and emotions.

⋖§ Extinguishing the Fire

The *Gemara* (*Kiddushin* 81a) relates that R' Amram *Chasida* (the pious one) once felt himself being overcome by an intense passion to sin. He spaced his feet apart and dug in his heels as he fought to resist taking another step, and shouted: נוּרָא בֵּי עַמְרָם!, "There is a fire in the house of Amram!" The sages who heard his cry came running, only to discover that there was apparently no fire at all. They told him, "You have shamed us (by causing us to come running without reason)." R' Amram replied, "Better to be ashamed in the house of Amram in this world than to be ashamed *of* him in the Next World." As *Rashi* explains, R' Amram was indeed being truthful when he shouted. The fire to which he had referred was the *yetzer hara* that had been burning within him. R' Amram needed the presence of his neighbors, for in their presence he would be ashamed to sin.

Would any of us have had the fortitude to react as R' Amram did? He sought a situation whereby he would be too embarrassed to sin. In all likelihood, we would have refrained from shouting as he did, because *that* would have caused us embarrassment. On the other hand, had a real fire broken out, we most assuredly *would* have shouted for help.

What is the difference between R' Amram and ourselves? *Chovos HaLevavos* (*Sha'ar Avodas Elokim*) provides the answer:

> ... *For physical pleasures, as opposed to man's intellect, are with him from his youth and his*

attachment to them is firm and increasing as they become more necessary to him. Therefore, the trait of physical desire is more powerful than his other characteristics, including his intellect — for which man was created. This blinds man's vision and causes his precious attributes to become wasted.

It is thus that man requires external forces to help him stand firm against the shameful trait of animalistic craving, so that his praiseworthy attribute, namely his intellect, be permitted to thrive. These forces are the teachings of the Torah, in which Hashem has taught His creatures the way of His service, through his emissaries and prophets, may they rest in peace.

Were a person's intellect *not* blinded by earthly passions and personal wants, he would be able to deduce the will of Hashem on his own. Avraham *Avinu* did in fact accomplish this, as he came to recognize Hashem while surrounded by a world of idolatry. Man's intellect has no pleasure from this world; its yearnings are purely spiritual. Avraham's physical being was dominated by his intellect to the extent that "*HaKadosh Baruch Hu* made his two kidneys like two teachers and they flowed with and taught him Torah" (*Bereishis Rabbah* 61:1).

It is for man to seek ways by which his intellect will rule over his desires. The initial step in this process is that one subjugate his desires by developing an almost tangible feeling for the destructiveness of sin. Then, one's physical being will gravitate toward the spiritual and his intellect will dominate. R' Amram Chasida perceived this. When he felt himself being overwhelmed by the fire of passion, he quickly sought to arouse his physical being against this passion. Thus he placed himself in a situation of potential humiliation, something which any person seeks desperately to avoid.

⋖§ More Potent Than Prophecy

Regarding the verse, "So the king took his signet ring from his hand and gave it to Haman, the son of Hammedasa, the enemy of the Jews" (*Esther* 3:10), the *Gemara* (*Megillah* 14a) comments:

> R' Aba bar Kahana said: The removal of the ring was
> more powerful than forty-eight prophets and seven
> prophetesses who prophesied for the Jews. For all of
> them could not return the Jews to the proper path,
> while the removal of the ring did.

We who do not live in an age of prophecy might be puzzled by the above. Prophecy can only be transmitted through an *ish kadosh*, a holy personage whose sublime way of life makes him or her worthy of transmitting the Divine word. We are sure that if only we were to merit hearing a prophet speak, surely we would immediately involve ourselves in an order of complete *teshuvah*, repentance! From the above *Gemara* we see that this is not necessarily so. All the words of rebuke which the prophets transmitted to their people in the name of Hashem did not accomplish what the transfer of King Achashveirosh's ring to Haman did. The prophecies entered the people's intellects, but were not enough to raise them out of the life which their physical beings found so gratifying. However, when Haman's decree became known and they realized that their lives were in danger, then their whole being was spurred toward fasting and a form of *teshuvah* that resulted in their salvation.

We can now understand the significance of בְּכָל דּוֹר וָדוֹר, חַיָּב אָדָם לְרְאוֹת אֶת עַצְמוֹ כְּאִלּוּ הוּא יָצָא מִמִּצְרָיִם. Remembrance is important, which is why the Torah obligates us to recall the Redemption from Egypt every day of our lives (*Devarim* 16:3). However, on the first night of *Pesach*, the celebration of זְמַן חֵרוּתֵנוּ, the season of our freedom, the obligation goes further. Then, the spiritual radiance of freedom that was attained during the Exodus returns in all its strength and we are obliged to make ourselves fitting receptacles to receive that radiance. For this, intellectual awareness will not suffice. Rather, it is necessary that we actually sense the feelings that our ancestors experienced at that time. As we involve ourselves emotionally in the redemption experience, our intellect is naturally affected. We must begin by reliving the עַבְדוּת, *slavery*, for a person can appreciate fully the taste of freedom only after he has experienced bondage. Once this has been accomplished, we move on to the purpose of the *seder* night: reliving — and absorbing the spiritual light of — that great moment in our history when we emerged from bondage to a חֵרוּת עוֹלָם, *eternal freedom*, as a nation of Hashem.

Transformations of the Spirit[1]

◄§ From Idolatry to Purity

וַיִּקְרָא מֹשֶׁה לְכָל זִקְנֵי יִשְׂרָאֵל וַיֹּאמֶר אֲלֵהֶם: מִשְׁכוּ וּקְחוּ לָכֶם
צֹאן לְמִשְׁפְּחֹתֵיכֶם וְשַׁחֲטוּ הַפָּסַח.
Moshe summoned all the elders of Israel and said to them: Draw close and take for yourselves sheep, according to your families, and slaughter the Pesach sacrifice (12:21).

Because they were steeped in idolatry, he [i.e., Moshe] said to them, מִשְׁכוּ וּקְחוּ לָכֶם, *Withdraw (*מִשְׁכוּ*) your*

---

1. This discourse was delivered at Beth Medrash Govoha in Lakewood, N.J. HaRav Segal prefaced his address with the following:

"The *Gemara* [*Berachos* 8a] states, '*HaKadosh Baruch Hu* does not reject the *tefillos* of a רַבִּים (assemblage).' The strength of a רַבִּים is such that even when it is not deserving, its entreaties are answered. The larger the רַבִּים, the greater is its power.

"I am not accustomed to lecturing in public, nor am I sure that I am qualified for it. However, the Torah commands us: וְהָלַכְתָּ בִּדְרָכָיו, "And you shall go in His ways" (*Devarim* 28:9), meaning that we are required to emulate the ways of Hashem. Therefore, I find it impossible to reject the request of this רַבִּים — a multitude of *bnei Torah* and *gedolei Torah* — that I speak.

"Whenever one studies *mussar*, he fulfills four *mitzvos*: Torah study; הוֹכֵחַ תּוֹכִיחַ אֶת עֲמִיתֶךָ ("You shall rebuke your fellow man" — *Vayikra* 19:17), where the word אֶת can be understood to include the obligation of self-rebuke; אֶת ה' אֱלֹקֶיךָ תִּירָא ("You shall fear Hashem, your God" — *Devarim* 10:20); and וּמַלְתֶּם אֵת עָרְלַת לְבַבְכֶם ("You shall remove the barriers of your heart" — *Devarim* 10:16). Today, I am also fulfilling the *mitzvah* of וְהָלַכְתָּ בִּדְרָכָיו. It is my hope that through the merits of this רַבִּים, my words will flow from the heart and enter your hearts."

hands from idol worship and take for yourselves (וּקְחוּ
לָכֶם) sheep of mitzvah (Rashi to 12:6).

וַיֹּאפוּ אֶת הַבָּצֵק אֲשֶׁר הוֹצִיאוּ מִמִּצְרַיִם עֻגֹת מַצּוֹת כִּי לֹא חָמֵץ,
כִּי גֹרְשׁוּ מִמִּצְרַיִם וְלֹא יָכְלוּ לְהִתְמַהְמֵהַּ וְגַם צֵדָה לֹא עָשׂוּ לָהֶם.
They baked unleavened bread with the dough that they
had taken with them from Egypt, for it was not
leavened, because they were driven out of Egypt and
could not tarry there; nor had they prepared for
themselves any provisions for the way (12:39).

This tells the praise of the Israelites, that they did not
say, "How can we go out to the desert without
provisions?!" Rather, they had faith and went. It is
regarding this that the prophet states (Yirmiyhau 2:2),
"[So said Hashem:] I remember for your sake the
kindness of your youth, the love of your bridal days,
how you followed Me in a wilderness in an unsown
land." What reward is stated afterward? "Israel is
sanctified before Hashem, the choicest of His crop"
(Rashi ibid.).

With these comments, Rashi expresses so beautifully the incredible spiritual transformation that Israel underwent at the time of
the Exodus. From a people that was steeped in idol worship, they
became a nation whose pure, unquestioning faith earned them their
Creator's praise. More than one million men, women and children
headed for the Wilderness without provisions, not knowing how
they would survive. They followed Hashem's command in the way
of a young child who unquestioningly accompanies his father on his
travels. The child does not worry how he will survive, for he has
complete faith in his father's judgment. Such was the pure faith of
the Jewish nation which had previously worshiped heathen idols.

How did such a turnabout occur?

No matter how far a Jew falls, the holiness of his neshamah, soul,
is never totally eradicated, ר"ל. Rather, it lies dormant, buried beneath
the layers of impurity brought about by sinful acts and midos ra'os,
destructive traits. It is like a massive underground spring that lies
concealed beneath the ground, covered by layers of rock and earth.
When the spring finds its way to the earth's surface, it gushes forth
with tremendous force, hurling aside the rocks and dirt that stand in

its path. Such is the strength of a *neshamah* that has undergone a spiritual awakening. The holiness of the *nishmas Yisrael* can suddenly shine forth in all its glory, shedding the layers of impurity that have hidden its inner beauty.

↜§ The Catalyst

What was the catalyst for this awakening? Another comment of Rashi provides the answer:

> *"And it shall be for you for a safekeeping"* (12:6) — this denotes examination, that it [i.e., the Pesach lamb] requires examination for blemishes four days prior to its being slaughtered.
>
> Why did it have to be set aside for slaughter for four days, which was not the command regarding the Pesach offerings of later generations? R' Masya ben Charash explained: It is written, "I passed over you and I saw you" (Yechezkel 16:8) — 'Behold, the moment was one of love; the time had come to [fulfill the] oath that I had sworn to Avraham that I would redeem his children.' But they had no mitzvos with which to involve themselves so that [in their merit] they could be redeemed! — as it is written, "...but you were naked and bare" [i.e., devoid of the merit of mitzvos].
>
> He therefore gave them two mitzvos, the blood of the Pesach offering and the blood of milah, as they were circumcised on that night. Thus it is written, "[I passed over you and I saw you] wallowing in your bloods [בְּדָמָיִךְ]" — in two bloods.[2] (Rashi 12:6).

The Jews surely did have *mitzvos* to their credit, but these were not sufficient to merit their redemption, considering their having been mired in impurity. Thus were they given the *mitzvos* of *Pesach* and *milah*, both of which demanded *mesiras nefesh*, self-sacrifice. Sacrificing the *Pesach* lamb meant slaughtering the animal which the

---

2. The verse continues, וָאֹמַר לָךְ בְּדָמַיִךְ חֲיִי, וָאֹמַר לָךְ בְּדָמַיִךְ חֲיִי, "And I said to you, 'Through your blood you shall live'; and I said to you, 'Through your blood you shall live.' "

Egyptians worshiped as their god. As Moshe asked Pharaoh at one point, "Were we to slaughter [thus doing] that which is abominable to the Egyptians, would they not stone us?" (8:22). As an additional self-sacrifice, they were required to set aside their offerings four days before the slaughter, allowing plenty of time for the Egyptians to learn of their plans.

The performance of *bris milah* was an act of *mesiras nefesh* particularly at that point when they knew that the Exodus was impending. Travel is dangerous for the newly circumcised.[3] While it is usually wrong to place oneself in danger, in this case the *Ribono shel Olam* was demanding that they perform this *mitzvah* — of course, for good reason. *Mesiras nefesh*, by definition, means that one performs a given deed at all costs, regardless of the obstacles involved. Thus, acting with *mesiras nefesh* is a great demonstration of faith and therefore the performance of *korban Pesach* and *bris milah* transformed Israel from a people steeped in idol worship to a nation of Hashem.

Given the above, yet another comment of *Rashi* is particularly enlightening:

וַיִּשָּׂא הָעָם אֶת בְּצֵקוֹ טֶרֶם יֶחְמָץ, מִשְׁאֲרֹתָם צְרֻרֹת בְּשִׂמְלֹתָם עַל שִׁכְמָם.

The people took up their dough before it became leavened, their kneading-troughs bound up in their clothes upon their shoulders (12:34).

Their kneading-troughs — [which contained] the remnants of matzoh and maror. Though they brought many animals [of burden] along with them, they cherished the mitzvos [and therefore carried these items on their shoulders] (Rashi).

Bnei Yisrael carried upon their backs the remnants of *matzoh* and *marror* which they had eaten together with the *Pesach* offering earlier that night. They cherished those objects, for they realized that it was their *mitzvah* performance at that time which uplifted them to so sublime a level.

Prior to the performance of most *mitzvos*, we recite a blessing in which we offer praise of Hashem אֲשֶׁר קִדְּשָׁנוּ בְּמִצְוֹתָיו, *Who has sanctified us with His mitzvos*. Performing a *mitzvah* infuses a Jew

---

3. See *Rashi* to *Shemos* 4:24.

with *kedushah*, holiness. The Jews who left Egypt were able to sense this *kedushah*.

◈ Chonyo's Fall

W e have seen how it is possible for those in a very low spiritual state to undergo a complete positive transformation virtually overnight. An incident in the *Gemara* demonstrates vividly how the opposite is also possible, ל"ר :

> *When Shimon HaTzaddik (the Righteous One) was about to depart this world, he told the Sages, "Chonyo my son should serve [as Kohen Gadol] in my stead." However, Chonyo would not accept the position, for Shimi his brother was two-and-one-half years his senior. Even so, Chonyo became envious of Shimi. Chonyo told Shimi, "Come, I will teach you the order of the [Temple] service." He dressed him in a woman's garment and belt and stood him near the altar. Then he said to the other Kohanim, "See how this one [i.e., Shimi] has honored the vow which he made to his beloved [i.e., his wife], for he told her, 'On the day that I will ascend to the High Priesthood, I will don your garment and belt.'" The Kohanim sought to kill Shimi [for attempting to perform the service while wearing such garments]. Shimi told them the entire story. They then sought to kill Chonyo, and he fled (Menachos 119b).*

This incident is astounding. *Tosafos* (ibid.), citing an exegesis in *Toras Kohanim*, maintains that Chonyo's *yiras shamayim*, Heavenly awe, was akin to that of his father, for if not, his father could not have designated him as his successor. It was not without cause that Chonyo's father, Shimon, was known as "the *Tzaddik*." His *yiras shamayim* was of an awesome level — and Shimon deemed Chonyo worthy in this regard. Moreover, we see that Chonyo initially was exceedingly sensitive to the feelings of his brother. Though Shimon *HaTzaddik* had designated Chonyo as his successor, Chonyo's concern for his older brother's feelings impelled him to transfer to

Shimi the mantle of the High Priesthood. Yet, Chonyo later tricked Shimi into donning women's clothing, fully aware that his fellow *Kohanim* would consider Shimi deserving of death for this. Chonyo, with all his *yiras shamayim*, with all his sensitivity, had turned murderer!

Where did Chonyo go wrong? נִתְקַנֵּא חוֹנְיוֹ בְּשִׁמְעִי, *Chonyo became envious of Shimi.* Envy lay dormant in Chonyo's heart. Negative traits can lay dormant for years, unprovoked and undetected. Then, an incident can come along that will cause the lion to arise from its slumber, resulting in destruction that one would not have dreamed possible.

A person can possess *yiras shamayim* and be fluent in all of *Shas*, yet this will not preclude his sinking — in an instant! — to the very nadir of human behavior if he does not make a conscious effort to rid himself of *midos ra'os*, destructive traits.

The nature of such an effort can be derived from a *Mishnah* in *Pesachim*, which offers a vital lesson in *avodas Hashem*.

✎ A Matter of Outlook

הַפִּגּוּל וְהַנּוֹתָר מְטַמְּאִין אֶת הַיָּדַיִם.

Pigul and leftover [sacrificial meat] contaminate the hands (Mishnah Pesachim 10:9).

Pigul refers to sacrificial meat that was disqualified by an improper intent on the part of the *Kohen* who performed the blood service of a given sacrifice. To eat such meat is forbidden by the Torah, the punishment being *kares*, excision.

That *pigul* contaminates the hands is a Rabbinic injunction. According to the *Gemara* (*Pesachim* 85a; see *Rashbam*), this enactment was intended as a deterrent against a *Kohen* intentionally disqualifying an offering through a wrong intent during the blood service — because of a personal antipathy for the owner of that offering. The knowledge that his hands would become *tamei*, ritually impure, upon touching *pigul* and would subsequently disqualify other sacrificial meat upon contact would deter a *Kohen* from rendering a sacrifice *pigul*.

It is possible to study this *mishnah* a thousand times without realizing the lesson that it indirectly conveys. A *Kohen* who intentionally renders an offering *pigul* through an improper intent is guilty of three transgressions: (1) He is a *mazik*, damager, having caused someone else a monetary loss; (2) he has transgressed the prohibition of הַמַּקְרִיב אֹתוֹ לֹא יֵחָשֵׁב לוֹ, פִּגּוּל יִהְיֶה, "The one who offers it may not intend this — it is *pigul*" (*Vayikra* 7:18); (3) he has intentionally blemished an offering unto Hashem. Now, what did *Chazal* do to deter a *Kohen* from intentionally transgressing these three Torah prohibitions? They enacted a single Rabbinic decree! How can it be that a person — who is willing to transgress three Torah commandments because of personal enmity — will withdraw his intentions because of a Rabbinic decree? The answer to this is found in a passage in *Yeshayahu*:

יַעַן כִּי נִגַּשׁ הָעָם הַזֶּה, בְּפִיו וּבִשְׂפָתָיו כִּבְּדוּנִי וְלִבּוֹ רִחַק מִמֶּנִּי,
וַתְּהִי יִרְאָתָם אֹתִי מִצְוַת אֲנָשִׁים מְלֻמָּדָה.
Because this nation has approached Me, honoring Me with their mouths and lips, but their heart was far from Me, and their fear of Me was by force of habit (*Yeshayahu* 29:13).

Every Jew has his *chumros* and *hidurim*, halachic stringencies and enhancement of certain *mitzvos* in whose performance he is particularly meticulous. On the other hand, there are certain *mitzvos*, which though major in their significance, are often not accorded proper attention. They are performed in a manner which the prophet Yeshayahu termed מְלֻמָּדָה, *by force of habit*. The Sages understood that the same *Kohen* who had a lethargic, complacent attitude toward severe Torah prohibitions might nevertheless be alarmed at the thought of his hands becoming *tamei*, ritually contaminated, for *tumah* is something which people find repulsive and are careful to avoid.

If we examine our own Divine service we will find that we too are guilty of a warped sense of spiritual values, a result of the complacency born by מְלֻמָּדָה. A man is mortified — and rightfully so — when he suddenly glances at his watch and realizes that the sun has already set and he has not *davened Minchah*. But is that same man mortified after having mouthed the words of the *Shemoneh Esrei* while his mind is elsewhere? *Yesod V'Shoresh Ha'Avodah* (2:2) writes that for pronouncing the name of Hashem without *kavanah*, intent, one transgresses the grave Torah prohibition against using God's Name in vain! People can go through the motions of a single

Shacharis and pronounce the Name in vain scores of times, and not contemplate their misdeeds for even a moment — for they are in the habit of *davening* this way and do not see the matter as the serious offense that it is.[4]

This is the message that we must derive from that *mishnah* in *Pesachim*. If we are to succeed in our mission to carry out Hashem's will on this earth, then we must actively seek to develop a stringent outlook for matters which truly stand בְּרוּמוֹ שֶׁל עוֹלָם, *at the pinnacle of the universe*. With regard to *tefillah*, this requires studying the laws of *tefillah* and delving into those works that will infuse us with a proper appreciation of *tefillah*. Of course, the *yetzer hara* who is "experienced in slyness" (see *Mesilas Yesharim* ch. 2) has his ways of convincing us not to seek improvement in this area. Maintaining proper concentration during *tefillah* is no simple task. Some may see it as impossible, thus they see no point in trying.

I have come across a letter from the *Rambam* to his son, in which the *Rambam* cautions regarding the need for proper *kavanah* when reciting the first blessing of *Bircas HaMazon*. The *Rambam* was instructing his son to insure *initially* that he had proper intent during the first blessing, the ultimate goal being proper *kavanah* throughout *Bircas HaMazon*. This advice provides the key to attaining proper concentration in *tefillah*. One must strive to improve his *kavanah* gradually, working on one small portion of the prayers at a time. In

---

4. To illustrate the gravity of pronouncing the Holy Name without intent, *Yesod V'Shoresh Ha'Avodah* offers the following:

The author of *Zera Yitzchak*, of blessed memory, fell into a faint and heard a great tumult in the Heavenly Court: "Clear the way for _____, a *tzaddik* who has died." The Court received the *tzaddik* with great honor and placed a *sefer Torah* in his arms. They asked him, "Have you fulfilled all that is written herein?" He replied in the affirmative ... They asked him, "Who will testify on your behalf?" Whereupon the countless angels which had been created through his performance of *mitzvos* came forward and testified ... They then brought before him the four sections of *Shulchan Aruch* and asked him, "Did you fulfill the Oral Law?" He replied in the affirmative and again angels came to testify for him. They then asked, "Were you careful not to utter the Holy Name in vain?" He did not respond. They asked the question again, and again he remained silent. They then called for witnesses, whereupon contingents of *malachai chabalah* (angels of destruction) cloaked in black came forward to testify against him. One said, "I was created on this-and-this day when he uttered the Name so-and-so many times during *tefillah* without *kavanah*." Another came forward and offered similar testimony ... and so it went. The members of the Heavenly Court all rent their garments. They told him, "Putrid drop! Where was your fear...?" It was decreed that he must either enter *Gehinnom* or return to this world as a *gilgul* (reincarnation). He chose *Gehinnom*.

Shemoneh Esrei, one should begin his efforts with the opening blessing; having mastered it, he should proceed on to the second one, and so on. With regard to the remainder of the *davening*, one should begin with *Shema*, then *Ahavah Rabah*, until he eventually masters all of *tefillah*.

With regard to *midos*, the only way to improve is through the study of *mussar*. Only through *mussar* can one come to view *midos ra'os* as the destructive forces that they are and be inspired to dedicate himself toward their refinement. Otherwise, he will be in constant danger of stumbling, ח״ו, in the way of Chonyo.

Shlomo *HaMelech* declared: הַחֲזֵק בַּמּוּסָר, אַל תֶּרֶף! נִצְּרֶהָ — כִּי הִיא חַיֶּיךָ, *Grasp steadfastly to mussar, do not loosen your grip! Guard it — for it is your life* (*Mishlei* 4:13). A person who can breath only with the aid of an oxygen support system would not for a moment consider disconnecting himself from it, for his life depends on it. *Mussar* study is not something reserved for the exceedingly pious. It is our life, for without it we are lost.

Sharing Another's Burden[1]

וַיָּבֹא עֲמָלֵק, וַיִּלָּחֶם עִם יִשְׂרָאֵל בִּרְפִידִם . . . וְהָיָה כַּאֲשֶׁר יָרִים מֹשֶׁה יָדוֹ וְגָבַר יִשְׂרָאֵל, וְכַאֲשֶׁר יָנִיחַ יָדוֹ וְגָבַר עֲמָלֵק. וִידֵי מֹשֶׁה כְּבֵדִים וַיִּקְחוּ אֶבֶן וַיָּשִׂימוּ תַחְתָּיו וַיֵּשֶׁב עָלֶיהָ, וְאַהֲרֹן וְחוּר תָּמְכוּ בְיָדָיו מִזֶּה אֶחָד וּמִזֶּה אֶחָד, וַיְהִי יָדָיו אֱמוּנָה עַד בֹּא הַשָּׁמֶשׁ.

Amalek came and did battle with Israel in Refidim . . . And it happened that when Moshe raised up his hands, Israel prevailed, and when he let down his hands, then Amalek prevailed. Moshe's hands felt heavy, so they took a stone and placed it beneath him and he sat upon it, while Aharon and Chur supported his hands, one from this side and one from the other side. His hands remained steadfast until the setting of the sun (17:8-12).

◆§ For Our Iranian Brethren

My brethren! Are you aware of what is currently transpiring in Iran? I was recently in Vienna, where I encountered precious Iranian *bachurim* (mature boys). They are broken, totally broken. They beg for our compassion. They requested a *brachah* (blessing) that their parents escape that land of persecution and that they and their parents be reunited.

We are obligated to concern ourselves with their welfare. As to the

1. This discourse is based on an address by HaRav Segal to a gathering in New York for the benefit of Iranian Jewry.

nature of that obligation, let us study a passage in *Masechta Ta'anis* (11a):

> At a time when the community is suffering, a man should not say, "I will go to my house and eat and drink — and peace will be unto me!" ... rather, he should suffer along with the community. We find this with Moshe Rabbeinu, as is written (Shemos 17:12), "Moshe's hands felt heavy, so they took a stone and placed it beneath him and he sat upon it." Did not Moshe possess a cushion or pillow upon which to sit? However, Moshe said, "Since Israel is immersed in suffering, I shall suffer along with them."
>
> Whoever suffers along with the community will merit to see the community's consolation. Now, perhaps a man will say, "Who will bear witness against me [if I do not share in their suffering]?" The stones and beams of his house will bear witness against him, as is written (Chavakuk 2:11): "For a stone from the wall will cry out, and a knot from a beam will respond." In the academy of R' Shilah it was said, "The two Heavenly angels who escort that man will bear witness against him, as is written (Tehillim 91:11), 'He will charge His angels for you.'"

Note that the *Gemara* expresses itself in both a positive and negative sense: "A man should not say, 'I will go to my house and eat and drink ...'; rather, he should suffer along with the community." It would seem that *Chazal* could have stated simply that we are to share in the suffering of the community, leaving us to draw the obvious conclusion that one is not to think, "Peace will be unto me!" To resolve this, we must first understand how one fulfills the obligation to suffer along with the community.

⊷§ A Lesson From Moshe

וַיִּגְדַּל מֹשֶׁה, וַיֵּצֵא אֶל אֶחָיו וַיַּרְא בְּסִבְלֹתָם, "Moshe grew older, and he went out to his brethren and took note of their burdens" (2:11). *Rashi* comments, "He set his eyes and heart toward agonizing over them."

The *Midrash (Shemos Rabbah* 1:27) relates:

> *He took note of their burdens — in what way? He would
> see their suffering and weep, saying, "Woe is to me for
> you! If only I could die for you!" There is no labor more
> strenuous than molding bricks and he used to shoulder
> the burdens and help each one of them.*

Moshe's conduct epitomized the obligation that one be מְצַעֵר עַצְמוֹ
עִם הַצִּבּוּר, *suffer along with the community.* More than being content to commiserate with his brethren, Moshe strove to imagine himself in their situation and actually sense their pain. Thus did he weep
over their plight and express his willingness to die for them. Thus did
he offer his shoulder to share in the burden of their bondage.

Such an attitude is implied in the *Gemara* to which we earlier
referred. The first step in sharing in the community's suffering is that
one not be at peace with himself, content with his own comfortable
situation. However, this alone falls far short of what is actually
required of us, which is why the *Gemara* expressed itself in a
two-fold manner. A Jew must be מְצַעֵר עַצְמוֹ עִם הַצִּבּוּר in a real sense,
imagining himself as one of those who are in fact suffering. This
approach applies both to community and individual suffering. The
requirement to be נוֹשֵׂא בְּעוֹל עִם חֲבֵרוֹ, *share his friend's burden,* also
requires this kind of emotional involvement. For example, if one hears
that a neighbor's child has been stricken by illness, ר"ל, he must
immediately ask himself, "How would I feel were it my child?"

My brethren! The Jews of Iran are suffering! We must imagine
ourselves in their situation, under the rule of that evil tyrant, the fear
of death hanging over us each day. The roads of escape are fraught
with danger. We must feel their pain and ask ourselves how we can
be of help to them. We must offer them whatever financial assistance
possible. And we must do more.

◆§ In Our Hands

In *Shemoneh Esrei*, we declare that Hashem מַתִּיר אֲסוּרִים, *releases
the confined,* and that He is גּוֹאֵל יִשְׂרָאֵל, *Redeemer of Israel.* Thrice
daily, we plead: תְּקַע בְּשׁוֹפָר גָּדוֹל לְחֵרוּתֵנוּ, וְשָׂא נֵס לְקַבֵּץ גָּלִיּוֹתֵנוּ, "*Sound
the great shofar for our freedom, and raise the banner to gather in our*

exiles." When offering these prayers, we should have in mind the plight of our Iranian brethren. "*Ribono shel Olam*, they are murdering our brothers and sisters! Please, have mercy on the remnants of Your people." We must shed tears and plead for mercy on their behalf.

Prior to praying, we must seek ways through which our *tefillos* will be effective in arousing Divine mercy. To this end, each one of us must confront himself with an awesome question: "Perhaps I am the guilty one? Perhaps I am to blame for these terrible troubles?" With this, I am referring to the following *Zohar* (*Parashas Pekudei*):

> *There is a certain Heavenly being which hovers over all habitual speakers of lashon hara (forbidden speech). When a group or individual is aroused to speak lashon hara then this evil impure being, which is called Sichsuchah, is aroused ... It ascends upward and brings about — through the 'stirring' caused by lashon hara — death, sword and murder to the world. Woe unto those who arouse this destructive force by not guarding their mouths and tongues, who are not concerned by this! They do not realize that Heavenly stirrings are contingent on earthly stirrings, whether for good or for bad ...*

When a person speaks *lashon hara*, he brings about an indictment of *Klal Yisrael* in Heaven and gives Satan added strength as our accuser. Additionally, he causes rejection of his own *tefillos*. Thus, when tragedy strikes, ר״ל, we must ponder our personal behavior, for it may well be that we are to blame. This applies to both personal and communal travail, including the current situation in Iran.

Conversely, *Chazal* have taught that whoever overlooks the pain which others cause him will have all his sins forgiven (*Rosh Hashanah* 17b). This reward comes measure for measure; one who is forgiving of the misdeeds done against him deserves to have his own misdeeds overlooked.

Moreover, the Chofetz Chaim (*Sha'ar HaZechirah* ch. 2) writes that when a Jew is forgiving and compassionate toward others, he arouses Heavenly mercy and compassion for the entire world.

It is in our power to arouse Heavenly mercy on behalf of our persecuted brethren. Let us do our share to ease their harrowing plight.

Seizing the Moment

וַיִּשְׁמַע יִתְרוֹ כֹהֵן מִדְיָן חֹתֵן מֹשֶׁה אֵת כָּל אֲשֶׁר עָשָׂה אֱלֹקִים
לְמֹשֶׁה וּלְיִשְׂרָאֵל עַמּוֹ, כִּי הוֹצִיא ה׳ אֶת יִשְׂרָאֵל מִמִּצְרָיִם.
Yisro, the priest of Midyan and the father-in-law of Moshe, heard of all that God did for Moshe and Israel His people, that Hashem took Israel out of Egypt (18:1).

What report did he hear that prompted him to come? That of the splitting of the sea and the war against Amalek (Rashi).

Did only Yisro hear and not the rest of the world? — It is written, "The nations heard and they trembled" (Sh'mos 15:14)! However, the entire world heard and was not affected, while this one heard and was affected, as he humbled himself before HaKadosh Baruch Hu and brought himself into His service (Zohar).

⋙ Changing Status

In relating that which prompted Yisro to join Israel in the wilderness, *Rashi* is actually citing two of three varying opinions. In *Masechta Zevachim* (116a) we find: "What report did he hear? R' Yehoshua said: 'The war with Amalek.' R' Elazar HaModa'i said: 'The giving of the Torah.' R' Eliezer said: 'The splitting of the Sea.' "

The opinion of R' Yehoshua seems difficult to understand. The war against Amalek was won without the benefit of open miracles. Ostensibly, it appeared to be a military victory in the way of normal warfare. Why should this have impressed Yisro more than the great, world-shattering occurrence of the splitting of the Sea?

With regard to the war with Amalek, the Torah implies that the Jews' fortune in battle was contingent on the hands of Moshe being raised — to which the *Mishnah* (*Rosh Hashanah* 3:8) comments:

> *Was it Moshe's hands that won the battle or lost the battle? Rather [the Torah] teaches you: As long as Israel looked heavenward and subjected their heart to their Father in Heaven, they would prevail; but when they did not, they would fall.* [1]

Apparently, the war lasted but a single day, for the Torah relates, "And his hands remained steadfast until the setting of the sun" (17:12). Within a single day, Moshe's hands were at times raised and at times lowered, reflecting the changing submission of the people's hearts to the will of Hashem. We see that a person can merit to achieve a spiritual awakening, only to regress to his previous status shortly thereafter.

This point can also be derived elsewhere in this *parashah*. As Israel triumphantly marched out of Egypt, the *Shechinah*, Divine Presence, led the way: "Hashem went before them by day in a pillar of cloud to show them the way, and by night with a pillar of fire, to travel by day and by night" (13:21). Israel was deserving of this guidance, as it had faithfully followed Moshe into the Wilderness, not having had time to prepare provisions for the way [see discourse to *Parashas Bo*]. Yet Hashem found it necessary to lead His people on a roundabout route that would make it difficult for them to return to Egypt should they later become frightened during battle. A people being led by the *Shechinah*, imbued with an awesome level of *emunah*, faith, had the potential to suddenly lose faith and attempt a hurried retreat back to the land whence they had been redeemed.

---

1. *Maharsha* explains that the raising and lowering of Moshe's hands reflected the prayers of the people. When they subjected their hearts to Hashem, Moshe felt strong enough to keep his hands aloft in prayer, but when they did not, his hands became weak and he was forced to lower them.

ᦔ The War's Message

Without question, Yisro was tremendously inspired by the wonders of the splitting of the Sea. Already then, he was convinced that Hashem was the true God and that He alone was to be served. However, Yisro saw no reason at that point to rush from his homeland and join Israel in the Wilderness. He had been inspired; uprooting himself could wait.

The war with Amalek changed Yisro's thinking. From there he learned that mere *hisorerus*, spiritual awakening, is not a guarantee against regression. The army of Israel had in the same day experienced moments of *hisorerus*, only to falter later in not dedicating their thoughts totally to their Father in Heaven. It then became clear to Yisro that *hisorerus* is not an end in itself, but merely a tool to spiritual achievement that must be acted upon immediately, lest its effects wear off and leave nothing behind. "What report did Yisro hear that made him come? R' Yehoshua said: 'The war with Amalek.' "

A Jew should seek means of *hisorerus*, as he forever strives to enhance his service of Hashem. However, when such *hisorerus* comes, one must not tarry in seizing the moment of opportunity and immediately using this awakening to improve his service in a practical way.

❅   ❅   ❅

Among other lessons to be gleaned from this *parashah* is the importance of paying heed to the advice of any person, regardless of the prominence of the one being advised and the relative lack of prominence of the adviser. Moshe *Rabbeinu* was the greatest prophet of all, while Yisro was a former idol-worshiper and a recent convert. Yet, when Yisro offered advice to Moshe for the improvement of Israel's judicial system (ch. 18), Moshe listened. This account precedes that of the giving of the Torah, for a willingness to overlook one's own pride and hear out the advice of others, whatever their station in life, is a prerequisite for success in Torah study and service of Hashem.

The Parameters of Falsehood

מִדְּבַר שֶׁקֶר תִּרְחָק.

Distance yourself from falsehood (23:7).

✥ In Speech and Deed

Mesilas Yesharim (ch.11) discusses at length the various levels of falsehood that exist among mankind. After delineating these levels in descending order of destructiveness, R' Moshe Chaim Luzzato writes:

> The Sage [Shlomo HaMelech] has informed us that all this is contrary to the will of the Creator, Blessed is He, and His pious ones, as is written (Mishlei 13:5), "A righteous one hates falsehood." It is regarding this that the admonishment "Distance yourself from falsehood" is written. Note that it does not say, "Guard yourself against falsehood;" rather, "Distance yourself." This is meant to alert us to the great extent to which we must distance ourselves and flee from falsehood . . .
>
> Our Sages have taught, "The seal of the Holy One is truth"(Shabbos 55a). Now, if truth is what Hashem has chosen as His seal, then how despicable must its converse be before Him! . . . Truth is one of the pillars

upon which the worlds exists (Avos 1:18); it follows,
then, that one who speaks falsehood is considered as if
he has destroyed the world's foundation.[1]

There is a common misconception that one violates מִדְּבַר שֶׁקֶר
תִּרְחָק only through speech. A lengthy *braisa* (*Shevuos* 30b-31a)
demonstrates how one can violate this admonition through deed:

A teacher tells his disciple: "You know of me that even
if I were to be offered one hundred maneh[2] I would not
say a lie. Now, so-and-so owes me a maneh but I have
only one witness [to support my claim]." From where
do we know that the disciple is not permitted to join the
witness [and thereby give the plaintiff his required pair
of witnesses]? It is thus that we are taught: מִדְּבַר שֶׁקֶר
תִּרְחָק.

[Asks the Gemara:] We derive this from מִדְּבַר שֶׁקֶר
תִּרְחָק*?! Surely, [were the disciple to do this] he would be*
saying an outright lie, thus transgressing, לֹא תַעֲנֶה בְרֵעֲךָ
עֵד שָׁקֶר, *"Do not bear false witness against your*
neighbor" (Shemos 20:13). Rather, the case is as
follows: The teacher tells his disciple: "I definitely have
one valid witness. Come and stand there [in court next
to the witness] and do not say a word, so that you will

---

1. On another occasion, HaRav Segal cited the following incident, as recorded in
Sefer Chassidim (§647):

   It happened once that a wicked person told a wise man: "If you were to guide me
   in the way of repentance for a single matter, I would do it, regardless of the
   difficulties involved." The wise man replied, "Do not ever lie; with this, your
   repentance will gain acceptance."

   When the man was about to rob, he told himself, "If they apprehend me and I
   admit to having robbed, then they will hang me; if I deny it, then I will have lied."
   Thus did he refrain from robbery. Another time, the king entrusted him with a
   vessel containing gold and silver. His evil inclination was inciting him to steal it.
   The man pondered: "If I utter a false oath, then I will have transgressed my
   teacher's word." Again, he restrained himself. On yet another occasion, he desired
   to commit an act of immorality, until he told himself: "If they catch me and I lie, I
   will have gone against my teacher's instructions." He restrained himself.

   In this way, he repented from all his sins. Thus it is written, "Falsehood and word
   of deceit — distance them from me" (Mishlei 30:8); also, it is written, "The
   remnants of Israel will do no iniquity, will utter no lie, and it will not be found in
   their mouths the language of deception" (Tzephaniah 3:13).

2. The *maneh* was a large coin worth one hundred *zuz* or *dinars*. *Chazon Ish* (*Yoreh*
Deah 192:19) calculates the *maneh* as 480 grams, or 15.5 troy ounces of silver.

not utter a falsehood. [By appearing as a valid pair, your joint presence will compel my opponent to admit to my claim (Rashi).]" Even this is forbidden, for it is written: מִדְּבַר שֶׁקֶר תִּרְחָק.

From here we see that מִדְּבַר שֶׁקֶר תִּרְחָק applies to both word and deed. One who wishes to emulate his Creator in ensuring that all his affairs bear the 'seal' of truth must be forever certain that his actions are not misleading; otherwise he will be guilty of living by that which the righteous hate and which corrodes the very foundation of the world.

✑§ Seeing Is Believing

The above-mentioned *braisa* offers yet another illustration of falsehood:

Two people [opponents] come before a court for judgment. One is clothed in rags while the other is wearing a tunic worth one hundred maneh. From where do we derive that we must tell the wealthy man, "Either dress like your adversary or clothe him like yourself"? It is thus that we are taught: מִדְּבַר שֶׁקֶר תִּרְחָק.[3]

The above passage is truly wondrous. An array of verses in the Torah admonish a judge to be scrupulous in his deliberations, unafraid of the rich and unbiased toward the poor. In short, a judge is responsible to insure that his judgment is accurate and free of all prejudice. The *Gemara* expresses this responsibility in awesome terms:

A judge should always picture himself as having a sword poised between his legs and Gehinnom open beneath him (Yevamos 109b).

This is the picture that a judge must envision every time he prepares to judge: A sword is poised between his legs, ready to pierce

---

3. While *Shulchan Aruch* (*Choshen Mishpat* 17:1) rules in accordance with this *halachah*, the commentators note that this is not the custom today.

him should he err in his judgment. At the same time, *Gehinnom* is already open beneath him; should he misjudge, his plummet into the abyss is immediate. Bear in mind that, in admonishing judges, the Torah is addressing men of the highest caliber: "... those who fear God, men of truth, who despise improper gain" (*Shemos* 18:21). No doubt, these judges take *Chazal's* admonishments literally, envisioning the retribution that awaits them should they be guilty of injustice.

Yet, *Chazal* feared that the contrast between the rags of one adversary and the silken garments of the other might influence a judge's thinking. Their method of remedying this is to clothe both in the same manner, though the judge knows very well who is in fact rich and who is poor. This is a striking illustration of the impact that seeing can have on a person. One can be sincerely dedicated to seeking out the truth, yet his mental vision may be blurred by a sight that he knows should have no bearing on the matter at hand.

How awesome is the power of sight! How important it is that we shield our eyes from that which a Jew should not see. The effect that such sights can have on a *neshamah* can be devastating, ר"ל. Each person must endeavor to guard himself in this regard to the fullest extent.

⇜ Mental Images

Elsewhere in this *parashah*, we learn how mental images can affect us in a positive sense. The Torah commands us to loan money to those in need:

אִם כֶּסֶף תַּלְוֶה אֶת עַמִּי אֶת הֶעָנִי עִמָּךְ . . .

When you will lend money to My people, to the poor among you . . . (22:24).

Rashi cites a homiletical interpretation of הֶעָנִי עִמָּךְ, *the poor among you:* "Look upon yourself (עִמָּךְ) as if you were poor (הֶעָנִי)." When someone is approached for a loan, he should imagine himself as being the prospective borrower: poor, ashamed, in need of assistance. He must picture in his mind how he would hope his prospective lender would act toward him — and live up to that mental image. In so doing, he will have fulfilled this *mitzvah* properly, while also fulfilling the *mitzvah* of וְאָהַבְתָּ לְרֵעֲךָ כָּמוֹךָ, "Love your neighbor as yourself" (*Vayikra* 19:18).

◆§ Reflection

A key factor in proper observance of any *mitzvah* is הַתְבּוֹנְנוּת, *reflection*, as to the inestimable value of fulfilling Hashem's will. Lack of such understanding is at the root of a well-known law found at the beginning of this *parashah*.

A נִרְצָע is an עֶבֶד עִבְרִי, *Jewish slave*, who desires to remain a servant even after his six-year period of slavery has elapsed. The Torah commands that prior to beginning his new period of service (which will last until *yovel*, the fiftieth year), the slave's ear must be pierced[4] with an awl at a door post. *Rashi* (citing *Kiddushin* 22b) relates the reasoning for this:

אֹזֶן שֶׁשָּׁמְעָה עַל הַר סִינַי, כִּי לִי בְנֵי יִשְׂרָאֵל עֲבָדִים, וְהָלַךְ וְקָנָה אָדוֹן לְעַצְמוֹ, תֵּרָצֵע.

The ear which heard at Sinai, "For unto Me are the Children of Israel servants" (Vayikra 25:55), and went and acquired for himself a master — let his ear be pierced.

R' Simchah Zissel of Kelm explains that the obligations of an עֶבֶד עִבְרִי to his master free him from certain *mitzvah* obligations. When such an עֶבֶד stands on the threshold of freedom and chooses instead to remain a slave, he demonstrates his lack of regard for those *mitzvos* which he cannot observe due to his servitude. This is a form of פְּרִיקַת עוֹל מַלְכוּת שָׁמַיִם, *removal of the yoke of the kingdom of Heaven*, and it is this which is the basis of the law of נִרְצָע: "The ear which heard at Sinai, 'For unto Me are the Children of Israel servants' — let it be pierced."

Mitzvah observance must not be stale. It requires proper reflection, both with regard to the immeasurable value of each *mitzvah* and the retribution for disobeying Hashem's command.

---

4. The term נִרְצָע stems from the command (21:6): וְרָצַע אֲדֹנָיו אֶת אָזְנוֹ בַּמַּרְצֵעַ, "And his master shall pierce his ear with an awl."

Make for Me a Sanctuary

וְיִקְחוּ לִי תְרוּמָה . . . וְעָשׂוּ לִי מִקְדָּשׁ וְשָׁכַנְתִּי בְּתוֹכָם.
And they shall take for Me an offering . . . And let them
make for Me a Mishkan (Sanctuary) so that I may
dwell among them (25:2,8).

◄§ The Primary Sanctuary

*"And they shall take for Me an offering": The One
regarding Whom it is written, "Hashem's is the earth
and its fullness" (Tehillim 24:1); "His is the sea and He
perfected it" (ibid. 95:5); "Behold, unto Hashem are
the Heavens" (Devarim 10:14) — He requires [the
offerings of] flesh and blood? Rather, He yearned to rest
His Presence amidst Israel in the way of a father who
yearns for his children. Thus it is written* וְיִקְחוּ לִי תְרוּמָה,
*Take for My sake an offering. From here we can
deduce: If to build a Mishkan, which is an honor and
atonement for Israel, Hashem said* דַּבֵּר אֶל בְּנֵי יִשְׂרָאֵל,
*Speak to the Children of Israel — an expression of
conciliation in the way of* דַּבְּרוּ עַל לֵב יְרוּשָׁלַיִם, *Comfort
the heart of Jerusalem (Yeshayahu 40:2), then what
[sort of retribution] awaits the nations of the world who
oppress Israel and deprive them of their possessions!
(Yalkut Shimoni, Terumah §25).*

The above *Midrash* demands clarification. Granted, the *Ribono shel Olam* yearns, as it were, to dwell among His chosen Nation. However, as the *Midrash* states, the *Mishkan* was of immeasurable benefit to Israel, bringing them honor and atonement. Since they stood to gain so much from having a *Mishkan* in their midst, why was it necessary for Hashem to speak to them in a manner of 'conciliation,' beseeching them, as it were, to grant His request?

In *Nefesh HaChaim* (footnote to 1:4), R' Chaim Volozhiner discusses the inner essence of the *Mishkan* and *Beis haMikdash*:

> For the Mishkan and [Beis Ha]Mikdash encompassed within them all the forces and Worlds and all the orders of kedushah (sanctity) in their entirety. All its [the Mikdash's] sections, hidden recesses, upper and lower chambers and all its holy vessels were a replica of that which is in the Upper Worlds, an image of the Holy Spheres and the order of the components of the Divine Chariot[1] ... Thus it is stated in Tanchuma (Parashas Pekudei) that the construction of the Mishkan corresponded to the creation of the universe. There, the Midrash lists in order the various stages of Creation and how their concepts were found in the Mishkan as well.
>
> Therefore, the Torah writes with regard to Bezalel [who led the Mishkan's construction]: "And I will infuse him with wisdom, understanding and knowledge" [Shemos 31:3], for the Worlds were created with these three attributes ... Thus did our Sages teach (Berachos 55a): "Bezalel knew how to arrange the holy letters through which heaven and earth were created."

It was in reference to a Jew's role in Creation that *Nefesh HaChaim* elaborates on the *Mishkan's* essence, for earlier he had stated, "*Man's heart should be gripped by awe regarding the 'sanctuary' that his being encompasses . . .*"

After concluding his discussion of the *Mishkan* per se, *Nefesh HaChaim* continues:

> Therefore, man, whose holiness comprises all the orders

---

1. The Divine Chariot is described in the esoteric first chapter of the Book of *Yechezkel*.

of Creation and the Divine Chariot — Creation in its entirety — is an image of the Mishkan and [Beis Ha]Mikdash and all their vessels. All this is the [hidden] intent within the order of connection between man's various limbs, sinews and all his innate strengths. So does the Zohar analyze the construction of the Mishkan and its vessels, showing how they are alluded to in man, each item in its proper place.

It is thus certain that the primary purpose of the Mikdash, and of God manifesting His presence there, is man. If man will sanctify himself appropriately through the observance of all the mitzvos, each of which is connected to a specific Heavenly root among the 'limbs' that form the 'body' of the totality of Spheres, as it were, then he is a Mikdash — literally — and the Divine Presence rests within him; as it is written, "The sanctuary of Hashem are they" (Yirmiyahu 7:4). As the Sages have taught: וְשָׁכַנְתִּי בְּתוֹכָם, " 'And I will dwell among them:' not בְּתוֹכוֹ, in it [i.e., in the Mishkan], but בְּתוֹכָם, in them, within each and every one of them."

... In this vein, we can interpret the words וְעָשׂוּ לִי מִקְדָּשׁ וְשָׁכַנְתִּי בְּתוֹכָם ... וְכֵן תַּעֲשׂוּ, "Make for Me a sanctuary so that I may dwell among them ... and so you shall do," to which our Sages comment (Sanhedrin 16b): וְכֵן תַּעֲשׂוּ – לְדוֹרוֹת, " 'And so shall you do' — for all generations." In light of the above, we can explain this as follows: [Hashem is saying,] "Do not think that My ultimate intention is the construction of the Mikdash edifice; rather, the entire purpose of My desiring the Mishkan and its vessels is merely so that you should infer from it how to mold yourselves; namely, that through your deeds you should be as desirable as the Mishkan and its vessels — all of you holy, fitting and prepared to be receptacles for My Presence in a literal sense."

The following citation from the final chapter of *Mesilas Yesharim* complements the above thoughts of *Nefesh HaChaim*:

When a person sanctifies himself with the holiness of

his Creator, then even his mundane actions become matters of kedushah, literally. Illustrative of this is the positive commandment to eat kodashim (sacrificial meat), regarding which the Sages have taught (Pesachim 59b): "The Kohanim eat and the [offering's] owners are thus forgiven."

... A kadosh (holy individual), who constantly clings to his God and whose soul soars among intellectual truths of love and awe of his Creator, is considered as walking before Hashem in the Land of the Living [i.e., the World to Come] while still on this world. Such a man is himself considered a Mishkan, a Mikdash, a mizbei'ach (altar). As the Sages have stated ... "The Patriarchs — they are the Divine Chariot"; and, "The righteous — they are the Divine Chariot," for the Shechinah (Divine Presence) dwells within them just as it did in the Mikdash.

Thus, the Mishkan was indicative of the capacity inherent in every Jewish soul to become a veritable sanctuary for the Shechinah. Moreover, the existence of the Mishkan and Mikdash were contingent on Israel's realizing its potential as a community of 'sanctuaries':

... And so did Hashem, Blessed is His Name, tell Shlomo after the completion of the [first] Beis HaMikdash: "This house that you are building, if you will follow My statutes and carry out My laws, and safeguard all My commandments ... then I shall dwell among the Children of Israel, and I will not forsake My nation Israel" (I Melachim 6:12-13). Therefore, when they ruined the inner Mikdash that resided within their beings, then the external Mikdash was of no use and its foundations were razed (Nefesh HaChaim ibid.).

The meaning of the Yalkut with which we began is now clear. True, the Mishkan brought honor and atonement to the Jewish Nation, but it also symbolized the awesome responsibility upon every Jew to transform himself into a living Mishkan. Awareness of this responsibility might have frightened some, especially when one considers that by nature man seeks the 'easy' life and does not want to shoulder that which requires intense effort. *Mesilas Yesharim* (ch. 4) writes that were this not man's nature, virtually every person would be spurred toward spiritual pursuits by the mere knowledge that honor in the Next World is dependent on the degree of one's *mitzvah* observance in this world. It is only man's desire to lighten his burden of responsibility which deludes him into thinking that he will be satisfied to have any portion at all in the World to Come.

Hashem therefore pleaded, as it were, to His people, "*Take for Me an offering . . . Build for Me a sanctuary, so that I shall dwell among You.*" The Nation responded to this call and it remains the responsibility and privilege of every Jew to this very day to transform himself into a *Mishkan* so that the *Shechinah* will dwell within him.

◄§ A Tzaddik's Zeal

The key to accomplishing such a self-transformation is that one not be satisfied with anything but the very best in his spiritual pursuits. Lethargy and complacency are the prime deterrents to one's creating his personal *Mishkan*. The Torah leaders in every generation attained their great spiritual levels through consistent effort and a constant awareness of their purpose in this world.

The Ponovezher *Rav*, R' Yosef Shlomo Kahaneman, studied in the Chofetz Chaim's yeshivah in Radin. He related the following:

The Chofetz Chaim and his family once journeyed to Vilna where the Chofetz Chaim's *rebbetzin* underwent surgery. On the day when they were to return home to Radin, R' Kahaneman stood waiting at the Chofetz Chaim's house, for he wanted to observe the Chofetz Chaim's behavior in the moments immediately following his return. This is what he saw: The Chofetz Chaim walked through the door, removed his coat, and immediately sat down to study the *Rambam*'s laws of *me'ilah*[2] with the serenity and concentration of one who had been immersed in his studies for hours. R' Kahaneman, swept with excitement by this sight, hurried across the road to where the Chofetz Chaim's saintly son-in-law, R' Tzvi Hirsh Levensohn, lived. "Come," he told R' Hirsh, "and see how the *rebbi* is already studying with awesome and wondrous diligence."

---

2. A term referring to unlawful benefit from consecrated property.

All of us should strive to emulate the Chofetz Chaim's zeal, to acquire his flaming passion to fulfill Hashem's will. If we will succeed in this, then surely we will realize our goal in becoming a living *Mishkan*.

A Proper Perception

⋽ Shattered

וְזֶה הַדָּבָר אֲשֶׁר תַּעֲשֶׂה לָהֶם לְקַדֵּשׁ אֹתָם לְכַהֵן לִי, לְקַח פַּר אֶחָד
בֶּן בָּקָר וְאֵילִם שְׁנַיִם תְּמִימִם.

This is the thing that you shall do for them to sanctify them so that they may serve Me: Take one young bull and two rams, unblemished (29:1).

One young bull — to atone for the Sin of the Golden Calf (Rashi).

The Sin of the Golden Calf (*Sh'mos* ch. 32) is one of the most dismal episodes in our people's history. The nation had ascended to incredible heights after experiencing the Splitting of the Sea and then receiving the Torah at Sinai, only to suffer a serious lapse of faith. The result was that Moshe *Rabbeinu* shattered the first *Luchos*, Tablets, those who worshiped the calf perished, and Israel suffered a tremendous descent from the awesome spiritual level that it had attained.

Yet, the Jews achieved atonement for this grievous sin. Moshe prayed on their behalf, the people repented and Hashem instructed them to bring offerings such as the one cited above[1] so that they could achieve forgiveness.

It seems, though, that even Hashem's informing Moshe that He

---

1. See also *Vayikra* 9:2 with *Rashi.*

had forgiven the nation was not sufficient consolation. The people needed something more. We find in *Parashas Pekudei*:

אֵלֶּה פְקוּדֵי הַמִּשְׁכָּן מִשְׁכַּן הָעֵדֻת ...
These are the accounts of the Mishkan (Sanctuary), the Mishkan of testimony ... (38:21).
The Mishkan of testimony — A testimony for Israel that HaKadosh Baruch Hu forgave them for the Sin of the Golden Calf, for He manifested His Presence among them (Rashi).

That they required a testimony of their forgiveness is indicative of how deeply broken the people were. They were shattered, mournful over what had occurred, despondent over their spiritual fall. So broken were they that, when they were informed by Moshe of their having been forgiven, they found it difficult to rejoice, for in the depths of their hearts they could not believe that forgiveness was attainable. Then came the command to prepare for the construction of the *Mishkan*, a place that would serve as an abode for the *Shechinah*, Divine Presence, that would dwell among them once again. Only then did the people rejoice, for this was surely a sign that Hashem had forgiven them.

We find a similar pattern with regard to the festival cycle, where *Rosh Hashanah* and *Yom Kippur* are followed by *Succos*, which is called זְמַן שִׂמְחָתֵנוּ, *the season of our gladness.* After a period of intense *teshuvah*, repentance, when one ponders his deeds, recognizes his sins and seeks to repent, the natural result should be that one is left broken and drained, shattered by the awareness of his iniquities of the past year. The joy of *Succos* is meant to strengthen our spirits by infusing us with a spiritual joy stemming from a renewed closeness with Hashem.

Unfortunately, we are far from such feelings. We do not take leave of the Days of Awe broken by an awareness of how we have sinned. We certainly are not shattered to the point where we feel a need to be comforted or to seek some sort of testimony to our having been forgiven. This is because we lack an awareness of the spiritual havoc wrought by sin, of the destructiveness brought about in the Upper Worlds through our misdeeds. Were we to have such an awareness, we would seek ways to avoid those sins that we have committed, no less than we seek to prevent the recurrence of dangerous accidents.

❧ R' Masya ben Charash

The way in which *Chazal* viewed sin can be seen from an incredible incident (*Yalkut Shimoni Vayechi* §161) involving the Mishnaic sage R' Masya ben Charash. R' Masya's face was radiant like the sun, his countenance akin to that of a Heavenly angel, for all his life he had meticulously avoided gazing upon anything that might entice him to sin. R' Masya spent his days and nights in the *beis midrash*, toiling in the study of Torah.

It happened once, as R' Masya was studying, that Satan took notice of his shining countenance. Satan said, "Is it possible that this man has never sinned?" Satan then went before *HaKadosh Baruch Hu* and asked, "R' Masya ben Charash — what is he considered in your eyes?" *HaKadosh Baruch Hu* replied, "He is a perfect *tzaddik*." Satan countered, "Grant me permission that I may incite him [to sin]." *HaKadosh Baruch Hu* replied, "You will not be able to prevail over him." Satan responded, "Even so [I wish to try]." "Go," *HaKadosh Baruch Hu* said. Satan went and appeared before R' Masya as a very beautiful woman. As soon as R' Masya noticed her, he turned around so that she was behind him. Satan then went and stood to R' Masya's left, whereby R' Masya turned to his right. Satan confronted him every which way. R' Masya said to himself, "I am fearful, lest my *yetzer hara* (evil inclination) overpower me and cause me to sin." R' Masya then went and blinded himself! When Satan saw this, he was shaken and fell backwards. *HaKadosh Baruch Hu* then summoned the angel Raphael [the angel of healing] and told him, "Go and heal R' Masya ben Charash." The angel went and presented himself before R' Masya. "Who are you?" R' Masya asked. The angel replied, "I am the angel Raphael whom *HaKadosh Baruch Hu* has sent to heal you." R' Masya told him, "Let me be; whatever has occurred has occurred." The angel returned before *HaKadosh Baruch Hu* and repeated R' Masya's words. *HaKadosh Baruch Hu* told him, "Go and tell him that I am his guarantor that the *yetzer hara* will not have dominion over him." R' Masya allowed the angel to heal him and his eyesight returned.

Let us ponder this amazing incident. Hashem bore witness that R' Masya ben Charash was a צַדִּיק גָּמוּר, a perfect *tzaddik*, and that Satan would be unable to induce him to sin. Surely R' Masya realized that he was not a person who was accustomed to falling victim to temptation. Why then did he feel it necessary to blind himself? The answer is that despite his stature, R' Masya realized that he was human and was therefore capable of being swayed after his inclination, however remote the possibility might have been. He also understood the tremendous blemish that he would bring upon himself and upon the world were he to sin. Thus, with Satan tempting him every which way, he found it necessary to act as he did.

We live in a society where the streets abound with immoral sights virtually everywhere we turn. Yet there are many who gaze casually at their surroundings as they walk, deluding themselves into thinking that they will be unaffected by all this. What they are actually doing is causing their *yetzer hara* to incite them to sin. Such behavior is the very opposite of that of R' Masya ben Charash.

◄§ Nachum Ish Gamzu

Another illustration of the way in which our Sages viewed sin can be seen from the following *Gemara* (*Ta'anis* 21a):

> They said of Nachum Ish Gamzu[2] that both his eyes were blinded, both his hands and feet were amputated, and that he lay in a tenuous structure with the legs of his bed in basins of water so that ants could not crawl upon him.
>
> His disciples once asked him, "Our teacher: Since you are a perfect tzaddik, why has all this befallen you?" He told them, "Once, I was traveling on the road to my father-in-law's house and I had with me three donkeys, one laden with food, the second with drink and the third with all sorts of delicacies. A poor man came and stood near me on the road. 'Rebbi,' he begged, 'feed me.' I responded, 'Wait while I unload [some packages] from the donkey.' Before I had unloaded the donkey, his soul had already left him. I fell

---

2. He was called נַחוּם אִישׁ גַּם־זוּ because no matter what befell him he would always say גַּם־זוּ לְטוֹבָה, "This, too, is for the good" (see *Ta'anis* 21a).

upon his face and said, 'My eyes which did not take pity on you — let them be blinded. My hands which did not take pity on you — may they be cut off. My feet which did not take pity on you — may they be cut off.' My spirit was not calmed until I said, 'Let my entire body be covered with boils . . .' "

Nachum Ish Gamzu sinned in having the poor man wait while he unloaded a food package from his donkey. Had he simply ripped open a package and quickly handed the man something to eat, the man might not have died. For this, Nachum asked that he be deprived of his eyes, hand, and feet — all of which, he said, 'did not pity' the poor man.

Judging from the punishment that he brought upon himself and the way in which he spoke, one would have thought that Nachum acted toward the poor man with cruelty. We know that this was not the case at all.

Nachum faulted himself for not having considered the unlikely possibility that the man was on the verge of death, which in fact was the situation, though the poor man made no mention of this. Nachum considered this an offense so serious that it could be atoned for only by the terrible punishments that he requested.

Such an approach can only come from perceiving the gravity of sin.

⊷ Consider Three Things

The *Mishnah* in *Avos* (3:1) states:

Akavia ben Mehalalel said: "Consider three things and you will not come into the grip of sin: Know whence you came, whither you go, and before Whom you will give justification and reckoning. 'Whence you came?' — from a putrid drop; 'Whither you go?' — to a place of dust, worms and maggots; 'and before Whom will you give justification and reckoning?' — before the King Who reigns over kings, HaKadosh Baruch Hu."

Rabbeinu Yonah, in his commentary to *Avos*, explains:

> For the purpose of Creation is that man fear Hashem.
> Now, how can man sin when he considers before Whom
> he will have to give justification and reckoning — and
> even more so when he considers the punishments and
> trials that will be visited upon him for
> his sins? [When he will come to the Next World] he
> will feel intense shame ... for the shame which the
> soul experiences after it is separated from the body
> is greater than that which it feels when it re-
> sides within the body. The nature of the body is that
> it forgets, so when a man does something disgraceful
> he might feel shamed in front of others for a year or
> two, but as time goes on, the matter will become
> forgotten and the shame will leave him. However, when
> the soul is no longer in the body, it forgets nothing, for it
> is wholesome and pure and has no corporeal traits
> within it. [Therefore,] when it is shamed before the King
> Who reigns over kings, HaKadosh Baruch Hu, it will
> feel that shame eternally just as the moment when it
> stood before Him. As it was shamed in that instant, so
> it will remain shamed forever ...

Were we to take these words of *Rabbeinu Yonah* to heart, ponder
them *and be ever mindful of them,* then surely we would think twice
before doing that which is contrary to Hashem's will. Man's nature,
however, is that he does forget easily.

An amazing story is recorded involving R' Yosef Shmuel of
Frankfurt, who served as *Av Beis Din* of his famous city. He was a
gaon of towering stature and disseminated Torah to many disciples.
He is the compiler of *Hagahos HaShas.*

After R' Yosef Shmuel died, his *talmidim* continued their studies
in his *beis midrash* in the same manner as when their *rebbi* was alive.
One day, as the *talmidim* were learning, R' Yosef Shmuel suddenly
appeared to them, standing near his place in the *beis midrash!*
The *talmidim* were, of course, speechless with astonishment. After
some time had elapsed, R' Yosef Shmuel began to speak. "Do not
be afraid," he told them. "I will now explain why I have returned to
you.

"When I came before the Heavenly Tribunal, they decreed that I be accorded a place in *Gan Eden* next to the *Sh'lah haKadosh*.[3] When the *Sh'lah* learned of this, he said, 'True, R' Yosef Shmuel studied and knows all of Torah, and he also taught Torah to the masses. However, I [in addition to all this] have spread teachings of *mussar* and *yiras shamayim* (Heavenly fear) and I also authored a work on these subjects — while he did not.'

"The Heavenly Tribunal agreed with the *Sh'lah*, and thus they decreed that I return to my *talmidim* to arouse them to the enormous importance of studying works of *mussar* and *yiras shamayim*. Therefore," R' Yosef Shmuel concluded, "I have come before you now. I ask that you all resolve to study such works."

The *talmidim* made a verbal resolution to this effect and R' Yosef Shmuel disappeared.

We must learn from this story and strengthen our own study of *mussar*. Why must you wait for me to return from the World of Truth to exhort you to study *mussar*? I am informing you right now that this study is of paramount importance!

Klal Yisrael, whom Hashem described as a "stiff-necked people" (*Sh'mos* 32:9), sinned so grievously with the Golden Calf that they themselves did not imagine that forgiveness was possible. Yet they were forgiven, to the point where Moshe asked Hashem:

וּבַמֶּה יִוָּדַע אֵפוֹא כִּי מָצָאתִי חֵן בְּעֵינֶיךָ אֲנִי וְעַמֶּךָ, הֲלוֹא בְּלֶכְתְּךָ עִמָּנוּ.

For with what shall it be known that I and Your people find favor in Your eyes, if not in that You will accompany us (Sh'mos 33:16)?

The people had accepted the reproof of Moshe, and returned to Hashem with a whole heart. As a result, they once again reached a point where they found favor before Hashem. Any Jew who engages in sincere *teshuvah* likewise finds favor in His eyes. To what degree we return to Him is entirely in our hands.

---

3. R' Yeshayah Horowitz, famous sixteenth-century Kabbalist. He is known as *Sh'lah HaKadosh* (The Holy Sh'lah) after the name of his *magnum opus* שְׁנֵי לוּחוֹת הַבְּרִית, the initials of which form the acronym של"ה, *Sh'lah*. In this extensive work, *halachah*, *kabbalah* and homiletics are combined to form a work that spans the spectrum of ethical Jewish living.

Shabbos: Day of Return

וְשָׁמְרוּ בְנֵי יִשְׂרָאֵל אֶת הַשַּׁבָּת לַעֲשׂוֹת אֶת הַשַּׁבָּת לְדֹרֹתָם בְּרִית
עוֹלָם.

And the Children of Israel shall keep the Shabbos, to make the Shabbos an eternal covenant for their generations (31:16).

◆§ The Day's Essence

"R' Chiyah bar Aba said in the name of R' Yochanan: 'Whoever keeps the Shabbos in accordance with its laws will be forgiven [of his sins] — even if he worshiped idols as in the generation of Enosh' "[1] (*Shabbos* 118b). The above can be understood with an insight attributed to *Rokeach*,[2] explaining why Shabbos had no *korban chatas*, sin offering, as part of its *Mussaf* offering in the *Beis HaMikdash* (as opposed to *Yom Tov*). The reason for this, according to *Rokeach*, is that the very essence of Shabbos atones; there is no need for sacrificial atonement.

That Shabbos is in itself a source of atonement should be no cause for wonder if one sees the gift of Shabbos in its proper light.

As is well known, when a Jew observes Shabbos he is bearing witness that Hashem created the world in six days and rested, as it

---

1. See *Bereishis* 4:26.
2. R' Eliezer Rokeach of Worms, a twelfth-century Halachist and Kabbalist.

were, on the seventh. There is, however, another symbolism in Shabbos, that of the Exodus from Egypt. In the Friday-night *Kiddush*, the seventh day is described as both a זִכָּרוֹן לְמַעֲשֵׂה בְרֵאשִׁית, "remembrance of Creation," and a זֵכֶר לִיצִיאַת מִצְרַיִם, "remembrance of the Exodus from Egypt." In fact, this duality finds its origin in the Ten Commandments. In the first reading of the Commandments (*Sh'mos* 20:11), Creation is the focus of the *mitzvah* of Shabbos; while in the second reading (*Devarim* 5:15) the redemption from Egypt is mentioned. *Rambam* (ibid.) resolves this apparent contradiction by saying that the two concepts are intertwined with one another. The Exodus was Hashem's demonstration to the world that He controls all of Creation, takes note of man's behavior and manipulates nature accordingly. Thus, the Exodus bore witness to His creation — and hence, mastery — of the universe. Shabbos, symbolic of creation, must perforce serve as the backdrop of the Exodus because it represents how the events of the Exodus became possible.

Imagine an enormous mansion whose benevolent owner welcomes one and all to his home. The owner cares for his guests' every need; in return, he asks that for the duration of their stay, the guests adhere to his code of conduct. Would the guests have any choice other than to obey their host's wishes?

This earth is but a huge mansion, created by an omnipotent Master. More than a mere host to his guests, the Master is the Source of every soul. His every act is perfect and affects every one of us in a way that is ultimately to our benefit.

This is the message of Shabbos, symbol of Creation, symbol of Redemption. If one ponders these concepts as he experiences the Shabbos, he will inevitably enjoy an uplifting of the spirit. He will surely take leave of the Shabbos having attained some degree of *teshuvah*, a return to Hashem.

That Shabbos is a day auspicious for *teshuvah* became apparent soon after Creation.

◄§ Decree and Reprieve

When the jealousy of Kayin, son of Adam, was aroused against his brother Hevel, the result was murder [see discourse to *Parashas Bereishis*]. Hashem informed Kayin that as punishment, he, the tiller of soil, would no longer find the ground as productive as it had been; he would wander from place to place in search of fertile farmland. Tranquility would elude him.

Kayin viewed his punishment as a death sentence, for his wanderings would leave him vulnerable to attack. He exclaimed, "My iniquity [i.e., punishment] is too great to be borne! Behold, You have driven me from the face of the land and from Your countenance I will be hidden; I must become a vagrant and a wanderer on earth — whoever meets me will kill me" (*Bereishis* 4:14).[3] In response to Kayin's entreaties, Hashem gave him a sign of protection and declared that should Kayin be murdered, his death would be avenged.

According to *Rabbeinu Yonah* (*Sha'arei Teshuvah* 4:1), death was, in fact, decreed against Kayin. However, Kayin repented,[4] and in the merit of his *teshuvah*, the death sentence was commuted.

Midrash relates:

מִזְמוֹר שִׁיר לְיוֹם הַשַּׁבָּת. טוֹב לְהֹדוֹת לַה' ...

A psalm, a song for the Shabbos. It is good to thank Hashem ... (Tehillim 92).

R' Levi said: "This psalm was first sung by Adam. Adam encountered Kayin and asked him, 'What became of the judgment against you?' Kayin replied, 'I repented and was granted clemency.' Striking himself on the face [in amazement], Adam exclaimed, 'The power of teshuvah is so great and I did not know!' Adam immediately stood up and recited this psalm" (*Yalkut Shimoni* 4:38).

Without a doubt, Adam had reason to be amazed. Kayin had committed murder; and as *Rashi* (4:10) comments to the words, "[Hashem said,] '... the blood of your brother cries out to me from the ground,'" murder is more than the slaying of a single soul. Kayin was also held accountable for the blood of Hevel's potential descendants; their blood, along with the blood of Hevel, cried out to the Heavens for retribution. Yet, Kayin had been granted a reprieve.

There is more. The level of Kayin's *teshuvah* does not seem commensurate with either the nature of his sin or his own spiritual

---

3. Our translation follows *Ramban* as well as other commentators; *Targum* and *Rashi* offer a somewhat different interpretation.

4. *Ramban* understands the above-cited verse as Kayin's confession.

level. Kayin was akin to a *navi*, prophet, in that Hashem spoke directly to him. His sin was the result of nothing more than unbridled jealousy; and Hashem had admonished him to repent *before* he had killed his brother. Furthermore, why did Kayin repent? "... whoever meets me will kill me." His repentance was a *teshuvah mi'yirah*, repentance for fear of retribution, a *teshuvah* which *Mesilas Yesharim* (ch. 24) speaks of in most disparaging terms. Yet Kayin's *teshuvah* had saved him from death.

No wonder that Adam had cause for amazement. "So great is the power of *teshuvah!*" Adam then applied this revelation regarding *teshuvah* to Shabbos, a day whose essence is atonement and whose purpose inspires *teshuvah*. It was this insight which caused Adam to sing the praises of this lofty day.

◄§ Meriting the Blessing

" **W**hoever keeps the Shabbos *in accordance with its laws* will have all his sins forgiven." For Shabbos to atone it must be observed properly. This can only be achieved with a thorough knowledge of *hilchos Shabbos*; without such knowledge, it is virtually impossible to avoid unintentional transgression.[5]

We should take a lesson from the dread which *tzaddikim* have always felt for even unwitting *chillul Shabbos*. It is told that the Vilna *Gaon* once inadvertently touched a food shell on Shabbos and immediately fainted for having moved an item which is *muktzah*. Those present managed to revive him, but when he noticed the shell and recalled what had happened, the *Gaon* again fainted! When he came to a second time, the *Gaon's* wife immediately took the shell and began to chew it, thereby demonstrating that the shell was edible *besha'as ha'dechak*, in case of dire need; the shell was therefore not *muktzah*, since it had some permissible use. Only then was the *Gaon* calmed.

We can be sure that the *Gaon's* fainting had nothing to do with physical weakness. He was a man of incredible strength. My father,[6] of blessed memory, related in the name of elders in his generation

---

5. This observation is found in *Ya'aros D'vash*, as cited by the Chofetz Chaim in his preface to the third volume of *Mishnah Berurah*.
6. R' Moshe Yitzchak Segal, late *Rosh Yeshivah* of the Manchester Yeshivah.

that doctors who examined the *Gaon* declared his physical condition to be such that he could conceivably have lived well past one hundred years[7] — though he hardly ate or slept. His fainting stemmed from nothing more than the thought of his having inadvertently transgressed the Rabbinic prohibition of *muktzah*.

Of course, there is much more to Shabbos than adherence to prohibitions. A *ben Torah* must be ever mindful that he utilize the Shabbos as would be expected of one who is immersed day and night in Torah study. This thought lies in the very words of the Talmudic passage cited above: כָּל הַמְשַׁמֵּר שַׁבָּת כְּהִלְכָתוֹ, literally interpreted: "Whoever keeps the Shabbos in accordance with its laws," but which can be understood homiletically: "Whoever keeps the Shabbos in accordance with his personal dictates;" i.e., in accordance with his own spiritual level.

To perceive the awesome *kedushah* which is the essence of Shabbos, one must sanctify himself before and after the day is ushered in. One's readiness in this regard should be commensurate with his own spiritual level, for the greater his level, the greater should be his perception of the day's *kedushah*. With this approach, one will surely merit atonement of sins through his Shabbos observance.

⋅§ A Meaningful Order

In arranging his monumental *Yad HaChazakah*, the *Rambam* codified the Torah's laws in a very precise order. There is much to be learned from the arrangement of *Sefer HaMada*, The Book of Knowledge, the opening section of *Yad HaChazakah*.

This section opens with *Hilchos Yesodei HaTorah*, fundamentals of Jewish faith. It is obvious why these laws are listed first; without *emunah*, faith, one has nothing.

Next come *Hilchos Dei'os*, which focus on *midos* and an approach to living as dictated by Torah. These chapters precede any and every ritual-related law; and even the laws of Torah study appear only later. Proper *midos* are a prerequisite for ritual observance as they are

---

7. The *Gaon* died at age seventy-seven.

for the study of Torah. If one is lacking in *midos*, then his Torah and *mitzvos* are lacking as well.

In *Shiras Ha'azinu* (*Devarim* 32:2), Moshe *Rabbeinu* says, יַעֲרֹף כַּמָּטָר לִקְחִי, תִּזַּל כַּטַּל אִמְרָתִי, "May my teaching drop like the rain, may my utterance flow like the dew." The Vilna *Gaon* (*Even Sheleimah* 1) explains that rain nurtures and gives growth to whatever has been planted; so it is with Torah. If a person holds fast to those character traits which are destructive, then the Torah which he learns will actually lend strength in a negative sense. If he works to overcome his character deficiencies, then the Torah will nurture and give growth to the positive traits that have taken root within him.[8]

Hilchos Dei'os are followed by *Hilchos Talmud Torah*, Laws of Torah Study. *Hilchos Avodah Zarah*, laws pertaining to the sin of idol worship, are next. The juxtaposition of these laws with those preceding teaches that when proper effort is not expended toward correcting one's *midos ra'os*, negative traits, the result can even be idol worship, ר"ל.

Following the section on idol worship comes the conclusion of *Sefer HaMada* — *Hilchos Teshuvah*. With this order, *Rambam* teaches us that with proper recognition of Hashem's omnipotence and providence in all our affairs, and with proper effort, a Jew can repent fully from even the most severe transgressions. With faith and determination, even an idol worshiper can purify his sullied soul. Such is the power of *teshuvah*.

מִזְמוֹר שִׁיר לְיוֹם הַשַּׁבָּת . . .

---

8. This concept is found in the *Gemara* (*Yoma* 72b): "If he is worthy, then it [the Torah] becomes for him a potion a life; if he is unworthy, then it becomes for him a potion of death."

For Hashem, and with Alacrity

◆§ Meriting a Miracle

וְהַמְּלָאכָה הָיְתָה דַיָּם לְכָל הַמְּלָאכָה לַעֲשׂוֹת אֹתָהּ, וְהוֹתֵר.
And the bringing of the materials [for the Mishkan] was enough for all the work that had to be done — and more than enough (36:7).

*O*hr HaChaim (ibid.) notes the apparent contradiction in the above verse. First, we are told that the bringing of the materials was דַיָּם, *enough*, implying that the people brought whatever was necessary to build the *Mishkan* (Sanctuary), but not more than that. Then, the verse concludes with וְהוֹתֵר, *and more than enough*. In *Ohr HaChaim's* words, "If it was דַיָּם, it was not הוֹתֵר; if it was הוֹתֵר, it was not דַיָּם!" He offers the following resolution:

> *Perhaps the Torah is informing us of how beloved the Children of Israel were in the eyes of the Omnipresent; because they brought more than was necessary, Hashem therefore concerned Himself with the honor of each individual who troubled himself to bring something, and He insured that everything was included in the construction of the Mishkan. This is the intent of the verse: And the work, through which Hashem commanded that the Mishkan be built, sufficed (דַיָּם) to encompass all that the Children of Israel brought, even though it was more than was necessary (וְהוֹתֵר).*

Through a miracle, the receptacle was able to receive more than it could actually contain.

Two factors contributed to the people's meriting this miracle. Their giving of their own valuable possessions for the construction of the *Mishkan* and its vessels was done purely *lesheim shamayim*, for the sake of Heaven, free of any personal motives. Additionally, the people performed this *mitzvah* with *zerizus*, alacrity. Both these points are expressed by *Ohr HaChaim* earlier in the *parashah* (35:20): "They all took leave of Moshe [to bring the materials] as one, with *zerizus*, and not one was held back by his neighbor [i.e., no one tried to selfishly deter his friend so that he could bring a given item instead]."

◆§ Immeasurable Reward

An act that is performed *lesheim shamayim* is never forgotten Above. It can be performed in the utmost secrecy, without another soul knowing what has transpired. Whatever the case, it is taken note of and recorded in Heaven, and its rewards are everlasting.

There are times when years, even generations, can pass before the reward for such a deed is realized.

Bezalel received a Divine appointment to head the *Mishkan's* construction. In stating this selection, the Torah traces Bezalel's lineage to his grandfather Chur. *Da'as Zekeinim* (35:30) relates:

> When HaKadosh Baruch Hu told Moshe, וְעָשִׂיתָ, *And you shall do*, regarding the construction of the *Mishkan*, Moshe thought that he himself would construct everything. Said HaKadosh Baruch Hu to him: "It will not be as you imagine; rather, the grandson of the tzaddik, meaning Chur, who was killed because of the Sin of the Golden Calf, will come and construct it, for the Mishkan is an atonement for that sin." Therefore, the Torah states, "Observe! I have selected by name Bezalel, son of Uri, the son of Chur . . ."

As *Rashi* (32:5, citing *Midrash*) relates, Chur, who was the son of Miriam, rebuked those who were involved with the Golden Calf. The people responded by murdering Chur. For this act of *mesiras nefesh*, self-sacrifice, Chur merited that his grandson be granted the awesome privilege of constructing the abode for Hashem's Presence on this earth.

Elsewhere, we find an instance where an act of *mesiras nefesh* resulted in incredible reward, though the act was lacking in wholesome intent. Haran, brother of Avraham *Avinu*, was cast into a furnace and killed by King Nimrod for siding with Avraham when the latter challenged the king's worship of idols. To quote *Rashi* (*Bereishis* 11:28):

> *Midrash Aggadah relates that on account of his own father [Terach] did Haran die. Terach complained about his son Avram before Nimrod regarding Avram's destruction of his idols. Nimrod then cast Avram into a fiery furnace. Haran said to himself: "If Avram prevails then I am with him; if Nimrod prevails then I am with him." When Avram was saved, they asked Haran, "To which side do you belong?" He responded, "I am on Avram's side." They then cast him into the furnace and he was burned to death.*

Haran died because he allowed himself to be hurled into the fire on the assumption that he would merit the same miracle as his brother. Nevertheless, he did allow himself to be cast into the flames, having rejected Nimrod's idol worship and having joined the camp of Avram. Thus, he performed an act of *kiddush Hashem*, sanctification of Hashem's Name. For this, says *Sfas Emes* (*Lech Lecha*), Haran merited that the Davidic dynasty — and ultimately *Mashiach* — descend from him.[1] Hashem does not deny anyone the reward due him for even the most insignificant deed; this is certainly true of a deed performed for His sake.

All this should serve as a source of inspiration to those who battle their *yetzer hara*, striving and struggling to refine their *midos*, subjugate their desires, and become better servants of Hashem. People often anticipate an almost tangible spiritual uplift as a result of such efforts. When 'Divine Inspiration' is not forthcoming, they become disappointed and frustrated. There is no reason for such despair,

---

1. Haran was the father of Lot, whose daughter gave birth to Moav. Rus (Ruth), who descended from Moav, was the great-grandmother of David *HaMelech*.

for no effort that is expended *lesheim shamayim* is ever for naught. The most minuscule deed, verbal expression, or thought that is directed toward self-improvement does not go unnoticed. Though decades or even centuries may pass without a given act having borne fruit, one can rest assured that it *will* bear fruit at some point in time.[2]

The converse of the above is true as well. When one is indolent in his service of Hashem, the resulting loss may not become apparent for quite some time, but it *will* surface eventually.

✎§ The Error of the Nesi'im

In *Parashas Vayakhel* (35:27), we find that the *Nesi'im* (Tribal princes) brought the precious stones for the *Kohen Gadol*'s vestments as their contribution to the *Mishkan*. *Rashi* cites the *Midrash*:

> *Why did the Nesi'im see fit to be the first contributors at the dedication of the altar, while they did not do so for the Mishkan's construction? [At the time of the construction] the Nesi'im said, "Let the people donate whatever they wish to donate, then we will supply whatever is lacking." However, when the people*

---

2. On another occasion, HaRav Segal cited a *Sifra* (see *Rashi* to *Vayikra* 5:17) in which R' Yosei makes the following observation: We can see from Adam how much reward awaits those who observe the *mitzvos*. Adam had only one commandment: not to eat from the Tree of Knowledge; because of his failure, death was decreed upon his descendants for generations on end. Since Hashem's kindness is far greater than His strict justice, we cannot even imagine the rewards earned by those who observe numerous commandments, day in and day out.

R' Yosei offers three commandments as examples: *pigul*, the prohibition against consuming sacrificial meat whose blood service was performed with improper intent; *nosar*, sacrificial meat that cannot be eaten because the time span for its consumption has expired; and the requirement to fast on *Yom Kippur*. HaRav Segal noted that none of these three commandments involve great personal trials. While fasting on *Yom Kippur* is not easy, it is done on the most solemn day of the year, is a great source of atonement, and is so accepted that it is even observed among many who are for the most part non-observant. This is precisely why R' Yosei chose to mention these commandments. Even an act of self-control that is not a great test earns one immeasurable reward.

contributed all that was needed, as is written, "And the bringing of the materials was enough," the Nesi'im said, "What is there left for us to do?" They brought the Shoham and Miluim stones.[3] Therefore, they were the first to contribute at the dedication of the altar.

Because they were initially indolent, a letter is missing from their name — thus it is written (ibid.) וְהַנְּשִׂאִם [with a י omitted].

While *Rashi* says of the *Nesi'im*: לְפִי שֶׁנִּתְעַצְּלוּ מִתְּחִילָה, *Because they were initially indolent*, we must understand that these *tzaddikim* were not guilty of indolence as we know it. To be sure, their intentions *were* meritorious. They had no idea how much or how little would be needed to supplement the people's contributions, yet they generously offered to provide any missing item. Nevertheless, this approach was found wanting.

Midrash (*Bereishis Rabbah* 47:1) relates that when the name of שָׂרַי, *Sarai*, was changed to שָׂרָה, *Sarah*, the letter י that was taken from the Matriarch's name needed to be appeased, as it were, by later being used to change the name of הוֹשֵׁעַ בֶּן נוּן to יְהוֹשֻׁעַ. Thus, the omission of this letter in the word נְשִׂאִם indicates a significant lapse, according to their exalted level of service. While everyone else rushed home with *zerizus*, they remained in their places. Apparently, they should have taken note of the people's alacrity and realized that there existed a possibility that there would be nothing left to be brought. This oversight is recorded for eternity — for us to learn from — by the omission of a letter from their name.

◆§ Alacrity vs. Indolence

In discussing the attribute of *zerizus*, *Mesilas Yesharim* (ch. 6) writes:

Man's nature is extremely sluggish because of the grossness of his corporeal being. It is thus that man does not desire exertion or work. One who seeks to merit

---

3. These stones were worn upon the shoulder-straps and breast-plate (*choshen*) of the *Kohen Gadol*, respectively.

serving his Creator, Blessed is He, must strengthen himself against his own nature and act with alacrity, for if he remains with his natural sluggishness then he will certainly not succeed. Thus does the Tanna [Mishnaic sage] say: "Be bold as a leopard, light as an eagle, swift as a deer, and strong as a lion, to carry out the will of your Father in Heaven" (Avos 5:23) . . . It is plainly stated in Scripture, "Be exceedingly strong and courageous to safeguard to do according to all the teachings that Moshe, My servant, commanded you" (Yehoshua 1:7).

In the above-cited verse, Hashem is exhorting none other than Yehoshua bin Nun: חֲזַק וֶאֱמַץ מְאֹד, *Be exceedingly strong and courageous!* Dare we consider ourselves superior to Yeshoshua? If he needed to strengthen himself in carrying out his charge, then certainly we must do the same.

Mesilas Yesharim continues:

Shlomo [HaMelech] repeatedly cautions in this regard, for he took note of the evil of indolence and the great loss that results from it. He declared (Mishlei 6:10): "A little sleep, a little slumber, a little folding of the hands in order to retire. Then poverty will come upon you like a surprise visitor, your wants [will spring upon you] like a man who shields." For even though an indolent one does not actively do evil, he nevertheless brings evil upon himself in a passive way.

As *Rashi* (ibid.) explains, the above verse is referring to indolence associated with Torah study. Indolence inclines a person to sleep late in the morning ("Only five minutes more") and then approach his studies in a manner that will demand little effort on his part. His learning sessions will be sprinkled with idle conversation — which completely alters the nature of the learning itself. Moreover, indolence breeds a learning that is very superficial, leaving the student without any clarity in that which he has attempted to study. *A little sleep, a little slumber . . . then poverty will come upon you . . .*

Mesilas Yesharim offers another citation from *Mishlei*:

עַל שְׂדֵה אִישׁ עָצֵל עָבַרְתִּי וְעַל כֶּרֶם אָדָם חֲסַר לֵב, וְהִנֵּה עָלָה

כְּלּוֹ קִמְּשֹׁנִים כָּסוּ פָנָיו חֲרֻלִּים וְגֶדֶר אֲבָנָיו נֶהֱרָסָה. וָאֶחֱזֶה אָנֹכִי,
אָשִׁית לִבִּי, רָאִיתִי לָקַחְתִּי מוּסָר.

I passed by the field of a lazy man, and by the vineyard
of a man devoid of understanding, and lo, it had become
overgrown with thorns, briars had covered it over, and
its stone fence had been destroyed. I perceived this and
considered it well, I looked upon it and took from it a
lesson (Mishlei 24:30-32).

Shlomo *HaMelech*, the wisest of men, took note of a field which
he chanced upon, pondered it and learned from it a lesson to carry
through life. What had once been a vineyard had become a plot of
earth barren of everything but thorns and briars. Shlomo realized that
this did not happen overnight. "I perceived this and considered it
well" — *I pondered this matter and saw the great harm [borne of*
indolence], for it is like a poison that spreads through the body little
by little, its effects unnoticed until death occurs (Mesilas Yesharim
ibid.).

This brings us once again to our earlier comment, that just as the
positive effects of *zerizus* and acting *lesheim shamayim* are not
always immediately apparent, so are the detriments of indolence
often unnoticed at first — but they are present nonetheless. If not
conquered, indolence can be totally destructive until one is left with
virtually nothing at all.

As we study Torah, let us emulate Shlomo who knew how to
ponder a matter and draw out the lesson inherent in it. When
studying *Parashas Vayakhel*, we must ponder the *zerizus* of the
nation and the criticism directed at the *Nesi'im* for their lack of
alacrity. Such contemplation is genuine *mussar* study and will
certainly lead to a strengthening of our *avodas Hashem*.

ויקרא
Vayikra

The Message of Korbanos

◄§ Beyond Our Grasp

Rambam, in *Yad HaChazakah* (*Hilchos Me'ilah* 8:8), writes:

> ... *Mishpatim are mitzvos whose reasons are obvious and the practical benefits of which are well known; examples include the prohibitions against robbery and murder and the commandment to honor one's father and mother. Chukim are mitzvos whose reasons are not known. As the Sages put it, [Hashem says,] "I have issued decrees and you have no right to question them." One's evil inclination is troubled by them and the nations of the world speak against them. Examples include: the prohibition against eating swine and the laws regarding milk and meat; eglah arufah [Devarim 21], parah adumah [Bamidbar 19]; and the azazel goat [Vayikra 16].*
>
> *How much did David HaMelech suffer because of the heretics and idol worshipers who spoke against the chukim! [Yet,] all the while that they were pursuing him with false refutations, contrived in accordance with their narrow-mindedness, his attachment to Torah was becoming strengthened, as is written (Tehillim 119:69), "Willful sinners piled falsehood on me, but I cherish Your precepts with all my heart." It is*

also written (ibid., v. 86), "All Your commandments are faithful; they pursue me with lies — help me!"

All korbanos (offerings) fall under the category of chukim. The Sages have said that the world exists because of the service of korbanos [Megillah 31b]. For through the observance of chukim and mishpatim the upright merit the World to Come; and the command regarding chukim precedes that of mishpatim, as is written (Vayikra 18:5), "You shall heed My chukim and mishpatim which a person shall perform and live by them."

Various reasons for the *korbanos* are given by the classic commentators. With all that has been written, it is still beyond us to grasp just why the slaughter of a sanctified animal, the placing of its blood and the burning of its flesh upon the altar, should bring Hashem's Presence down to earth. It is impossible to fathom the ramifications of each particular service, be it an animal offering, meal-offering, wine libation or any of the other aspects of the Temple sacrificial service. *Ritva (Sefer Zikkaron)* writes that the reason for *korbanos* is so profound that, in its entirety, it is beyond human comprehension and the best efforts of our greatest thinkers are only a drop in the ocean of Hashem's intent. Therefore, *Rambam* places *korbanos* in the category of *chukim*, commandments whose reasons are not known to us.

When a Jew offers a *korban*, he is demonstrating his unquestioning submission to Hashem's will. It is as if he is saying, "I do not understand *why* this offering will accomplish great things for myself and for the world, but I know that it *will* accomplish great things, for that is what Hashem has taught us by way of His Torah." Thus, the bringing of a *korban* is a great declaration of faith. It is through this approach to Torah and *mitzvos* that a Jew earns himself a portion in the World to Come. This is what *Chazal* mean in saying that the world exists because of the service of *korbanos*.

Today, our recital of the Scriptural order of the *korbanos* service takes the place of the actual offerings. As we say during *Shacharis* when reciting the order of *korbanos*:

יְהִי רָצוֹן מִלְּפָנֶיךָ, ה' אֱלֹקֵינוּ וֵאלֹקֵי אֲבוֹתֵינוּ, שֶׁיְּהֵא שִׂיחַ ...
שִׂפְתוֹתֵינוּ חָשׁוּב וּמְקֻבָּל וּמְרֻצֶּה לְפָנֶיךָ, כְּאִלּוּ הִקְרַבְנוּ קָרְבַּן
הַתָּמִיד ...

*. . . May it be Your will, Hashem, our God, and the God
of our forefathers, that the prayer of our lips be worthy,
favorable and acceptable before You, as if we had
brought the tamid offering . . .*

When a Jew utters these words he is in effect saying the following:
"I know that in this world there are *chukim* which I do not
understand, but I accept them nevertheless for they are an expression
of Your will." One should carry this message with him throughout
each day; then, he will have the fortitude to weather whatever trials
the day may bring.

◄§ One Man Alone

Elsewhere in *Yad HaChazakah* (*Hilchos Avodah Zarah* 1:1-3),
Rambam traces Avraham *Avinu's* beginnings:

*In the days of Enosh [Bereishis 4:26], the people fell into
gross error, and the wise men of the generation began to
give foolish counsel. Enosh himself was among those
who erred. Their error was as follows: "Since God
created the stars and spheres to guide the world, set
them on high and allotted them honor, and since they
are ministers who serve before Him, they deserve to be
praised and glorified, and honor should be rendered
them . . ." This was the root of idolatry, and this was
what the idolaters, who knew its fundamentals, said . . .*

*In the course of time, false prophets arose who
asserted that God had commanded and explicitly told
them, "Worship that particular star, . . . offer such and
such sacrifices to it. Erect a temple to it. Make a statue
of it, to which all the people shall bow down . . ."*

*So gradually the custom spread throughout the
world to worship figures with various types of worship
. . . As time went on, the honored and revered Name of
God was forgotten by mankind. It vanished from their
lips and hearts and was no longer known to them. All
the common people, including women and children,
knew only the figures of wood and stone . . . Even their*

wise men, such as priests and the like, also fancied that there was no God save for the stars and heavenly spheres for which the figures were made.

The Creator of the universe was known to none and recognized by none, save a few solitary individuals, such as Enosh, Mesushelach, Noach, Shem, and Ever. The world moved on in this fashion until the Pillar of the World, the Patriarch Avraham, was born.

As soon as this mighty one was weaned, his mind began to ponder, though he was but a small child. He would meditate day and night and wonder: How is it possible that this sphere, which functions ceaselessly, can be without a Guide? Who causes it to revolve? — for it is impossible that it is self-revolving! He had no teacher, nor anyone to make him cognizant of anything; rather, he was mired in Ur Kasdim among the foolish idol worshipers. His father, mother, and all the people worshiped idols — and he worshiped along with them, while his heart pondered and perceived until it ascertained the true path and his proper logic realized that which is correct. He realized that there exists one God and it is He Who guides the spheres and it is He Who created everything and that there is no power whose source is external of Him. He understood that all the world was in error and that the cause of all this was their worship of the stars and images until the truth had been completely lost from their minds. At age forty, Avraham recognized his Creator.

As soon as he recognized and perceived [all this], he began to refute the people of Ur Kasdim and debate them, saying, "This path that you are treading is not a true one." He smashed their images and began to make the people aware that it is improper to worship anything, save for the God of the universe . . . Once he triumphed over them with his proofs, the king [Nimrod] sought to kill him and a miracle was wrought for him.

To *Rambam's* statement that Avraham recognized his Creator at age forty, *Ra'avad* raises an apparent contradiction from the Aggadic teaching (*Nedarim* 33a) that Avraham perceived this truth at age three. In fact, *Rambam* seems to contradict his own earlier statement that "as soon as this mighty one was weaned, his mind began to ponder ..." *Kesef Mishneh* (citing *Hagahos Maimoniyos*) resolves the difficulty by explaining that Avraham's quest for truth began at age three, but it was not until age forty that his clear perception of Hashem as the Source of all existence was complete.

Note that *Rambam* writes, "He would meditate day and night." Day after day, night after night — for thirty-seven years! — Avraham strove to uncover the light of truth that had been all but forgotten in those generations of spiritual darkness. He tread this path alone, one man against an entire world. As the *Midrash* (*Bereishis Rabbah* 42:13) tells us, "The whole world was on one side and he [i.e., Avraham] was on the other."

How did Avraham view his encounter with death at the hand of Nimrod in Ur Kasdim? He saw it as a *chok*, a royal decree of the King of kings, the reason for which he did not know. This, too, was Avraham's view of the *Akeidah*, when he was commanded to make the ultimate sacrifice and offer his beloved son Yitzchak on the altar before God. The command regarding the *Akeidah* was an apparent contradiction to two other Heavenly utterances. Hashem had promised Avraham (*Bereishis* 21:12), "... that through Yitzchak will offspring be considered yours," meaning, that only Yitzchak (and not Yishmael) would be considered Avraham's genuine offspring and heir to his spiritual legacy. What would become of that promise now? Also, Avraham observed all 613 *mitzvos* (*Kiddushin* 20a), one of which specifically prohibits the idol worshiping of *Molech* where fathers would offer their children as sacrifices (*Vayikra* 18:21; see *Ramban*). Why, then, was Hashem commanding that Yitzchak be offered as a sacrifice? Avraham did not allow these questions to deter him as he calmly headed toward Mount Moriah.

Whence did Avraham derive the spiritual strength to withstand such tests? There is but one answer. Avraham's *emunah*, faith, was pure and complete. It was unshakable. Nothing, not even the most enigmatic order from Above, could sway Avraham from his belief in Hashem, in His perfection and in the ultimate goodness of His ways. Not for a moment did Avraham consider disobeying Hashem's commands, ר״ל. He had questions, but they did not disturb him.

Through his behavior, Avraham taught the message of *korbanos*, namely, that one must accept the Divine will with pure faith, without question. How one accepts the *chukim* of life will depend on the strength of his *emunah*.

⋙ In Our Own Lives

It is impossible for us to grasp the workings of Providence with regard to our nation as a whole, especially in these days of *hester panim*[1] when all that occurs is veiled in layers of concealment. The same is true on an individual level; our personal lives are fraught with *chukim*, occurrences and situations that are unexpected, inexplicable and often not to our liking. When Providence sends such events our way we must see them for what they are: Heaven's method of instructing us in the chapter of *chukim*. We do not have to understand everything, but we are obligated to accept all that occurs as the Divine will. As *Ramban* (*Shemos* 13:12) writes:

> From the great, famous miracles [i.e., the Exodus from Egypt] one comes to recognize the hidden miracles which are the foundations of the entire Torah. For a person has no share in the Torah of Moshe Rabbeinu unless he believes that all events and occurrences are miracles; they are not natural or simply the way of the world, both with regard to the community and the individual . . . all is decreed from Above.[2]

---

1. Lit., "concealment of [His] Countenance," a metaphor used when describing a period in which the manifestation of Providence is difficult to discern.
2. This passage from *Ramban* is the subject of the discourse to *Parashas Re'eh*.

A Time for Caution

⊷§ Warning Signs

צַו אֶת אַהֲרֹן וְאֶת בָּנָיו לֵאמֹר זֹאת תּוֹרַת הָעֹלָה.

Command Aharon and his sons saying: "This is law of the olah offering" (6:2).

R*ashi* (citing *Sifra*) notes the use of the emphatic term צַו, *command*,[1] to introduce the laws of the *olah* offering. He explains that the *Kohanim* are being urged to be especially zealous in performing this service and that this exhortation must be stressed to future generations as well. *Rashi* concludes with a comment of the Mishnaic sage R' Shimon, that an exhortation to be zealous is especially important with regard to *mitzvos* where there exists a possibility of monetary loss, as is the case here.[2]

We can liken this to a warning sign on a road where there is a remote possibility of mishap. The fact that an accident is unlikely does not dispel the need for a warning sign. In a similar vein, the Torah cautions us when there exists even a remote possibility of weakness related to performance of a *mitzvah*. Though we would not expect a *Kohen*, or any Jew for that matter, to let monetary loss affect his service, such a possibility exists nevertheless. Thus, the use of צַו, *command* — a warning for all generations.

---

1. As opposed to אֱמֹר, *say*, or דַּבֵּר, *speak*.

2. Various explanations are given for the monetary loss associated with the *olah* offering. See, for example, *Ramban*, *Chizkuni*, and *Gur Aryeh*.

◆§ Crossing the Threshold

There are periods in a person's life when the need for caution is especially urgent. To better understand this, we cite the following passage in *Midrash Tanchuma* (*Naso §12*):

> וַיְהִי בְּיוֹם כַּלּוֹת מֹשֶׁה לְהָקִים אֶת הַמִּשְׁכָּן, *And it was on the day that Moshe completed setting up the Mishkan (Sanctuary)* [*Bamidbar 7:1*]: וַי בְּיוֹם כַּלּוֹת מֹשֶׁה, *Woe on the day when Moshe completed setting it up!*
>
> *This can be likened to a king who had a quarrelsome wife. He therefore told her: "Make for yourself a royal garment." She began work on it. As long as she was busy with it she did not quarrel. She finally completed her work and brought it to the king, who examined it and found it very much to his liking. Suddenly the king began to moan, "Woe, woe!" Said his wife to him, "What is this, my master? I troubled myself to fulfill your wishes and you respond with 'Woe, woe?!' " Replied the king, "Your work is exceedingly pleasing to me ... However, as long as you were busy with it, you did not become angry and did not torment me. Now that you are without work, I fear that you will once again anger me."*
>
> *So did HaKadosh Baruch Hu say: "As long as My children were busy building the Mishkan, they did not complain. Now that their work is complete, they will begin [to complain]."*

During the years when a *ben Torah* engages in full-time study of Torah, his responsibility to follow the yeshivah schedule and curriculum ensures that his days and nights will be utilized properly. When the moment comes that he steps out into the world as his full-time study comes to an end, a warning signal must be flashed, for the possibility of danger exists. Then, he is on his own and must rely on his own fortitude to live up to the title 'ben Torah' that his yeshivah years have earned him.

In truth, the above is also highly relevant to those still involved in full-time study, for they too step out into the world, in a sense, when *bein haz'manim*, intersession, arrives. It is important to spell out what *bein haz'manim* should and should not be.

⋸§ Bein HaZ'manim

Bein haz'manim serves an important purpose in that it allows a student to rest up from the pace of the yeshivah schedule, thereby renewing his strength for the coming semester. However, it must not be a time of *hefkeirus*, irresponsibility. While one should take time to relax, he must make sure to set aside a significant, fixed period of time each day for Torah study. As always, the learning should be without any unnecessary interruption. The Chofetz Chaim writes that one does not see fruit from Torah study that is interrupted by idle conversation.

Most ideal is the establishing of '*bein haz'manim yeshivos*' where students organize themselves to assemble at one meeting place for their daily study sessions. "There is no comparison between a few who fulfill the Torah to a multitude that fulfills the Torah" (*Toras Kohanim, Bechukosai* 26:8). A *mitzvah* performed by a רַבִּים, *multitude*, is a different *mitzvah* entirely.

One should not neglect his *mussar* study during *bein haz'manim*, nor the daily study of *Sefer Chofetz Chaim* on the laws of *shemiras halashon* (guarding one's tongue). Anyone who studies the Chofetz Chaim's works perceives the resultant impression made upon his soul, for the Chofetz Chaim's words are *kodesh kodashim*, holiest of holies.

Along with the title '*ben Torah*' comes an awesome responsibility. A *ben Torah* must never forget that he is viewed by others as an embodiment of Torah — as he ought to be. Always, his behavior should inspire others to exclaim, "Fortunate is his father who taught him Torah! Fortunate is his teacher who taught him Torah! Woe to those who do not study Torah! He who studies Torah — how beautiful are his ways and how proper are his deeds!"[3]

Unfortunately, there are those who do not appreciate the individual and communal benefits of having our young men dedicate

---

3. *Yoma* 86a.

themselves to the full-time study of Torah. When such people observe a *ben Torah* conducting himself in a negative manner, they see this as support for their views. Thus, a *ben Torah* must realize that his behavior has far-reaching ramifications.

The *ben Torah* must carry this recognition with him every day of the year, including *bein haz'manim*. During *bein haz'manim*, one should exercise his usual *zehirus*, cautiousness, in matters of *tefillah* regardless of which sort of *minyan* he finds himself in. This includes not speaking during the recitation of *Kaddish*, the *chazzan's* repetition of *Shemoneh Esrei*, or the Torah reading. A *ben Torah* who is not cautious in this regard is guilty of *chillul Hashem*, aside from transgressing the *halachah*. Also, one should not adopt the practice of common vacationers who sleep into the late hours of the morning, even if he will still be able to *daven* with *minyan* within the halachically proscribed time-frame. Rather, a *ben Torah* should live up to the opening statement of *Shulchan Aruch* (*Orach Chaim* 1:1) that a Jew should "strengthen himself like a lion" and rise early and with a freshness to serve his Maker.

When a *ben Torah* does his vacation-time shopping, he must take care to deal with the proprietor in a most befitting manner and speak in a most refined way. Wherever he goes, his behavior should be a *kiddush Hashem* and inspire others to exclaim, "Praiseworthy is he who studies Torah!"

As a *ben Torah* spends much of his *bein haz'manim* at home, this is a most opportune time for fulfilling the *mitzvah* of honoring one's parents. In advent of *Yom Tov*, mothers are especially in need of their sons' help and such help should be offered generously. One will have thus fulfilled both the *mitzvah* of *kibud eim* and *gemilas chesed* (performing acts of kindness), for assisting a parent is no less a *chesed* than assisting anyone else. When providing such assistance, one should have in mind the fulfillment of these two *mitzvos*.

There is one area in which one must *not* obey his parent's wishes. Under no circumstances should anyone oblige his parents by joining them to watch television. Words cannot describe the awesome spiritual dangers of watching television. When confronted with such an invitation, one should imagine that he is being asked to blind himself in both eyes! Watching television is clearly forbidden by *halachah* and is inexcusable. However, when refusing such invitations, one should take care to speak to his parents in a respectful manner, as always.

✑ Daily Admonition

At the outset of our discussion, we spoke of the need for 'warning signals' when the threat of spiritual danger exists. In fact, we are cautioned in this regard twice daily. In the second portion of *Shema* (*Devarim* 11:13-21), we read:

וְהָיָה אִם שָׁמֹעַ תִּשְׁמְעוּ אֶל מִצְוֹתַי אֲשֶׁר אָנֹכִי מְצַוֶּה אֶתְכֶם הַיּוֹם,
לְאַהֲבָה אֶת ה' אֱלֹקֵיכֶם וּלְעָבְדוֹ בְּכָל לְבַבְכֶם וּבְכָל נַפְשְׁכֶם.
וְנָתַתִּי מְטַר אַרְצְכֶם בְּעִתּוֹ יוֹרֶה וּמַלְקוֹשׁ, וְאָסַפְתָּ דְגָנֶךָ וְתִירֹשְׁךָ
וְיִצְהָרֶךָ. וְנָתַתִּי עֵשֶׂב בְּשָׂדְךָ לִבְהֶמְתֶּךָ וְאָכַלְתָּ וְשָׂבָעְתָּ.

And it will come to pass that if you continually hearken to My commandments that I command you today, to love Hashem your God, and to serve Him with all your heart and with all your soul — then I will provide rain for your land in its proper time, the early and late rains, that you may gather in your grain, your wine, and your oil. I will provide grass in your field for your cattle and you will eat and be satisfied.

To serve Hashem בְּכָל לְבַבְכֶם, *with all your heart*, is to weigh every thought, word, and deed to see if it is in full consonance with Hashem's will. Thus, this verse speaks of the highest form of *avodas Hashem*, service of Hashem. The reward for such service is bountiful material blessing, for such blessing will allow its recipient to devote his days and nights to spiritual pursuits.

The Torah continues with a warning:

הִשָּׁמְרוּ לָכֶם, פֶּן יִפְתֶּה לְבַבְכֶם, וְסַרְתֶּם וַעֲבַדְתֶּם אֱלֹהִים אֲחֵרִים
וְהִשְׁתַּחֲוִיתֶם לָהֶם. וְחָרָה אַף ה' בָּכֶם וְעָצַר אֶת הַשָּׁמַיִם וְלֹא יִהְיֶה
מָטָר, וְהָאֲדָמָה לֹא תִתֵּן אֶת יְבוּלָהּ. וַאֲבַדְתֶּם מְהֵרָה מֵעַל הָאָרֶץ
הַטֹּבָה אֲשֶׁר ה' נֹתֵן לָכֶם.

Beware lest your heart be seduced and you turn astray and serve gods of others and bow to them. Then the wrath of Hashem will blaze against you. He will restrain the heaven so there will be no rain and the ground will not yield its produce. And you will swiftly be banished from the good land which Hashem gives you.

Rashi (ibid.) explains that this warning is sounded as a follow-up to the promise of וְשָׂבָעְתָּ, *and you will be satisfied*, for in a time of prosperity one needs particularly to be on guard against disloyalty to Hashem. The Torah warns specifically against idol worship, says *Rashi*, for once a person neglects the Torah he begins a course that will end in idolatry — though he initially served Hashem with all his heart!

A *Mishnah* in *Avos* sums up the Torah's message here:

אַל תַּאֲמִין בְּעַצְמְךָ עַד יוֹם מוֹתָךְ.

Do not believe in yourself until the day of your death (Avos 2:5).

There is no room for complacency in the spiritual realm. No one, no matter how impressive his spiritual achievements, can assume that he will be unaffected by a laxity in behavior. This is true in both an active and passive sense. Earlier we discussed the need for constant vigilance with regard to *tefillah*, Torah study, and our dealings with others. Vigilance is equally vital with regard to what we read, where we go and what our eyes see as we walk among today's immoral society. Let no one delude himself into thinking that a look in the wrong direction or the reading of today's secular literature will not affect him. It will. And once a person begins to slide, there is no telling how far he may go. This we see in the second portion of *Shema*, where those who serve Hashem with a full heart are cautioned lest they start on a path that will result in idol worship — from the zenith of Divine service to the nadir of impurity.

The Torah then continues:

... וְשַׂמְתֶּם אֶת דְּבָרַי אֵלֶּה עַל לְבַבְכֶם וְעַל נַפְשְׁכֶם

Place these words of Mine upon your hearts and upon your souls ...

We may suggest that "these words" (דְּבָרַי אֵלֶּה) refers to the message of אַל תַּאֲמִין בְּעַצְמְךָ עַד יוֹם מוֹתָךְ that is implicit in this chapter. It is this which we are to 'place upon our hearts,' all our days. No matter how much we achieve, we must awaken each dawn with a freshness, forever striving to grow and forever watchful against possible deterrents to our spiritual goals. Having taken this message to heart, we will surely see success from our efforts and soar ever higher in our service of Hashem.

The Kashrus Laws

❧ A Dulled Heart

A major portion of this *parashah* deals with מַאֲכָלוֹת אֲסוּרוֹת, *forbidden foods;* specifically, those creatures which the Torah prohibits a Jew to eat. Near the *parashah's* conclusion, the Torah stresses the reason for these laws in powerful terms:

וְלֹא תְטַמְּאוּ בָּהֶם וְנִטְמֵתֶם בָּם.

Do not contaminate yourselves through them lest you become contaminated through them (11:43).

Mesilas Yesharim (ch. 11) explains:

> *One who is lenient [regarding kashrus] in a situation where the Sages require stringency is destroying his own soul. In the words of Sifra [to the above-quoted verse]: "If you will contaminate yourselves through [eating] them, you will in the end become defiled [spiritually] through them." This means that forbidden foods bring impurity into the heart and soul of a person — literally — until the sanctity of the Omnipresent, Blessed is He, removes itself and distances itself from him. This is also the intent of the teaching (Yoma 39a): "וְנִטְמֵתֶם בָּם — Do not read it וְנִטְמֵתֶם (lest you become contaminated); rather, [understand it as if it would say] וְנִטַּמְתֶם (lest you become dulled)," for sin dulls a*

person's heart, as it removes from him true wisdom and the intellectual spirit which HaKadosh Baruch Hu confers upon His pious ones ... The person thus remains beastly and earthy, immersed in the grossness of this world. Forbidden foods are worse in this regard than other sins, for they literally enter a person's body and become a part of his flesh.

⋘ From Infancy — and Earlier

When, as a three-month-old, Moshe *Rabbeinu* was taken from the water by the daughter of Pharaoh, he would not nurse from the Egyptian women. As the *Gemara* (*Sotah* 12b) comments, the mouth that was destined to speak with the *Shechinah*, Divine Presence, could not nurse from a non-Jewess. *Rashi* (ibid.) explains that a mother's milk has in it the flavor of those foods that she consumes. In this case, the Egyptian women had certainly consumed foods forbidden to a Jew, therefore Moshe could not drink of their milk.

Such concern over מַאֲכָלוֹת אֲסוּרוֹת is not limited to those who converse with the *Shechinah*. *Rama* (*Yoreh Deah* 81:7) writes that though the *halachah* permits a Jewish infant to be nursed by a heathen woman, this should nevertheless be avoided, "For the milk of a heathen dulls the heart and instills in the infant a bad nature." Moreover, adds *Rama*, if a Jewish mother's failing health forces her to partake of מַאֲכָלוֹת אֲסוּרוֹת[1], she should not nurse her child during this period.

Note that all this is said of mother's milk, which is but a by-product of מַאֲכָלוֹת אֲסוּרוֹת!

The *Gemara* (*Chagigah* 15b) tells of Acher [Elisha ben Avuyah], the Mishnaic sage who in the end turned heretic. *Tosafos* (ibid.) cites *Talmud Yerushalmi* where a number of opinions are offered as to the source of Acher's astonishing decline. According to R' Nassan, "When Acher's mother was pregnant with him, she passed before a place of idol worship and smelled the aroma of that sort [of offering]. She ate of [the offering] and it seethed inside her like a serpent's venom."

---

1. Of course, such matters must be decided upon by a competent halachic authority.

Here is a vivid illustration of how deeply מַאֲכָלוֹת אֲסוּרוֹת can affect a Jewish soul. The food consumed by an expectant mother resulted in her child becoming a heretic. While this is not to say that such will be the result whenever a mother partakes of that which is unkosher, it nevertheless underscores the importance of zealousness in matters of *kashrus*. The *neshamah* is affected whenever unkosher food is consumed, and the affects can be devastating, ר"ל.

What can one do to counteract the spiritual harm caused by unwitting consumption of מַאֲכָלוֹת אֲסוּרוֹת? He must seek additional *kedushah*, sanctity, through the performance of *mitzvos*. In the blessing recited prior to the performance of most *mitzvos*, we say: אֲשֶׁר קִדְּשָׁנוּ בְּמִצְוֹתָיו . . . , *Who has sanctified us through His mitzvos*. Every *mitzvah* endows its performer with added *kedushah*.[2]

❀ ❀ ❀

The *Mishnah* in *Avos* (3:4) states:

רַבִּי שִׁמְעוֹן אוֹמֵר: שְׁלשָׁה שֶׁאָכְלוּ עַל שֻׁלְחָן אֶחָד וְלֹא אָמְרוּ עָלָיו דִּבְרֵי תוֹרָה, כְּאִלּוּ אָכְלוּ מִזִּבְחֵי מֵתִים.
R' Shimon said: "If three have eaten at the same table and have not spoken words of Torah there, it is as if they have eaten of offerings to dead idols."

A table where Jews eat is likened to a sacred altar upon which offerings are brought. It is through the words of Torah spoken during the meal that the mundane act of eating becomes a means of attaining *kedushah*. However, when Torah is not discussed, then the meal is nothing more than a means of satisfying one's physical desires. It is devoid of *kedushah* and may even be spiritually detrimental; thus, it is likened to a meal of מַאֲכָלוֹת אֲסוּרוֹת.

⮜§ Forbidden Foods of a Different Sort

There is a form of food that is not included in the dietary laws, but can nevertheless be termed מַאֲכָלוֹת אֲסוּרוֹת. In one of his works, the author of *Bnei Yissaschar* relates the following in the name of his teacher, the *Rebbe* of Rimanov: We sometimes find that Jewish

---

2. See discourse to *Parashas Bo.*

children who, although endowed with a special חֵן (charm and graciousness) in their early youth, lose their charm as they grow older. While this can be attributed to a variety of factors, the *Rebbe* maintained that a prime factor could very well be that these children are fed unkosher food, meaning food that was purchased with money that was earned dishonestly. As the years go on, and a given child continues to be fed such food, more and more of his or her חֵן disappears.

As in every area of life, a Jew's monetary affairs must be conducted in strict accordance with *Shulchan Aruch*. He must be scrupulously honest in his dealings with Jew and gentile alike. *Shulchan Aruch* explicitly prohibits *gezel akum*, robbing a gentile. This prohibition also applies to government funds. The noblest intentions do not permit taking a single dishonest cent from either the government or a private individual. In fact, the noblest goal of all is to be *mekadeish sheim shamayim*, to sanctify God's Name. The way to accomplish this is by strictly adhering to Torah, so that others will come to admire those who emulate Hashem's ways and observe His teachings.

Avoiding Self-Destruction

৺§ Naaman's Arrogance

The *haftarah* of *Parashas Tazria* (from *II Melachim* ch. 5) opens with the story of Naaman, general of the army of Aram, stricken with *tzaraas*[1] and desperate for a cure. At that time, a young Jewish girl captured in battle against Israel was a servant to Naaman's wife. Noting the general's illness, the girl informed her mistress that the 'prophet in Shomron' — a reference to Elisha (the disciple of Eliyahu HaNavi) — had the power to effect Naaman's cure.

Eventually, Naaman arrived outside Elisha's door, accompanied by a retinue of riders and chariots. After being told of the general's arrival, the prophet sent a messenger outside with the following instructions: Namaan was to immerse himself seven times in the Jordan river and he would be cured. Hearing this,

> *Naaman became enraged and he left, saying: "Behold, I had thought that he [Elisha] would come out to me, that he would stand and call out in the name of Hashem, his God, and lift up his hands to the area [of my malady] and the afflicted one would be healed! Are not Amanah and Pharpar, the rivers of Damascus, better than all the waters of Israel? Can I not immerse in them and be*

---

1. While צָרַעַת, *tzaraas*, is somewhat similar in appearance to leprosy, it is by no means related to that physical ailment. This is obvious from a study of these two *parshios*. For further discussion, see the commentary of R' Samson Raphael Hirsch.

healed?" And he left in a rage (II Melachim 5:11-12).

While the main source of Naaman's fury seems to have been Elisha's advice, which Naaman saw as ludicrous, a careful study of Naaman's words reveals what actually triggered his rage. His opening words were: הִנֵּה אָמַרְתִּי אֵלַי יֵצֵא יָצוֹא, "Behold, I had thought that he would come out to me." *Metzudos* explains:

> *"I had thought that due to my importance, he would come out to me and stand erect in the way of honor that people normally accord esteemed officers."*

Here was a man stricken with a malady for which there existed no natural cure. He had placed all his hope in this Jewish prophet who was said to perform miracles. Now, he was ready to head home and live out his life with his affliction, because he had not been accorded the honor he felt was due him!

Such behavior is not surprising to anyone familiar with the following words of *Mesilas Yesharim* (ch. 4): "One who is still bound up in the chains of his evil inclination cannot see nor perceive the truth, for his inclination blinds his vision, literally."

When a person is afflicted with the need for honor, this craving will make everything else — even lifelong physical affliction — seem trivial by comparison.

৵§ Geichazi's Deceit

The *haftarah* to *Parashas Metzora* (II *Melachim* ch. 7) tells of four Jewish *metzora'im* (i.e., those afflicted with *tzaraas*) who according to *Chazal* were Geichazi (the prime disciple of Elisha) and his three sons. Geichazi's affliction was directly connected to that of Naaman.

In the end, Naaman had been convinced by a subordinate to follow Elisha's instructions. He immersed himself in the Jordan seven times and emerged with the smooth, unblemished skin of a young child. He then returned to Elisha and presented the prophet with a tribute, which was refused. In fact, Elisha swore that he would not accept any gifts from the general, for he held it wrong to derive personal gain from a miracle, except in extenuating circumstances.[2] He swore in the way of *tzaddikim*, who undertake oaths when they perceive something as wrong but fear that their *yetzer hara* may later convince them otherwise.[3]

Geichazi, noting his teacher's refusal of the tribute, uttered an oath of a different sort.

> And Geichazi, disciple of Elisha the man of God, said [to himself]: "Behold, my master has refrained from accepting that which Naaman the Aramean has brought. I swear in the Name of Hashem that I shall chase after him [Naaman] and take something from him."
>
> He pursued Naaman ... and he said: "Peace! My master has sent me, saying, 'Two youths have just now come to me from the hills of Ephraim from among the sons of prophets. Please give for them a talent of silver and two changes of clothing.'"
>
> Naaman replied, "Swear [that your master did indeed send you (Rashi)] and then take two talents." He pressed him [to accept two talents[4]], then he bound two talents of silver in two satchels, and along with two changes of clothing, gave it to his [Naaman's] two youths; and they carried it before him [Geichazi] (II Melachim 5:20-23).

Thus far, Geichazi had lied outright to Naaman and then covered his lie with a false oath. That Naaman insisted that he swear is no cause for wonder. The general had only a short while earlier heard Elisha, whom he recognized as a true man of God, swear that he would not accept anything from him. He was therefore suspicious of Geichazi. Though Geichazi probably anticipated this, he was not deterred.

Geichazi arrived at home with his treasures and hid them, then presented himself before Elisha.

> Elisha said to him: "Whence do you come, Geichazi?"

---

2. According to *Metzudos*, v. 26.

3. See discourse to *Parashas Lech Lecha*.

4. Geichazi feigned unwillingness to accept 'more than my master has requested.' Thus, Naaman saw it necessary to press him to accept two talents instead of one (*Metzudos*).

Geichazi replied: "Your servant has not gone any-
where." Said Elisha: "Did not my thoughts accompany
you when the man [Naaman] turned around in his
chariot to face you? And at the time when you
accepted the silver with which to purchase clothing,
olive trees, vineyards, sheep, cattle, servants and
maids?

"The tzaraas of Naaman shall cling to you and your
children forever." And Geichazi left from before him, a
metzora like snow (ibid. 25-27).

Geichazi's response to Elisha reveals to what depths he had fallen.
He had been Elisha's prime disciple and knew well that Elisha was
the leading prophet of that generation. How could he dare deny the
truth? Did he not realize that Elisha, the man of God, could perceive
what had really occurred?

Again, we refer to the above citation from *Mesilas Yesharim*:

One who is still bound up in the chains of his evil
inclination cannot see nor perceive the truth, for his
inclination blinds his vision, literally.

In the case of Naaman, a desire for honor was almost his undoing.
In the case of Geichazi, a lust for wealth was his undoing.

רַבִּי אֶלְעָזָר הַקַּפָּר אוֹמֵר: הַקִּנְאָה וְהַתַּאֲנָה וְהַכָּבוֹד מוֹצִיאִין אֶת
הָאָדָם מִן הָעוֹלָם.
R' Elazar HaKappar says: Jealousy, lust and a desire
for honor remove a man from this world (Avos 4:28).

Geichazi's materialistic cravings ruined him in this world, while
other sins (see *Sanhedrin* 107b) caused him to forfeit his share in the
World to Come.

The case of Geichazi is particularly noteworthy. Whereas Naaman
was a gentile warrior, Geichazi was not only Elisha's prime disciple
but a גְּבוֹר בַּתּוֹרָה, *a warrior of Torah scholarship* (*Yerushalmi
Sanhedrin* 10:2). We see from here that superior Torah scholarship
without proper *midos* is of no substance. Moreover, if a person does
not place importance on refining his *midos*, then no amount of Torah
scholarship will insure him against spiritual decadence — and his
potential for decline will be without limit, ר"ל.

✒⊷ A Torah Perspective

Let us cite one illustration of the destructiveness of *midos ra'os*, negative character traits, and the Torah's expectations of us with regard to *midos*.

In *Parashas Ki Seitzei* (*Devarim* ch. 22), we find the case of מוֹצִיא שֵׁם רַע, where a husband slanders his newly married wife, accusing her of immorality and bringing false witnesses so that she will be sentenced to death by *beis din*. When a second pair of witnesses prove the husband's treachery, he is punished by מַלְקוּת, *lashes*, in addition to a fine. The Torah states:

> וְעָנְשׁוּ אֹתוֹ מֵאָה כֶסֶף וְנָתְנוּ לַאֲבִי הַנַּעֲרָה, כִּי הוֹצִיא שֵׁם רָע עַל
> בְּתוּלַת יִשְׂרָאֵל.
>
> *And they shall fine him one hundred [shekel of] silver and give them to the father of the maiden, for he has slandered a virgin in Israel (Devarim 22:19).*

In *Sha'arei Teshuvah* (3:111), *Rabbeinu Yonah* comments:

> *The Torah does not mention his sin of having sought to cause her death in beis din through the false witnesses he brought regarding her alleged immorality; rather, it mentions the sin of slander ["for he has slandered a virgin in Israel"], because this is a greater sin than seeking to take a person's life, for the pain of being shamed is worse than death.*

Thus we gain a better understanding of the gravity of shaming someone else. Now, how are we to react when *we* are the ones being shamed? *Chazal* extol the merits of those who bear their shame in silence, saying that this will cause one's sins to be forgiven (*Yoma* 23a). At the very least, we are prohibited from seeking to avenge the hurt that others have caused us, as is written (*Vayikra* 19:18): לֹא תִקֹּם, *Do not take revenge*. This may prove difficult at times, especially when one's pride has been deeply wounded. *Sefer HaChinuch*'s explanation of this *mitzvah*[5] places matters in a different perspective:

---

5. This explanation is also cited in the discourse to *Parashas Behar-Bechukosai*, though in a different context.

Among the roots of this mitzvah is that a person know and take to heart that whatever happens to him, whether for good or for bad, is brought about by Hashem, Blessed is He, for nothing can occur that is contrary to His will. Therefore, when one is pained or annoyed by another, he should realize that his sins have caused this and it has been decreed by Hashem. He should thus not turn his thoughts to revenge, for this person is not the real cause of his hurt; rather, his sins are the cause.[6]

Assimilating these words of *Sefer HaChinuch* into one's psyche is not easy, but those who succeed in doing so will find tolerating hurt and injustice a much lighter task. Conversely, when one does not engage in conscious effort to overcome a desire for vengeance, there is no telling where this urge might lead him.

Certain traits need to be channeled toward a proper goal. For example, curiosity can be terribly destructive, as it can easily lead to *lashon hara* and a variety of other sins. One who is curious by nature should channel this urge toward discovering the wisdom of Hashem.

The Chasam Sofer is said to have remarked that the source of his vast knowledge was his powerful desire to know all of Torah. Let us strive toward that same goal.

---

6. This explanation does not discount the fact that the one who caused hurt did so of his own free will and will be held accountable for his misdeed.

The Road to Return

⋖§ Do Not Despair

כִּי בַיּוֹם הַזֶּה יְכַפֵּר עֲלֵיכֶם לְטַהֵר אֶתְכֶם, מִכֹּל חַטֹּאתֵיכֶם לִפְנֵי ה׳
תִּטְהָרוּ.

For through this day he will atone for you, to cleanse you; from all your sins before Hashem you will be cleansed (16:30).

It is a positive Torah commandment that a person arouse his spirit to return [to God] through teshuvah on Yom Kippur, as it is written, ". . . from all your sins before Hashem you will be cleansed" (Sha'arei Teshuvah 2:14).

While *teshuvah*, repentance, is demanded of us on *Yom Kippur* and is especially effective during the Ten Days of *Teshuvah* beginning with *Rosh Hashanah* and ending with *Yom Kippur*, a Jew must constantly seek to better himself and mend his errant ways. Thrice daily we pray:

הֲשִׁיבֵנוּ אָבִינוּ לְתוֹרָתֶךָ, וְקָרְבֵנוּ מַלְכֵּנוּ לַעֲבוֹדָתֶךָ, וְהַחֲזִירֵנוּ
בִּתְשׁוּבָה שְׁלֵמָה לְפָנֶיךָ.

Bring us back, our Father, to Your Torah, and bring us near, our King, to Your service, and influence us to return in perfect repentance before You.

Every person has his tranquil moments when he is granted a respite from the rigors of life. These times are most opportune for reflection and soul-searching. However, such spiritual awakening can swiftly be quelled by feelings of desperation: "I have sinned heinously, doing that which the Torah deems despicable. I can never cleanse myself of such impurity and wickedness."

יֵאוּשׁ, despair, is a prime deterrent to *teshuvah*. Such thoughts are purely the work of one's *yetzer hara*. As *Rambam* writes in *Hilchos Teshuvah* (1:3):

> Today, when there is no Beis HaMikdash and there is no altar of atonement, we have nothing save for teshuvah. All sins can be forgiven through teshuvah. Even one who has been wicked all his days and repents at the very end will not have his wickedness mentioned [in the Next World], as it is written, "The wicked one will not stumble through his wickedness on the day when he will repent from that wickedness" (Yechezkel 33:12). And the day of Yom Kippur is itself an atonement for those who repent, as it is written, "For through this day he will atone for you . . ."

These words of *Rambam* are complemented by the following excerpt from *Rabbeinu Yonah's Yesod HaTeshuvah*:

> O person who has willfully sinned or erred and seeks to take refuge under the wings of the Divine Presence and to enter the paths of repentance, I will make you wise and enlighten you in the proper path to travel.
>
> On that day let him cast off all the sins he has committed and consider himself as though he were newly born on that very day, and he is with neither merit nor guilt . . . Let him map out his ways so that he will not veer from the path of good . . .
>
> Let not his thoughts confound him and restrain him from repenting, on the grounds that he is ashamed of his sins. He may think, "How can I be so brazen as to repent, when I have erred, been iniquitous, and willfully sinned! I have done such and such; I have transgressed over and over countlessly. How can I come before Him again, ashamed, like a thief who has been caught; for I am ashamed to stand before Him!"
>
> . . . Let him not think this way, for the seducer [the

yetzer hara] lurks like a fly at the entrances of the heart. He renews his offensive every day. He scrutinizes and seeks ways to trip him up and convince him of his evil counsel.

◄§ A Lesson in Teshuvah

The *Gemara (Bava Metzia* 85a) relates:

> *Rabbi [R' Yehudah HaNassi] arrived in the city of R' Elazar ben R' Shimon. He said to the people, "Does that tzaddik [R' Elazar] have a son?" They told him, "He has a son. Every harlot who hires herself out for two coins, hires him for eight" [for he was exceptionally handsome (Rashi)]. Rabbi went and ordained this son with the title 'Rabbi' and gave him over to his mother's brother, R' Shimon ben Isi ben Lekunia [to study Torah]. Every day, he [the son] would say, "I am returning to my city [to resume my wayward behavior]." His teacher would tell him, "They made you into a scholar, spread a golden cloak over you and even called you 'Rabbi' — and you say, 'I am returning to my city'?!" The son finally said, "I swear that I am forsaking this [and will no longer seek to return to my city and pursue my errant ways].''*
>
> *When the son grew older, he went and seated himself in the academy of Rabbi. Hearing his voice, Rabbi said, "That voice is similar to that of R' Elazar!" They told him, "He is his son." Rabbi applied to him the following: "The fruit of a tzaddik is a tree of life, and one who acquires souls is a wise man" (Mishlei 11:30). "The fruit of a tzaddik is a tree of life" — this ['a tzaddik'] refers to R' Elazar ben R' Shimon; "and one who acquires souls is a wise man" — this ['a wise man'] refers to R' Shimon ben Isi ben Lekunia [who acquired a 'son' by rearing the son of R' Elazar to become a Torah scholar (Rashi)].*

A number of important lessons can be derived from this. First, we see that z'chus avos, ancestral merit, is of no value when a person does not strive to live up to his ancestors' legacy. R' Elazar was the son of the holy Tanna (Mishnaic sage) R' Shimon bar Yochai; together they spent twelve years in a cave studying Torah, their sustenance provided through miracles (see Shabbos 33b). R' Shimon once declared, "I [through the merits of my years in the cave (Maharsha)] can exonerate the entire world from judgment from the time I was created until today — and were my son Elazar to join me [we could exonerate the entire world] from the time of Creation until today" (Succah 45b). Yet, all this did not prevent R' Elazar's son from becoming mired in the tumah, impurity, of immorality.

When Yaakov was heading for his encounter with a vengeful Eisav, he began his prayer, "God of my father Avraham, God of my father Yitzchak ..." (Bereishis 32:9). Midrash Rabbah (ibid. 76:4) questions why Yaakov invoked the merit of his grandfather and father, since they were grandfather and father to Eisav as well. The Midrash answers:

> [Hashem says:] I stand by those who choose to go in their [ancestors'] ways and do as they did; I do not stand by those who do not choose to go in their ways and who do not do as they did.

A person cannot live a life of sin and expect to fall back on the merits of his ancestors when he is in need of Divine assistance. First and foremost, he must help himself by engaging in a sincere effort to return to Hashem.

∽§ The Impetus

In the case of R' Elazar's son, a change for the better did eventually occur. The impetus for this turnabout came from R' Yehudah HaNassi, who accorded the son a title he had not yet earned, in the hope that a competitive spirit would inspire him to equal those who bore the same title and possessed the Torah knowledge that he did not (Rashi to Bava Metzia 85a).

Torah should be studied lishmah, for its own sake, solely for the purpose of acquiring a knowledge of Hashem's will and fulfilling His commandments. The concept of lishmah applies to all other mitzvos as well. However, in treading the path of *mitzvah* observance, a preliminary step is often needed. *Chazal* tell us: "R' Yehudah said in the name of Rav: 'A person should [initially] occupy himself with Torah and *mitzvos* not for their own sake, for through [a service that is] not for its own sake, one will eventually attain [a service that is] for its own sake' " (*Pesachim* 50b).[1] *Nefesh HaChaim* (introduction to ch. 4) explains:

> It is virtually impossible to attain a desired degree of lishmah as soon as one commits himself to Torah study. The purpose of toil in Torah that is not lishmah is so that one will eventually study lishmah, just as it impossible to go from ground level to a second story without climbing a ladder. Therefore, one who studies in this manner is likewise beloved by HaKadosh Baruch Hu.

In *Ruach Chaim* (3:1), R' Chaim Volozhiner offers a parable of a king who commands his servant to climb up to a roof for some purpose. Surely the king does not expect his servant to leap from the ground to the roof! He must use a ladder. However, if the king notices the servant moving to and fro on one of the ladder's rungs instead of climbing upwards, he will surely be incensed. Similarly, the goal of שֶׁלֹּא לִשְׁמָה must be to attain a study that is לִשְׁמָה; then, the student will be 'beloved by *HaKadosh Baruch Hu.*'

The 'ladder' concept can be applied to all areas of service of Hashem. For example, someone who is hot tempered cannot be expected to harness this trait in an instant. The improvement must be gradual, as one works on his self-control day after day. A person who has mastered his temper only a bit, but *strives* to control it entirely, likewise endears himself to Hashem.

R' Yehudah *HaNassi* employed the benefits of שֶׁלֹּא לִשְׁמָה to rescue R' Elazar's son from a life of sin. To what degree he succeeded can be seen from the continuation of that passage in *Bava Metzia*:

---

1. HaRav Segal cited R' Simchah Zissel of Kelm (*Chochmah U'Mussar*, vol. 2: p. 239), who explains that when one engages in Torah study steadily, day in and day out, he grows accustomed to it and it becomes easy for him, relatively speaking. With this having been accomplished through studying שֶׁלֹּא לִשְׁמָה, one's primary task ahead is to alter his mental approach to study, namely to make the transition from שֶׁלֹּא לִשְׁמָה to לִשְׁמָה.

When that son died, they brought him to the cave of his father. A serpent encircled the cave. Someone called out, "Serpent, serpent, make way and allow a son to be brought near his father." The serpent would not make way. A Heavenly voice came forth and said, "It is not because one [the father] is greater than the other [the son]; rather, it is because one suffered in the cave [for twelve years] while the other did not."

"Not because one is greater than the other . . ." — A son who had veered so far from the path of Torah returned to a level where he was compared to his illustrious father, one of the great *Tannaim* of the *Mishnah*. Such is the power of *teshuvah*.

Love Your Fellow Jew

לֹא תִקֹּם וְלֹא תִטֹּר אֶת בְּנֵי עַמֶּךָ, וְאָהַבְתָּ לְרֵעֲךָ כָּמוֹךָ. אֲנִי ה׳.
Do not take revenge and do not bear a grudge against the members of your nation; love your neighbor as yourself. I am Hashem (19:18).

◄§ Hillel and the Gentile

The *Gemara* (*Shabbos* 31a) relates the famous incident of the gentile who came before Hillel seeking to convert on condition that he be "taught all of Torah while standing on one foot." Hillel told him: דְּעֲלָךְ סְנֵי לְחַבְרָךְ לָא תַעֲבֵיד. זוֹ הִיא כָּל הַתּוֹרָה כֻּלָּהּ; וְאִידָךְ פֵּירוּשָׁה הוּא – זִיל גְּמוֹר., "What is hateful to you, do not do to your fellow. This is the entire Torah; the rest is commentary — go and study it."

Maharsha explains that in presenting his request, the gentile was seeking to learn one dictum that would serve as a foundation for all of Torah. Let us attempt to understand Hillel's response.

Ostensibly, the dictum דְּעֲלָךְ סְנֵי לְחַבְרָךְ לָא תַעֲבֵיד is the inverse of וְאָהַבְתָּ לְרֵעֲךָ כָּמוֹךָ, "Love your fellow as yourself." Why did Hillel not tell the gentile these words from the Torah, or at least their Aramaic translation as found in *Targum Onkelos*, since that was the language which the gentile understood? *Maharsha* raises this question and comments that in Hillel's opinion, the Torah does not demand of us that we literally love every Jewish soul as ourselves in a positive sense;

rather, the dictum of וְאָהַבְתָּ לְרֵעֲךָ כָּמוֹךָ is related to the first part of the verse: One should not seek revenge nor bear a grudge, but should rather love his fellow and bear him no ill will for any harm he has caused. Thus, Hillel told the gentile the intent of this *mitzvah* as he understood it: *What is hateful to you, do not do to your fellow.* Indeed, as *Maharsha* points out, this is exactly how *Targum Yonasan* interprets this *mitzvah*.

We may suggest a different resolution to the question of *Maharsha*. In *Tehillim*, David *HaMelech* exhorts us:

סוּר מֵרָע וַעֲשֵׂה טוֹב, בַּקֵּשׁ שָׁלוֹם וְרָדְפֵהוּ.
Turn from evil and do good; seek peace and pursue it (34:15).

The path to self-improvement is gradual. First, one must turn from evil; that is, he must refrain from doing that which is contrary to Hashem's will. When this has been accomplished, one must proceed to עֲשֵׂה טוֹב, *do good*, as he strives to fulfill His will in a positive sense.

Indeed, there *is* a positive aspect to וְאָהַבְתָּ לְרֵעֲךָ כָּמוֹךָ. A Jew should strive to love and admire his fellow Jew's every redeeming quality while overlooking his faults; he should rejoice in his success as he would in his own, while feeling the pain of his neighbor's misfortunes; and he should express his love by actively seeking to improve his fellow's lot in any and every way. However, there is a step that precedes all this: First, one must avoid doing to others that which he himself detests. In responding to the gentile, Hillel told him only the initial step of this precept.[1]

·§ Foundation of Torah

A major question remains: How is this *mitzvah* a foundation of the entire Torah? *Rashi* (*Shabbos* 31a), in one interpretation, understands Hillel's use of לְחַבְרָךְ, *to your fellow*, in consonance with a verse in *Mishlei* where רֵעֲךָ, *your fellow*, refers to Hashem. Hillel was thus saying: Just as you do not want others to go against your will [דְּעֲלָךְ סָנֵי], so, too, do not go against the will of Hashem [לְחַבְרָךְ]

---

1. *Chiddushei HaRim* offers a very similar explanation: Hillel knew that the mind of a non-Jew could not comprehend the positive aspect of loving one's fellow, so he translated the concept into negative terms, which the gentile did understand.

לָא תַעֲבֵיד]. In his second interpretation, in which לְחַבְרָךְ is understood as referring to one's fellow man [the standard interpretation], *Rashi* writes that Hillel's admonition encompasses all the many *mitzvos* that involve a Jew's dealings with his neighbor. Still, this does not explain how Hillel's words serve as a foundation to 'the entire Torah,' including the scores of *mitzvos* that are בֵּין אָדָם לַמָּקוֹם, between ourselves and Hashem.

The *Mishnah* in *Avos* (4:1) states:

בֶּן זוֹמָא אוֹמֵר — ... אֵיזֶהוּ מְכֻבָּד? הַמְכַבֵּד אֶת הַבְּרִיּוֹת, שֶׁנֶּאֱמַר:
כִּי מְכַבְּדַי אֲכַבֵּד, וּבֹזַי יֵקָלּוּ.

Ben Zoma says — ... "Who is honored? He who honors others, as it is said: 'For those who honor Me I will honor, and those who scorn Me shall be degraded' " (I Shmuel 2:30).

Ben Zoma speaks of the honor that one must accord his fellow man; to prove his point, he cites a verse which speaks of those who honor *HaKadosh Baruch Hu*. To honor another human being is to honor Hashem, for man was created בְּצֶלֶם אֱלֹקִים, *in the image of God*. If one has proper reverence for Hashem, then he will naturally not do hateful things to those who were created in His image — and surely he will not transgress a מִצְוָה בֵּין אָדָם לַמָּקוֹם, which would be a direct affront to His honor! In telling the gentile, דַּעֲלָךְ סְנֵי לְחַבְרָךְ לָא תַעֲבֵיד, Hillel conveyed the underlying premise of this dictum, which is indeed a foundation of the entire Torah.

⊱ One Nation, One Soul

We cited above the opinion of *Maharsha*, that Hillel understood the *mitzvah* of וְאָהַבְתָּ לְרֵעֲךָ כָּמוֹךְ in a negative sense, and as relating to the negative commandments of לֹא תִקֹּם and לֹא תִטֹּר which precede it. *Talmud Yerushalmi* (*Nedarim* 9:4) takes an opposite approach, explaining the prohibitions of לֹא תִקֹּם and לֹא תִטֹּר in light of the requirement to love a fellow Jew as oneself. *Yerushalmi* offers a parable of a man who has accidentally cut one of his hands with a knife held by his other hand. Would the man consider 'wreaking vengeance' on the hand that inflicted the wound? To do so would be to hurt himself further. If a Jew truly loves his fellow Jews and sees all of *Klal Yisrael* as a multitude of limbs connected to the same body, then he will never seek revenge nor bear a grudge against others.

In discussing the prohibitions of לֹא תִקֹּם and לֹא תִטֹּר, the Chofetz Chaim (*Sha'ar HaTevunah* 6) comments that when the seventy souls descended with Yaakov *Avinu* to Egypt, they were referred to as נֶפֶשׁ, a soul (*Bereishis* 46:27). It is in this vein that he interprets the verse, מִי כְעַמְּךָ יִשְׂרָאֵל גּוֹי אֶחָד בָּאָרֶץ?, "Who is like Your people Israel, one nation on earth?" (*I Divrei HaYamim* 17:21). The Jewish nation is אֶחָד, *one*, a single inseparable unit, a myriad of souls that stems from one Heavenly source. "Therefore," says the Chofetz Chaim, "be exceedingly careful not to take vengeance or harbor a grudge against your fellow, for you would actually be taking vengeance or bearing a grudge against *yourself!*" [2]

The epitome of the love that can and should exist between Jews was that of David and Yehonasan, the son of Shaul *HaMelech* (see *Avos* 5:19). Though each knew that the other stood in the way of his ascension to the throne, their souls were bound up with one another. The *Mishnah* (*Avos* 5:19) describes this as אַהֲבָה שֶׁאֵינָהּ תְּלוּיָה בְדָבָר, *love that is not dependent on anything.* Attaining such love for our fellow Jews should be our ultimate goal. As in other areas of our Divine service, we must climb the ladder of *ahavas Yisrael* rung by rung, the initial step being the fulfillment of דַּעֲלָךְ סְנֵי לְחַבְרָךְ לָא תַעֲבֵיד.

---

2. See the conclusion of the discourse to *Parashas Tazria-Metzora* for further discussion of the prohibition of לֹא תִקֹּם.

Chillul Hashem

וְלֹא תְחַלְּלוּ אֶת שֵׁם קָדְשִׁי . . .
And you shall not profane My holy Name . . . (22:32).

⁓§ Rabbi Akiva's Disciples

Each year, during the days of *Sefiras HaOmer* (the Omer Counting), we observe the days of mourning for the twenty-four thousand disciples of R' Akiva, who died during this period some two thousand years ago. The *Gemara* (*Yevamos* 62b) relates:

> There were twelve thousand pairs of disciples of R'
> Akiva, [residing] between Givas and Antiphras. They
> all died during a single period because they did not
> accord one another proper respect. The world became
> [spiritually] desolate [for the Torah became forgotten
> (Rashi)], until R' Akiva came to our Sages in the south
> and taught them. [They were:] R' Meir, R' Yehudah, R'
> Yosi, R' Shimon, and R' Elazar ben Shamua. It was they
> who preserved the Torah at that time.

It is certain that the spiritual level of R' Akiva's disciples was great and their sin must be understood in this context. They surely did accord one another proper respect by our standards. *Tzaddikim*, however, are judged according to their own exalted level of service; it was thus that the disciples of R' Akiva were found guilty of sin.

Still, the depth of the judgment against them demands some explanation, for the impact of their deaths was of mammoth proportions. *The world was desolate, for Torah had become forgotten.* The *Ribono shel Olam* deemed it necessary to deprive the world of all the Torah that these students would have transmitted, thrusting all of creation into a spiritual situation for which *Chazal* — who were exacting in their terminology — found שְׁמָמָה, *desolation,* an apt description. All this was a result of their not having accorded one another the degree of respect expected of them. The severity of this sin must have been extremely great to have required such retribution. Let us understand the nature of this sin.

⋖§ Man and His Surroundings

Rambam, in *Yad HaChazakah*, writes:

> It is natural for man's thoughts and deeds to be patterned after those of his friends and neighbors and for him to conduct himself in the way of his community. Therefore, a person must attach himself to the righteous and forever sit among the wise so that he will learn from their ways; and he must distance himself from the wicked who go in darkness, so that he will not learn from their ways . . . If he is in a province whose customs are wicked and whose people do not go in an upright way, then he must go to a place whose people are righteous and who conduct themselves in a good way. If all the provinces that he knows and hears of do not go in a good way . . . or if he is unable to travel to a good place because of sickness or fear of marauders, then he should live in solitude . . . And if the people are so wicked and sinful that they do not allow him to live in their province unless he mingles with them and conducts himself in their wicked manner, then let him flee to the caves, crevices and wildernesses rather than conduct himself in the ways of sinners, as it is written

*(Yirmiyahu 9:1), "If that I could but be set in a
wilderness, in a lodging of wayfarers, so that I could
take leave of my people and go away from them"
(Hilchos Dei'os 6:1).*

Yad HaChazakah is a halachic work; thus, Rambam's words
constitute a halachic statement that one is required to flee negative
influences, even if this means living in caves or wilderness. Though
one may consider himself strong of spirit, he must not underestimate
the effects of his environment upon his soul. Negative surroundings
breed negative behavior.

There is another side to this matter. The fact that a *neshamah* can
be so affected by its environment places an awesome responsibility
upon every Jew to ensure that his behavior does not influence others
negatively. For those who dedicate themselves to the study of Torah,
this responsibility is particularly great, as we shall explain.

⊷§ A Mirror Image

Rashi in *Masechta Yoma* (86a) describes one who is guilty of
chillul Hashem, desecration of Hashem's Name, as חוֹטֵא וּמַחֲטִיא
אֲחֵרִים, *one who sins in a manner that influences others to sin.* The
Gemara cites Rav's illustration of *chillul Hashem:* "For example, if I
were to take meat from a butcher and not pay for it immediately." As
Rashi there explains, the butcher might suspect that payment had not
been offered because the buyer, in this case Rav, had no intention of
paying. These suspicions might influence the butcher to become lax
in his own monetary matters.

Mesilas Yesharim (ch. 11) elaborates on this theme:

> *The various aspects of chillul Hashem are numerous
> and significant, for man must be exceedingly concerned
> for the honor of his Master. One must carefully
> scrutinize and ponder all that he does so that a disgrace
> to the honor of Heaven should not result, God forbid.
> We have been taught: [R' Yochanan ben Beroka said:
> "Whoever desecrates the Name of Heaven in secret,
> they will exact punishment from him in public;]*

unintentional or intentional, both are alike regarding chillul Hashem."

... Each man, in accordance with his own spiritual level and his standing in the eyes of his generation, must exercise forethought so that he does not do something unbefitting a person of his stature. For man's alertness and meticulousness in service of Heaven must reflect his stature and wisdom; if not, then the Name of Hashem is desecrated through him, God forbid. It is an honor to the Torah when one who devotes himself exceedingly to its study is likewise devoted to correcting and refining his midos. To the extent that such refinement is lacking, the study of Torah is disparaged — and this is a disgrace, Heaven forfend, to the Name of Hashem, Who gave us His holy Torah and commanded us to toil in its study so that we attain spiritual perfection.

Chazal state: "For a person who has been guilty of *chillul Hashem*, there is no power in *teshuvah* to suspend his judgment, nor in *Yom Kippur* to atone, nor in affliction to cleanse; rather, all of these suspend the judgment and death cleanses" (*Yoma* 86a). With regard to cleansing of sins, death is not to be seen as a severe form of affliction, for if such were the case it would be difficult to understand why certain very severe afflictions, ר״ל, cannot accomplish that which death accomplishes. Death is unique in that it detaches the soul from its corporeal counterpart; it is only through this detachment that the soul can rid itself of the blemish caused by *chillul Hashem*.

In *Pirkei Avos* (4:15) we find:

רַבִּי אֶלְעָזָר בֶּן שַׁמּוּעַ אוֹמֵר: יְהִי כְּבוֹד תַּלְמִידְךָ חָבִיב עָלֶיךָ
כְּשֶׁלָךְ; וּכְבוֹד חֲבֵרְךָ כְּמוֹרָא רַבָּךְ; וּמוֹרָא רַבָּךְ כְּמוֹרָא שָׁמַיִם.

R' Elazar ben Shamua said: "Let the honor of your student be as dear to you as your own; the honor of your colleague as the reverence for your teacher; and the reverence for your teacher as the reverence of Heaven."

The above is required of any *talmid, chaver*, or *rebbi*. The disciples of R' Akiva, on their exalted level of service, were found wanting with regard to כְּבוֹד חֲבֵרִים. That their behavior in this area did not reflect their superior scholarship in Torah was a *chillul Hashem*. Thus, they had to die.[1]

⪥ 'Woe to Those Who Do Not Study Torah'

R' Yisrael Salanter is reported to have said: "I know that I am not the great redeemer of my people, but what can I do if people consider me as such? I am obligated to be meticulous with regard to Torah and *mitzvos* as is befitting a man of such stature — for if not, I will have been guilty of *chillul Hashem*."[2]

Bnei Torah must realize that their behavior is forever being noted and emulated and that they exert a profound influence on those around them. If their *midos* and general approach to life are not commensurate with their learning, then they are guilty of *chillul Hashem*. A *ben Torah* should always bear in mind the famous passage in *Yoma* (86a):

> *A Jew should study Scripture and Mishnah, serve Torah scholars and deal graciously with his fellow man. Then others will say of him, "Fortunate is his father who taught him Torah! Fortunate is his teacher who taught him Torah! Woe to those who do not study Torah! He who studies Torah — how pleasant is his behavior and how proper are his deeds!" To him may the verse be applied: "And He said to me: 'You are My servant Israel, in whom I will be glorified' " (Yeshayahu 49:3).*
>
> *However, if one studies Scripture and Mishnah and*

---

1. One should note that there *is* an alternative to death in cases of *chillul Hashem*. *Sha'arei Teshuvah* (4:16) states: ". . . For one who has been guilty of *chillul Hashem* . . . there is a restorative cure for his wound; namely, that he constantly sanctify the name of Hashem." *Kiddush Hashem* through speech and deed is an atonement, measure for measure, for *chillul Hashem*.

2. The Chofetz Chaim once told his son R' Leib not to engage in a certain practice as it was unbefitting a *talmid chacham*. R' Leib replied that he did not consider himself a *talmid chacham*. The Chofetz Chaim responded that modesty is out of place in such situations; rather, one should consider himself a *talmid chacham* and live up to that title.

*serves Torah scholars, but is not honest in his dealings
and does not converse pleasantly with people — what
do others say of him? "Woe to he who studies Torah!
Woe to his father who taught him Torah! Woe to
his teacher who taught him Torah! He who studies
Torah — how corrupt are his deeds and how ugly is
his behavior!" To him may the verse be applied:
"In that men said of them: 'These are Hashem's people
but they are departed from His land' " (Yechezkel
36:20).*

❧   ❧   ❧

There are additional lessons to be learned from the incident of the
talmidei R' Akiva. At the time of his disciples' death, R' Akiva was
well advanced in years. Surely his pain and sorrow over their deaths
were enormous and probably weakened his aged body. A lesser man
would have fallen prey to despair. Yet R' Akiva mustered his
strength of body and spirit and carried on his mission of spreading
Torah.

Furthermore, the kind of dissemination of Torah which R' Akiva
now undertook seemed insignificant in comparison to what he had
been involved in previously. From a teacher of twenty-four thousand
he now became a teacher of five. R' Akiva realized, however, that in
spiritual pursuits, particularly with regard to spreading Torah, no act
is insignificant. History proved him right, as those five disciples went
on to become the Torah leaders of the next generation. A desolate
world had once again become a world illuminated by the brilliance of
Torah.

R' Simchah Zissel of Kelm writes that were it not for the fact
that there is much for us to learn from the incident where Aharon
and Miriam spoke against Moshe *Rabbeinu* (*Bamidbar* ch. 12),
the Torah would never have recorded that which is dishonorable
to Aharon and Miriam. The same can be said of the deaths of
the *talmidei R' Akiva*. The *sefirah* period, when we mourn their
deaths, is a most auspicious time to learn from this incident, which
will be a source of merit for their *neshamos*. Let us strive to improve
our ways and seek to live a life that will be one continuous *kiddush
Hashem*.

The Key to Shemittah Observance

וּבַשָּׁנָה הַשְּׁבִיעִית, שַׁבַּת שַׁבָּתוֹן יִהְיֶה לָאָרֶץ, שַׁבָּת לַה'; שָׂדְךָ לֹא תִזְרָע וְכַרְמְךָ לֹא תִזְמֹר.

And in the seventh year, there shall be a Sabbath of complete rest for the land, a Sabbath for Hashem; you shall not sow your field, nor shall you prune your vineyard (25:4).

◆§ Of Warriors and Angels

בָּרְכוּ ה' מַלְאָכָיו; גִּבֹּרֵי כֹחַ עֹשֵׂי דְבָרוֹ, לִשְׁמֹעַ בְּקוֹל דְּבָרוֹ.

Bless Hashem, O His angels, the strong warriors who do His bidding, to obey the voice of His word (Tehillim 103:20) — R' Yitzchak Nafcha said: "This refers to those who observe Shemittah. It is common for a person to perform a mitzvah for one day, for one week, or for one month — but for an entire year? Yet this man sees his field lie fallow, his vineyard lie fallow — and he accepts all this in silence! Can there be a more powerful warrior than he?" (Yalkut Shimoni, Tehillim 860).

Every seven years for an entire year, the farmers of *Eretz Yisrael* must allow their land, their source of livelihood, to lie fallow. Moreover, the fruits that do grow during the *Shemittah* year are *hefker*, ownerless. The farmers must open the gates of their fields and orchards to allow free access for anyone who wishes to partake of their produce. A farmer may have spent years cultivating his orchard, yet during the seventh year the fruits are not his and he has no more right to them than does any stranger. It is not surprising that David *HaMelech* describes *Shemittah* observers as גִּבֹּרֵי כֹחַ, *strong warriors*, and מַלְאָכִים, *angels*.

The *mitzvah* of *Shemittah* is indicative of *Klal Yisrael's* exalted status as מַמְלֶכֶת כֹּהֲנִים וְגוֹי קָדוֹשׁ, *a kingdom of priests and a holy nation* (*Sh'mos* 19:6). However, this status carries with it the potential for severe retribution if we are neglectful in fulfilling our charge. *Parashas Bechukosai* delineates the terrible punishments that will befall the Jewish nation for their failure to live up to that which is expected of them. They will be exiled from their Land, cast among the nations and forced to endure fear, death and privation. After foretelling all of this, the Torah states:

אָז תִּרְצֶה הָאָרֶץ אֶת שַׁבְּתֹתֶיהָ כֹּל יְמֵי הָשַּׁמָּה וְאַתֶּם בְּאֶרֶץ
אֹיְבֵיכֶם; אָז תִּשְׁבַּת הָאָרֶץ וְהִרְצָת אֶת שַׁבְּתֹתֶיהָ.

Then the land will be appeased for its Sabbaths all the days of its desolation, while you are in the lands of your enemies; then the land shall rest and be appeased for its Sabbaths (26:34).

Rashi (ibid.) comments that the seventy years of exile following the destruction of the first *Beis HaMikdash* corresponded to the seventy years of *Shemittah* and *Yovel*[1] in which the Jews were neglectful in their observance of the relevant laws. Thus, while those who observe this *mitzvah* are likened to angels, those who are lax in its observance suffer severe consequences. Obviously, the proper observance of *Shemittah* is within everyone's reach, for Hashem does not command us to do that which is beyond our abilities. What is the key to proper *Shemittah* observance?

⋖§ 'We Will Do, We Will Listen'

Let us return to the verse from *Tehillim* with which we began, where *Shemittah* observers are called מַלְאָכִים and גִּבֹּרֵי כֹחַ.

---

1. The laws of *Shemittah* are also observed during *Yovel*, the fiftieth and final year of the cycle pertaining to Land-related *mitzvos*.

The *Gemara* (*Shabbos* 88a) cites this same verse in relation to *Klal Yisrael's* readiness to heed God's every command as they prepared to receive the Torah at Sinai:

> When Israel gave precedence to נַעֲשֶׂה ("We shall do") over נִשְׁמַע ("We shall listen"), a Heavenly voice exclaimed, "Who has revealed this secret of the angels to My children?" For it is written, "Bless Hashem, O His angels, the strong warriors who do His bidding, to obey the voice of His word." Angels first 'do' and then 'listen.'

As *Rashi* (ibid.) explains, a servant will usually not undertake a task unless he first hears what it involves and ascertains that he is capable of carrying it out. Angels do not have this problem, for every angel knows that it is endowed with whatever abilities are needed to perform its particular mission. At Sinai, Israel expressed a willingness to heed Hashem's every command, though they did not yet know the nature of those commands. That they gave precedence to נַעֲשֶׂה over נִשְׁמַע was indicative of their complete *emunah*, faith, in Hashem, their firm belief that all that transpires stems from Him and that He would never command them to do that which was beyond them. With proper faith, a person can soar to the level of angels.

We find elsewhere that in fulfilling his calling in this world, a Jew must garner his spiritual energy and conduct himself in a manner that seems angelic in nature. *Mesilas Yesharim* (ch. 11) states:

> It is exceedingly difficult for man's spiteful heart to be entirely free of hate and revenge, for man is extremely sensitive to insult and is deeply pained by it. Revenge is sweeter than honey, for that is the only thing that will put him at ease. [Being entirely free of such feelings] is easy only for ministering angels, in whom such traits do not exist.

Though ridding one's heart of hate and revenge is not easy, it is nevertheless our obligation. The key to accomplishing this is stated in *Sefer HaChinuch* where the prohibition of לֹא תִקֹּם, *Do not take revenge* (*Vayikra* 19:18), is discussed:[2]

> *Among the roots of this mitzvah is that a person know*

---

2. This prohibition is also discussed in the discourse to *Parashas Kedoshim*.

and take to heart that whatever happens to him, whether for good or for bad, is brought about by Hashem, Blessed is He, for nothing can occur that is contrary to His will. Therefore, when one is pained or aggravated by another, he should realize that his sins have caused this and that it has been decreed by Hashem. He should thus not turn his thoughts to revenge, for this person is not the real cause of his hurt; rather, his sins are the cause.[3]

The key to ridding oneself of hatred and revenge is *emunah*, a perception that all suffering, including mental and emotional pain, is decreed by Hashem. *Emunah* was likewise the key to the Jews' proclaiming נַעֲשֶׂה וְנִשְׁמַע at Sinai and to a farmer's steadfast year-long observance of *Shemittah*. It is through proper *emunah* that one can rise to the level of angels in surmounting all trials and obstacles on the road to achieving perfection as a servant of Hashem.

---

3. This citation from *Sefer HaChinuch* also appears in the discourse to *Parashas Tazria-Metzora*, though in a different context.

במדבר

Bamidbar

Preparing to Receive the Torah

◄§ A Lesson for All Time

As the days of *Sefirah* draw to a close, we should bear in mind the words of the holy *Sh'lah*[1] regarding the *Yom Tov* of *Shavuos*: יוֹם הַדִּין הוּא לְקַבָּלַת הַתּוֹרָה, *It is a day of judgment regarding the acceptance of the Torah.* On the day that marks the giving of the Torah at Sinai more than three thousand years ago, every Jew has the opportunity to renew his own attachment to Torah.

While there is a wonderful custom to beautify *shuls* with flowers and leaves in honor of *Shavuos*, a Jew's primary task during these days is to beautify his *neshamah*, making it a fitting receptacle for *kabalas haTorah*. Regarding this, we can take a lesson from the generation that received the Torah at Sinai. The *Midrash* relates a parable of an ill prince whose doctors ordered his education suspended until a two-month curative period had passed. During that period, the prince remained at home, eating an abundance of nourishing foods, as well as following other directives that helped restore his health. Similarly, before the Jews could receive the Torah, they needed to refine their souls so that they would be spiritually fit to hear the words of the Living God. It was during that period that the Jewish people began to partake of the מָן, *manna*, which Scripture refers to as *the bread of angels* (*Tehillim* 78:25), and drink from the miraculous well of Miriam. Their consumption of food and drink of

---

1. See discourse to *Parashas Tetzaveh*, footnote 3.

such spiritual quality was just one aspect of the process that infused them with *kedushah*, sanctity, readying them to receive the Torah.

⋴§ Our Preparation

In defining our own process of preparation, we begin with the well-known teaching in *Avos* (3:21): אִם אֵין דֶּרֶךְ אֶרֶץ, אֵין תּוֹרָה, *If there is no derech eretz, there can be no Torah*. *Rabbeinu Yonah* comments:

> *This means to say that one must first correct his midos (character traits). Then the Torah can dwell within him. For it [the Torah] will never dwell in someone who does not possess good midos.*

Any discussion of *midos* naturally relates to one's relationship with others. Let us select one area of this relationship, namely, *gemilas chassadim*, performing acts of kindness. Numerous anecdotes attest to our *gedolim* as being *gaonim*, geniuses, of benevolence, sensitivity, and concern:

The *rebbetzin* of R' Yehoshua Leib Diskin once accidentally put salt instead of sugar in her husband's tea. R' Yehoshua Leib had drunk almost the entire glass before his *rebbetzin* realized her mistake and rushed in to stop him. A student who was present later took a sip of what remained in the glass and felt forced to spit it out. R' Yehoshua Leib, realizing that his wife had erred, had calmly swallowed the awful concoction rather than cause his wife hurt and embarrassment.[2]

A similar story is told about R' Avigdor Halberstam, the brother of R' Chaim of Sanz. Once, when R' Avigdor was an honored Shabbos guest, his host placed before him the serving bowl of *cholent* when it was brought from the kitchen. R' Avigdor kept the bowl in front of him, eating every last morsel in it! When he had taken leave of his host, R' Avigdor explained to his disciples that as soon as the bowl had been placed in front of him, he smelled the scent of kerosene

---

2. HaRav Segal noted that R' Yosef Dov Soloveitchik (the *'Beis HaLevi'*) felt such awe for R' Yehoshua Leib that it would take him three months to complete a letter to him — for every time that he would lift his pen to continue, his hands would begin to tremble.

which had been mistakenly included in the *cholent*. Realizing that the cook, a poor orphan girl, might be berated should her error be discovered, R' Avigdor chose to suffer the shame and unpleasantness of consuming the bowl's entire contents.

As R' Yisrael Salanter lay on his death bed, a lone attendant stood at his bedside.[3] Realizing that his end was near, R' Yisrael used his remaining time on this world to calmly assure the attendant that one need not be afraid of being alone in a room with a dead body.

R' Yosef Chaim Sonnenfeld would spend a few weeks each summer at the Diskin Orphan Home on the outskirts of Jerusalem. The summer before his death, R' Yosef Chaim requested that he be taken back to his home in the Old City earlier than planned. He explained that he felt his end drawing near and did not want to burden others with having to transport his body back home for burial.[4]

Gaonim of *chesed!*

In the case of R' Yosef Chaim, the Day of Judgment, when one is called for an accounting before the Heavenly Court, was not far off. In the case of R' Yisrael, it was imminent. One would have expected R' Yisrael to have spent his remaining moments on this world deeply involved in *viduy*, confession, of (what he viewed as) his sins. Instead, the possible fears of another person were uppermost in his mind. It is obvious that there can be no better way to prepare to face Divine judgment than by performing kindness for one's fellow. Striving to help others is likewise a most desirable way to prepare for the judgment of *kabalas haTorah*.

The matter can be summed up concisely: A Jew is not to wait until the need for *chesed* on his part presents itself; rather, he must make a conscious effort to seek ways through which he can be of assistance to others. Through such contemplation, worlds of opportunities for *chesed* become revealed.

We have touched upon but one area of *midos*. We must also turn our attention to the many other traits of which our personalities are

---

3. R' Yisrael passed away in Konigsberg, Germany, far away from his disciples in Kovno, Lithuania.

4. Upon hearing this explanation, someone expressed fear that such mournful thoughts could prove harmful to R' Yosef Chaim's fragile health. The *tzaddik* replied, "Such thoughts do not depress me in the least. From the time I turned forty, the prospect of death has never been far from my thoughts and has absolutely no ill effect on my health."

comprised. Of particular importance is what we say and how we say it. It is imperative that a Jew train himself to speak in a refined manner. As we ready ourselves for *Shavuos*, let us accept upon ourselves to improve in these areas.

If there is no derech eretz, there can be no Torah.

◄§ The Primary Task

Once we have resolved to improve our *midos*, we can then turn our attention to the essence of our *kabalas haTorah*, namely, to strengthen our dedication to Torah study.

One should know that it is Torah study, more than anything else, that shields us from Divine retribution. This is vividly illustrated by the following *Midrash HaNe'elam* (ch. 2; cited by the Chofetz Chaim in *Sha'ar HaTorah* ch. 7):

Someone appeared to R' Zemira'ah in a dream. "Who are you?" R' Zemira'ah asked. The person replied that he had sinned grievously in this world and had passed on. In *Gehinnom*, he was being punished with three judgments each day and three each night. In response to R' Zemira'ah's inquiries, the soul revealed that it had resided in the Upper Galilee during its lifetime. R' Zemira'ah then made his way to that region.

He inquired among the local inhabitants regarding this man and was told that, indeed, he had lived in their area and had been known as a *rasha*, wicked person. Further inquiries revealed that the man had left behind an only son who was following in his father's errant ways.

R' Zemira'ah located the son and undertook the task of teaching him Torah. From reading *aleph-beis*, the son progressed to *davening* and *Shema*, then on to *Mishnah*, *Gemara*, *Halachah* and *Aggadah*, until he developed into a full-fledged *talmid chacham*.

One night, the father reappeared to R' Zemira'ah. "As you have comforted me," he said, "so may *HaKadosh Baruch Hu* comfort you. For on the day that you taught my son his first *pasuk*, one judgment against me was absolved. When you taught him the *Shema*, they absolved one judgment by day and one by night. On the day that he was permitted entry into an academy of higher learning, all remaining judgments were absolved. On the day that he was crowned with the title 'Rabbi,' they prepared for me a place among the tzaddikim in Gan Eden. Each day that he propounds a new insight in Torah, they adorn me with yet another crown with which the tzaddikim are adorned.

"All this," the father concluded, "is in your merit. This is the portion of one who leaves behind a son who toils in Torah."

If such is the reward of one whose son studies Torah, how much greater must the reward be for one who himself toils in Torah!

On Shavuos, we must strengthen our resolve to study diligently, with the goal of knowing Torah in all its breadth and depth.

May we merit a true kabalas haTorah.

The Struggle for Self-Control

דַּבֵּר אֶל בְּנֵי יִשְׂרָאֵל וְאָמַרְתָּ אֲלֵהֶם: אִישׁ אוֹ אִשָּׁה כִּי יַפְלִא לִנְדֹּר
נֶדֶר נָזִיר לְהַזִּיר לַה׳.

Speak to the Children of Israel and say to them: When a man or woman will express themselves to vow the vow of a nazir, to consecrate themselves to Hashem (6:2).

ঙ্গ From Servant to Master

*P*arashas Naso discusses the laws of the *nazir*, a person who, by making a vow, has willingly accepted upon himself a status which prohibits one from partaking of any grape derivative, from cutting his hair and from contracting *tumas meis*, defilement through contact with a human corpse. A number of commentators see the word יַפְלִא in the above verse as expressing the essence of the *nazir's* achievement. *Sforno*, who understands the word as connoting separation, comments:

> כִּי יַפְלִא — *He separates himself from the vanities and [earthly]indulgences of humanity.* לִנְדֹּר נֶדֶר נָזִיר — *To be removed and separated from common indulgences... in order to be committed to God, to occupy himself in His Torah, to walk in His ways and to cleave to Him.*

Ibn Ezra relates the word יַפְלִא to פֶּלֶא, *wonder:*

> *He [the nazir] will do something wondrous, for most people pursue their physical desires.*

Thus, the goal of the *nazir* is to become a master over himself. His means of accomplishing this is by abstaining from that which is permissible but unnecessary. In truth, the *nazir's* goal should be that of every Jew, as is summed up in the famous comment of *Ramban* to the words קְדֹשִׁים תִּהְיוּ, *You shall be holy* (*Vayikra* 19:2): קַדֵּשׁ עַצְמְךָ בְּמוּתָר לָךְ, *Sanctify yourself with that which is permitted to you.* *Ramban* explains that it is possible for a person to be lustful and overindulgent while technically staying within the confines of *Halachah.* Such a person is considered a נָבָל בִּרְשׁוּת הַתּוֹרָה, *a despicable person within the framework of Torah*, for such behavior is contrary to the refined conduct expected of Hashem's people. Thus we are commanded: קְדֹשִׁים תִּהְיוּ.

Through avoidance of תַּעֲנוּגִים, *earthly indulgences*, a person can attain lofty levels of spirituality. Regarding the *nazir*, the Torah writes: כִּי נֵזֶר אֱלֹקָיו עַל רֹאשׁוֹ, "For the crown of His God is upon his head" (6:7). *Ba'al HaTurim* offers an amazing comment: Through being a *nazir*, one can merit that the Divine Presence will come to rest upon him. However, some might misconstrue the *nazir's Ruach HaKodesh*, Divine inspiration, as a manifestation of the forbidden practice of communicating with the dead (see *Devarim* 18:11). Therefore, the Torah prohibited the *nazir* from having any contact with the dead for the duration of his *nezirus.*

By restraining one's earthly desires, one can attain *Ruach HaKodesh!*

Sforno, in explaining the qualities of the *nazir*, goes on to cite the teachings of *Chazal* that one is not to afflict himself in a manner that would impair his Divine service (*Ta'anis* 11b), nor torture his body as was the way of certain idolaters (*Sotah* 20a). By abstaining from wine, the *nazir* will learn to subdue his desires while not diminishing his strength. It is important to underscore *Sforno's* assertion that the way to subdue one's *yetzer hara* is not through self-affliction. *Mesilas Yesharim* (ch. 13), in discussing the benefits of פְּרִישׁוּת, *abstention*, also dwells on this point:

> ... *The undesirable way of abstention is that of the foolish gentiles, who not only abstain from that which is unnecessary, but even deny themselves necessities and also afflict their bodies with sufferings and strange practices for which Hashem has no desire at all. To the contrary, the Sages have taught, "It is forbidden for a person to afflict himself"* (*Ta'anis* 22b).

↝ The Dangers of
Unrestrained Indulgence

It is vital for a person to exercise self-control with regard to those תַּעֲנוּגִים in which the *Halachah* permits us to indulge. This is necessary not only to attain a heightened degree of spirituality. If we will not exercise self-control in that which is permissible, then we will find ourselves unprepared when faced with a test involving that which is clearly forbidden by *Halachah*. Moreover, one who pursues his earthly desires is never satisfied. A comment of *Ramban* in this regard is noteworthy:

> For when the heart of a satiated soul, which does not crave that which is bad for it, is possessed by a bit of craving and it satisfies that craving — then the soul will have an increased craving and be exceedingly thirsty for that thing . . . and it will desire bad things for which it originally had no craving at all (*Ramban, Devarim 29:18*).

One who seeks to rid himself of wrongful desires should take to heart the following words of R' Yisrael Salanter:

> One should know that the pain of retribution for a given sin is far greater than the pain of restraining one's desire to commit that sin. Certainly at the moment of trial [when one struggles to control his desires] one experiences great anguish, an anguish that his body literally feels. One should know, however, that in no way does this anguish compare to the pain of the punishment that will be inflicted against him should he transgress that sin, ח"ו (*Ohr Yisrael* §6).

One can gain added insight into the seriousness of sin from the ruling of *Rama* (*Orach Chaim* 656:1) that one is obligated to surrender his entire fortune rather than transgress a single לֹא תַעֲשֶׂה (negative prohibition). R' Akiva Eiger adds that this ruling includes rabbinically ordained prohibitions. A young millionaire, for example, is required to give away every cent he owns and live a lifetime of poverty rather than transgress a single rabbinic transgression — for such is the seriousness of sin.

⋖§ The Nazir and Shimon HaTzaddik

The story of a particular *nazir* (*Nedarim* 9b) provides added insight into the workings of the *yetzer hara* and the means through which it can and should be subdued:

> Shimon HaTzaddik said, ''. . . It happened once that a *nazir* from the south came [to the Beis HaMikdash to bring his offering]. He had beautiful eyes, a pleasing complexion and rows of wavy locks. I said to him, 'My son, what has impelled you to destroy your beautiful hair?' [At the conclusion of the period of nezirus, the nazir must have all his hair shorn.] He replied, 'I was a shepherd for my father in my city. It happened once that I went to a spring to fill my pail and I took note of my reflection [in the water]. I felt my evil inclination rush upon me — it sought to drive me from this world! I said to it: "Wicked one! Why do you take pride in a world that is not your own, in one who will in the end be [among the] worms and maggots! I swear that I will [become a nazir and] have you [i.e., his hair] shorn for the sake of Heaven.'' '
>
> ''I [Shimon HaTzaddik] immediately arose and kissed him on his head. I told him, 'May there be many more nezirim like you in Israel. It is regarding you that the Torah writes: 'When a man or woman will express themselves to vow the vow of a nazir, to consecrate themselves **to Hashem** [i.e., for Hashem's sake]' '' (6:2).

Rashi comments that as this young man observed how handsome he was, he felt himself being overcome by an urge to sin. He then perceived that his having become enamored with his own good looks was the work of his *yetzer hara*. His subsequent reaction is illustrative of a principle found in *Orchos Chaim L'HaRosh:* גְּעַר בְּיֵצֶר הָרַע, *Rebuke the yetzer hara.* The young man told himself, ''Why should I take pride in my beautiful hair and good looks? What good will all this do me when my life ends and I am buried among the worms and maggots? Wicked one! You are attempting to draw me after the vanities of this world, a world that is not my own, so that I will stray after falsehood and evil instead of truth and goodness. But you, my *yetzer hara*, will not succeed; I will become a *nazir*, cut off my beautiful locks for the sake of Hashem, and thereby subdue the passion that is urging me on toward sin."

A Jew must constantly be alert to the enticements and schemes of his evil inclination. Generally speaking, one must seek to uproot הֶרְגֵּל, *habit*; meaning, he must learn to think before he acts rather than act without thinking. By analyzing a given situation to arrive at a correct course of action, one develops a 'habit' for seeing matters in light of Hashem's will and for ignoring the urgings of his *yetzer hara*. Additionally, when one senses that he is being drawn by the enticements of his inclination, he should employ the young *nazir's* tactic of explaining to himself how false and empty such behavior is.

The incident of the *nazir* and Shimon *HaTzaddik* offers an additional lesson that is highly relevant in our times. The *Midrash* (*Bereishis Rabbah* 22:6) states:

> R' Ami said: "The yetzer hara does not walk on the 'side streets' [among the humble and modest who are not overly concerned with their outward appearance — Maharzu]; rather, he walks down the 'main thorough-fare' [after those who are concerned with their appearance]. When he sees someone fingering his eyes, fixing his hair, and adjusting his step, he says, 'This one is mine!' "

There is no question that a *ben Torah* must have a neat and clean appearance — but Heaven forfend that he seek to be 'in style,' clothing himself in the latest fashions designed by the gentile world. Nor should a *ben Torah* be so concerned with his appearance that he preens himself before a mirror, carefully combing every hair on his head! It is with regard to those who engage in such practices that Satan says, "They are mine!" One who finds himself struck by such whims should confront his *yetzer hara* head-on, challenging him as did that young *nazir*: "Why do you take pride in a world that is not your own?!" Those who live by this approach will surely be granted *siyata dishmaya* in mastering their desires.

The Right Desires

ঙ Aharon's Distress

דַּבֵּר אֶל אַהֲרֹן וְאָמַרְתָּ אֵלָיו: בְּהַעֲלֹתְךָ אֶת הַנֵּרֹת, אֶל מוּל פְּנֵי הַמְּנוֹרָה יָאִירוּ שִׁבְעַת הַנֵּרוֹת.

Speak to Aharon and say to him: "When you light the lamps, towards the face of the Menorah shall the seven lamps give light" (8:2).

Why is the chapter of the Menorah juxtaposed with the chapter of the Nesi'im? For when Aharon saw the dedication of the Nesi'im [i.e., the numerous offerings they brought at the dedication of the altar], he felt dispirited that neither he nor his tribe had participated in the dedication. Said HaKadosh Baruch Hu to him: "By your life, yours is greater than theirs, for you will kindle and prepare the lamps" (Rashi ibid. from Midrash Tanchuma).

Ramban wonders why Aharon should have felt dispirited, given that the number of offerings which he brought during the seven days of מִלֻּאִים, inauguration, far exceeded those of the *Nesi'im*. To resolve this, we may suggest the following:

In the Book of *Koheles*, Shlomo *HaMelech* declares: אֹהֵב כֶּסֶף לֹא יִשְׂבַּע כֶּסֶף, *A lover of money will never be satisfied with money* (*Koheles* 5:9). In the words of *Midrash Rabbah* (ibid. 1:13), "He who has one hundred wants two hundred, and he who has two hundred wants four hundred." That man can desire something to the point that no amount of it will ever satisfy him is a characteristic which can

— and should be — channeled toward spiritual pursuits. In fact, it is precisely for this purpose that Hashem instilled such relentless desire in man. One can develop within himself a relentless desire to fulfill the word of Hashem, to strive to perform *mitzvah* after *mitzvah* without ever wearying of this lofty service. Indeed, the *Midrash* states:

אֹהֵב כֶּסֶף לֹא יִשְׂבַּע כֶּסֶף, אֹהֵב מִצְוֹת לֹא יִשְׂבַּע מִצְוֹת.

A lover of money will never be satisfied with money; a lover of mitzvos will never be satisfied with mitzvos (*Midrash Rabbah to Koheles* 5:9).

Aharon *HaKohen* epitomized the latter half of the above *Midrash*. No matter how many *mitzvos* he performed, it was never enough. Though he had been anointed as *Kohen Gadol*, had already brought numerous offerings, and would be privileged to perform services that no other Jew could perform, he nevertheless experienced a חֲלִישַׁת הַדַּעַת, *dispirited feeling*, at not being included in the dedication of the *Nesi'im*.

◆§ Torah Study

While the above principle applies to all *mitzvos*, it is especially true with regard to the study of Torah. *Midrash Rabbah* says as much in a variant text of the above-cited teaching:

אֹהֵב כֶּסֶף לֹא יִשְׂבַּע כֶּסֶף, אֹהֵב תּוֹרָה לֹא יִשְׂבַּע תּוֹרָה.

A lover of money will never be satisfied with money; a lover of Torah will never be satisfied with Torah (*Vayikra Rabbah* 22:1).

It is easy to find excuses for lackluster study. A most common excuse is simply that one lacks חֵשֶׁק, *desire*, for his studies. There are those who actually delude themselves into thinking that desire for learning is an inborn gift and that a lack of desire excuses one from immersing himself in the study of Torah. Those who believe this could not be further from the truth. No one is excused from the obligation to study Torah and no one is denied the potential to grow in Torah. Desire for Torah study is likewise within everyone's reach. A lack of such desire in *avodas Hashem* is usually indicative of a lack of effort born of laziness. In the words of *Mesilas Yesharim* (ch. 9):

The factors which impede zerizus (alacrity) are those which promote laziness, the primary deterrents being a desire for relaxation, an aversion to exertion and the love of [earthly] pleasures to their very limits. A man with such traits will surely find serving his Creator extremely burdensome. For one who desires to eat his meals amid perfect tranquility, to sleep without anything on his mind, and to walk only at a relaxed pace, will find it difficult to rise early in the morning to go to the beis haknesses, to cut short his afternoon meal in order to daven Minchah, or to go to perform some other mitzvah when the time is not convenient. Certainly he will not want to rush to do a mitzvah or to study Torah.

One who habituates himself in these ways is not a master over himself to behave in an opposite manner when he so desires, for his will is already bound up in the ropes of habit which has become second nature to him.

Desire for Torah study can be attained through persistent effort. Persist we must, for when our time before the Heavenly Court will come, our accomplishments in Torah will be judged in accordance with our potential. This point is illustrated by a remarkable incident.

When the *Netziv*[1] completed his *Ha'aamek She'elah*, a classic study of *She'iltos D'Rav Achai Gaon*, he marked the occasion with a *siyum* (*mitzvah* banquet). At the *siyum*, he related the following:

As a young child, the *Netziv* was playful and did not seem to have much interest in his studies. His father offered him all sorts of rewards and incentives, but nothing worked. One day, he overheard a discussion between his father and mother. His father said that, while he had always dreamed that his son would grow to be a *talmid chacham*, it was apparent that this dream would not be realized. He had been unsuccessful in attempting to inspire his son toward study and was now resigned to having his son trained as a tradesman.

The *Netziv* was shaken by his father's words. He rushed into the room and promised his father that he would devote himself to the study of Torah.

---

1. נצי"ב, *Netziv*, is an acronym for נפתלי צבי יהודה ברלין.

Having concluded his story, the *Netziv* told his guests that had he not overheard his father's lament, and thus made that commitment and honored it, the result would have been that when his time would come to stand before the Heavenly Court, he would have been asked, "Why did you not compose a work on the *She'iltos D'Rav Achai Gaon?* You were capable of this!" The *Netziv* would have had nothing to say, and the Court would have found his service on this earth wanting.

❦ ❦ ❦

In the beginning of this *parashah*, Rashi cites *Sifri* (§59) which relates the word בְּהַעֲלֹתְךָ to מַעֲלָה, *step*, meaning that there were steps in front of the *Menorah* upon which the *Kohen* would ascend in order to prepare and kindle the lamps.

Chazal tell us that the *Menorah* was the conduit for the wisdom of *Torah She'be'al Peh*, the Oral Law, which flowed from Above.[2] We may suggest that the *Kohen's* ascending to kindle the *Menorah* symbolized the spiritual elevation in the World to Come that awaits those who study Torah. The key to meriting this reward is found in a *Mishnah* in *Avos*:

> כָּךְ הִיא דַרְכָּהּ שֶׁל תּוֹרָה: פַּת בַּמֶּלַח תֹּאכֵל, וּמַיִם בַּמְּשׂוּרָה
> תִשְׁתֶּה, וְעַל הָאָרֶץ תִּישָׁן, וְחַיֵּי צַעַר תִּחְיֶה, וּבַתּוֹרָה אַתָּה עָמֵל;
> אִם אַתָּה עוֹשֶׂה כֵּן, "אַשְׁרֶיךָ וְטוֹב לָךְ": "אַשְׁרֶיךָ" — בָּעוֹלָם הַזֶּה,
> "וְטוֹב לָךְ" — לָעוֹלָם הַבָּא.
>
> *This is the way of Torah: Eat bread with salt, drink water in small measure, sleep on the ground, live a life of deprivation — but toil in Torah! If you do this, "You are praiseworthy and all is well with you" (Tehillim 128:2). "You are praiseworthy" — in this world; "and all is well with you" — in the World to Come (Avos 6:4).*

Torah must be studied amid the tranquility born from being satisfied with one's lot, and *bitachon*, trust, that Hashem will continue to provide for one's needs in the future. The blend of these qualities with the diligent study of Torah will insure a life of joy in This World and the Next.

---

2. In commenting on the words בְּהַעֲלֹתְךָ אֶת הַנֵּרֹת, the *Netziv* (in *Ha'amek Davar*) writes that Moshe *Rabbeinu* would enter the *Mishkan* at night when the *Menorah* was lit to review portions of the Oral Law.

Taking a Lesson[1]

⁜ Downfall of the Spies

שְׁלַח לְךָ אֲנָשִׁים וְיָתֻרוּ אֶת אֶרֶץ כְּנַעַן.

Send out men for yourself that they may scout out the Land of Canaan (13:2).

Why was the portion [discussing] the Spies juxtaposed to that of Miriam? Because she was punished for slandering her brother, and these wicked people saw this but did not take a lesson (Rashi ibid.).

Rashi (v. 13) writes that the מְרַגְּלִים, *Spies,* were men of distinction and upright individuals before they embarked on their mission to spy out *Eretz Yisrael* on behalf of their brethren. *Midrash Rabbah* (*Shelach* §5) relates that in selecting one spy from each tribe, Moshe sought — and received — Hashem's approval for each of his choices:

"And I took from among you twelve men" (Devarim 1:23) — From here we learn that they were all righteous in the eyes of Moshe and the people; also, Moshe did not want to send them of his own volition until he sought the opinion of the Holy One regarding each specific choice and Hashem responded that all were indeed worthy.

---

1. Delivered at a gathering commemorating the one hundredth anniversary of the Gateshead Jewish community.

It was a desire for honor that was the Spies' undoing. In the words of *Mesilas Yesharim* (ch. 11):

> ... It is possible that a person will contain his inclination for money and other pleasures, yet still be pressed for honor, as he cannot tolerate being on a lower status than his friends ... It was this which, according to our Sages (Zohar, Bamidbar 3:13), caused the Spies to slander the Land and brought death upon them and their entire generation. For they feared, lest their honor be diminished when they would enter the Land, as they would no longer be princes among Israel and others would serve in their stead.

It was this personal interest which prevented them from recognizing the truth of the Land's superlative qualities and believing that with Hashem's help it surely could be conquered. Though this self-interest was an existent fact, it could have been overcome had they taken a lesson from Miriam, who was punished for having criticized her brother Moshe.

The righteousness of Miriam need not be dwelled upon. It is sufficient to mention the miraculous well which, in Miriam's merit, provided water for the Jews throughout their forty-year sojourn in the wilderness. As *Rambam* explains (*Sefer HaMitzvos* §7), her sin was far from the sort that we associate with the term slander:

> If Miriam, who spoke only in front of Moshe and in Moshe's interest and because of the esteem in which she held him and because of her concern for 'the building of the world' [i.e., that Moshe remain with his wife], was nevertheless punished in such a manner, then surely those who speak disparagingly of their neighbors in public [will face severe judgment for their misdeeds].

Because of her error, Miriam was afflicted with *tzaraas*. The Spies were indeed great people, but they erred — beginning with their reaction to Miriam's affliction. They viewed it as just another unfortunate occurrence instead of contemplating what had occurred and taking a lesson from it to carry through life. Had they done this, they might have had the fortitude to overcome their personal interests and refrain from speaking evil of the Chosen Land that was God's gift to the Chosen People.

⊰§ Gateshead

It is important that one learn to derive meaningful lessons from occurrences and relate them to his own personal life. This was Shlomo *HaMelech's* intent when he said (*Mishlei* 2:4): "If you seek it out as you seek silver and search for it as you search for buried treasures — then you will comprehend the fear of Hashem, and knowledge of God you shall find." When a person attains great wealth, people are quick to ask, "How did he do it?" They ask this both out of curiosity and in the hope that perhaps they can emulate his accomplishment. This should be our approach in spiritual matters. When, for example, we see others attain lofty heights of Heavenly fear, we must ponder their accomplishments, so that we can emulate them.

We, who are here to commemorate the one hundredth anniversary of the founding of the Gateshead Jewish community, are obligated to ponder the development of this *kehillah*. From a beginning of a mere handful of individuals sprouted forth a fortress of Torah and *mitzvah* observance that is a beacon of light to Jews everywhere. How did all this come about and what lesson can we learn from it?

In *Parashas Pekudei* (*Shemos* 38:22), the lineage of Betzalel, who led the *Mishkan's* construction, is traced to his grandfather Chur and the tribe of Yehudah. *Sforno* comments:

> The leaders of the craftsmen of the Mishkan's work were of noble lineage and were the tzaddikim of the generation, and therefore, the Divine Presence rested on the work of their hands and it did not fall into the hands of their enemies. However, the Beis HaMikdash of Shlomo (was built by) workers of the nations of the world (I Melachim 7:13), and although the Divine Presence did rest there, its sections deteriorated and it was necessary to 'repair the breaches of the House' (בֶּדֶק הַבַּיִת); and eventually, it all fell into the hands of the enemy.

Gateshead's phenomenal success as a Torah center is rooted in the sterling personalities of its founders and those leaders who joined the community as time went on. One of the community's founders was R' Eliezer Adler, whose fear of Hashem was awesome. R' Eliezer was extremely meticulous with regard to *Halachah*, particularly in the area of *kashrus*. There was a time when certain elements who did not conduct themselves in the traditional way sought to gain a foothold in the community. R' Eliezer fought these elements fearlessly and successfully. We all owe him a great debt of gratitude.

As time went on, a *shochet*, R' David Dryan, was hired by the *kehillah*. R' David proved to be far more than a *shochet*. A disciple of the Chofetz Chaim, he imbued the community with a new spirit, spreading Torah among the youth and influencing them in a most sublime manner. R' David had no children of his own, but he fathered thousands of children in a spiritual sense, for *Chazal* have taught: "One who teaches his friend's child Torah is considered as having given birth to him" (*Sanhedrin* 19b).

It was R' David who conceived of establishing a yeshivah in the city. For this, he brought to Gateshead two *talmidim* of Novaradok. First came R' Nachman David Landinsky (son of the Radiner *Rosh Yeshivah*) to serve as *Rosh Yeshivah*. He was later joined by R' Eliezer Kahan, who served as the yeshivah's *menahel*. The spirit of the Chofetz Chaim which was already permeating Gateshead was then blended with that of Novaradok.

Living in the city at that time was an upright Jew named R' Shlomo Zalman Kohen. In a time when *kollel* was still a foreign concept, R' Shlomo Zalman was determined that his daughter marry a *ben Torah* who would dedicate himself to the full-time study of Torah. Even more unusual at that time was that R' Shlomo Zalman's daughter desired to marry this sort of young man. She was an exceptionally pious, worthy young woman. R' Shlomo Zalman journeyed to the yeshivah in Mir, Poland, to find her[2] a suitable mate.

Mention must also be made of R' Ephraim Bloch, who selected a *ben Torah* from Telshe — R' Chaim Shmuel Lopian — to marry his eldest daughter. For his second daughter, he chose a *ben Torah* from Kaminetz, who is today known as *Dayan* Grossnas, *shlita*. These

---

2. Few among HaRav Segal's audience realized that he was referring to his own *rebbetzin*, who passed away some years ago. HaRav Segal lived in Gateshead after his marriage, devoting himself to the full-time study of Torah.

marriages introduced the community to the idea of seeking sons-in-law who were *bnei Torah*.

It was after the outbreak of the second World War that the community decided to retain the services of an official *rav*. A letter was sent to the Slabodker *Rosh Yeshivah*, R' Isaac Sher, requesting someone who was great in Torah knowledge and fear of Hashem, a *ba'al mussar* and an accomplished *darshan* (scholarly orator) whose words could inspire his listeners. R' Naftali Shakovitsky, son of the Minsker *Maggid* and an outstanding product of the famed Kovno *Kollel*, was chosen for this role. R' Naftali grew up in a home permeated with Torah and *chesed* and he inherited this legacy in abundance. His appointment as *rav* was yet another turning point for the *kehillah*. Upon his arrival, R' Shakovitsky immediately garnered support for the construction of a new *beis haknesses* and *mikveh*, both of which stand to this day. In this effort, he was ably assisted by the very dedicated Dr. Chalk, without whom the project could not have come about.

An unofficial *kollel* was formed, as the *rav* led the city's few married *bnei Torah* in organized study. However, R' David Dryan desired more than this for Gateshead, so he invited R' Eliyahu Dessler to come and undertake the task of establishing an official *kollel*. Later, three great personalities — R' Leib Lopian, R' Moshe Schwab, and R' Leib Gurwicz — joined the Gateshead Yeshivah. Their presence had a profound impact on the yeshivah, the *kollel*, and the entire community, which later saw the founding of its famous seminary for young women. The seminary's founder and principal for more than four decades was Mr. Avraham Kohn.

Chazal established specific blessings upon witnessing certain extraordinary sights. There is a blessing one recites upon seeing a gentile king, and another one said when seeing a Jewish king. There is a blessing to be said upon seeing a great Torah scholar and one recited when witnessing a gathering of six hundred thousand Jews. What blessing would be appropriate for this gathering in which we are now participating?

In my opinion, the blessing בָּרוּךְ הַמְקַדֵּשׁ שְׁמוֹ בָּרַבִּים, *Blessed is He Who sanctifies His Name among the multitudes*, is most appropriate. The Gateshead Jewish community is a great *kiddush Hashem*, an example of what can result from sincere, dedicated effort for Hashem's sake, and a living testimony to the promise that Torah will never be forgotten from among our people.

Maintaining a Proper Outlook

ᴇᔰ The Grandfather from Brisk

The following anecdote was related to me by a resident of Mir, Poland, during my years of study at that city's great yeshivah:

The man's grandfather had lived in Brisk, where he owned a textile shop. On the same street was another textile concern whose volume of business far exceeded that of the grandfather's shop.

One day, an army officer entered the second store and made a purchase. When the officer later arrived home and unwrapped the goods, it seemed to him that the material was less than the amount for which he had paid. He immediately suspected the Jew of deliberately cheating him. The officer contacted a government official who dispatched an inspector to check the store's weights and measurements.

Somehow, the grandfather learned of what was transpiring. While he could not be certain whether or not his competitor's weights and measurements were accurate, he was positive that his were. He also knew that should his competitor's tools prove inaccurate, the anti-Semitic officials would punish him severely. Without a moment's hesitation, the grandfather rushed to his competitor, informed him of his discovery, and gave him his weights and measurements before the inspector reached the store.

To some, the grandfather's act might seem incredible. A lesser man would have looked forward to being rid of his competition so that he could finally earn a decent living. The key to the grandfather's behavior was an awareness of man's true purpose on this earth and an ability to maintain this awareness when the moment of trial presented itself. Thus, such behavior is within everyone's reach.

✺§ Korach

It was a failure to maintain such an awareness that was the undoing of Korach and his assembly. Korach brazenly challenged the leadership of Moshe and the appointment of Aharon as *Kohen Gadol*. In response, Moshe said that all who considered themselves worthy of the High Priesthood should appear the next morning at the *Mishkan* carrying a *ketores*, incense, offering. Moshe warned (see *Rashi* 16:6) that only the one whom Hashem desired as the *Kohen Gadol* would survive this test and have his offering accepted; everyone else would perish. Yet the next day, Korach and two hundred and fifty followers stood ready with their offerings. *Rashi* (v. 7) asks, "Korach, who was a perceptive individual — what drove him to such foolishness?" Citing the *Midrash*, *Rashi* explains that Korach, through *Ruach HaKodesh*, saw great men of righteousness and distinction descending from him, including the prophet Shmuel. This knowledge caused Korach — a perceptive man — to believe that his offering would be accepted and that he would live, while everyone else, including Aharon, would perish!

For such a man to suffer such delusion, there had to have been some personal desire that blurred his vision and deprived him of his perception. In explaining what impelled Korach to embark on his campaign against Moshe and Aharon, *Rashi* states:

> What caused Korach to argue against Moshe? He was envious of the princeship of Elitzaphan ben Uziel, whom Moshe appointed prince over the family of Kehas by Divine command. Said Korach: "My father was one of four brothers...Amram, who was the eldest — his two sons took high positions; one [Moshe] is a king, while the other is Kohen Gadol. Who is fit to receive the next appointment [i.e., the princeship of Kehas] if not me, who is the son of Yitzhar, the second son after Kehas? — and he appointed the son of the youngest brother instead!"

Korach's folly is aptly summed up in the following citation from *Mesilas Yesharim* (ch. 11):

> *Envy is likewise rooted in a lack of understanding and foolishness, for being envious does not achieve any gain for oneself, nor does it cause any loss to the one who is the object of envy...There is a type whose foolishness in this regard is so great that if he sees his neighbor in possession of a good thing, he broods, worries and feels pained — to the point that he will not even enjoy his own good things because of the pain of seeing that which his neighbor possesses.*

Korach was not satisfied with being a distinguished member of the exalted tribe of Levi. His uncontrolled envy caused him to become a real-life illustration of a well-known teaching:

רַבִּי אֶלְעָזָר הַקַּפָּר אוֹמֵר: הַקִּנְאָה וְהַתַּאֲוָה וְהַכָּבוֹד מוֹצִיאִין אֶת הָאָדָם מִן הָעוֹלָם.

R' Elazar HaKappar says: Jealousy, lust, and glory remove a man from this world (Avos 4:28).

Returning to the story of the grandfather from Brisk: There is no doubt that his coming to the rescue of his competitor was a result of his having worked to refine his character traits. Thus was a simple man able to choose the correct course of action rather than be blinded by ill will and a desire for an improvement of his own financial position. On the other hand, envy and a desire for glory blurred the vision of a man as great as Korach.

◆§ The Wife of Ohn

A sidelight to Korach's dispute lends added insight to the above. The Torah lists Ohn ben Peles among the original cohorts of Korach; however, further in the recounting of the dispute there is no mention of him. The *Gemara (Sanhedrin 109b)* explains:

> *Rav said: "Ohn ben Peles was saved by his wife. She said to him, 'What difference is it to you [whether Moshe, Korach, or anyone else is our leader]? If this one*

is the teacher, then you are but a student, and if the other is the teacher, then you are still but a student!' Ohn told her, 'What can I do? I took part in their plans and swore to join them.' She said, 'I know that the entire nation is holy, as is written, "For the entire assembly is holy" (Bamidbar 16:3). Sit, and I will save you.' She then gave him wine until he was intoxicated and put him to sleep inside their tent. She sat herself at the entrance to the tent and uncovered her hair. Whoever saw her went away."

Ohn's wife used very simple logic: Why get involved in a dispute of such magnitude when you stand to gain nothing? It would seem that Ohn should have realized this himself. That he did not is yet another proof of the *yetzer hara's* prowess in beclouding our thinking and preventing us from recognizing obvious truths. Persuaded by Korach's arguments and perhaps afflicted with his own envy, Ohn was in the fore of the disgraceful challenge to Moshe's authority. His wife, however, was free of such influences and had no difficulty perceiving that which was obvious.

Noteworthy also is the means by which Ohn's wife saved her husband. In waging their dispute, Korach and his assembly transgressed a host of grievous sins. Nevertheless, Ohn's wife was sure that these same people would not compromise their personal *kedushah*, sanctity, and walk where they would be forced to see the uncovered hair of a married woman. If they were so concerned with their sanctity, why did they not contemplate the eternal blemish they were bringing upon their souls through their actions against Moshe and Aharon?

Such is the power of the *yetzer hara*.

Korach spoke as one whose intentions were noble and pure: "...for the entire assembly is holy and Hashem dwells among them; and why have you raised yourselves above the congregation of Hashem?" (16:3). However, his true intentions were actually apparent from the moment he joined forces with the wicked Dasan and Aviram, whose evil history dated back to the time when they informed on Moshe to Pharaoh, forcing Moshe to flee from Egypt (see *Rashi* to *Sh'mos* 2:16). One whose intentions are honorable does not invite men of ill repute to join his cause.

However, it is clear from *Chazal* that there was some underlying spiritual yearning in the demands of Korach and his assembly. After they put forth their initial complaint, Moshe responded: רַב לָכֶם בְּנֵי לֵוִי, Enough, sons of Levi (16:7). The Gemara (Sotah 13b) relates that this response was overly harsh, and as a result Moshe's prayers were ineffective in gaining him entry into Eretz Yisrael:

וַיֹּאמֶר ה׳ אֵלַי רַב לָךְ.

Hashem said to me, "It is enough" (Devarim 3:26).
R' Levi said: "Moshe told [Korach], 'Enough,' and he was told by Hashem [when he asked to enter the Land], 'Enough.' "

The many prayers which Moshe offered on High in the hope that he be permitted to enter Eretz Yisrael reflected his intense desire to reap the spiritual blessings of Hashem's Chosen Land. For responding somewhat harshly to the aspirations expressed by Korach and his assembly, Moshe was punished midah k'neged midah, measure for measure, in that his own spiritual yearnings were denied him.

The spiritual dreams of every Jew must be recognized and accorded due attention so that his yearning will remain strong, rather than wane.

The Need for Reflection

✍ The Sin of Not Thinking

In the *viduy* (confession) which we recite during the *Shemoneh Esrei* of *Yom Kippur*, we say: עַל חֵטְא שֶׁחָטָאנוּ לְפָנֶיךָ בִּבְלִי דָעַת, *For the sin that we have sinned before You without knowledge.* *Siach Yitzchak* explains that this refers to wrongful practices for which there are no specific prohibitions, but which man's intellect dictates as sinful. Man is held accountable for such practices and must seek atonement for them, for, as *Sefer Chassidim* (§153) states: "We find in the Torah that whoever is capable of deducing a given matter is punished for not having acted accordingly, though there is no command regarding it."

Sefer Chassidim offers two proofs for the above. The first is where Moshe faulted the military officers who directed the battle against Midian for having allowed the women captives to remain alive (*Bamidbar* 31:14-16). Though they had not been commanded to kill the women, Moshe had expected the officers to deduce this by way of a *kal v'chomer*: If the Jews were commanded (*Devarim* 20:16) to eradicate the Canaanite nations with whom they had thus far had no contact,[1] lest they be influenced by their sinful ways, then certainly

---

1. HaRav Segal mentioned parenthetically that this commandment underscores the dangers of living among the gentiles and the need to insulate oneself from their negative influences. He remarked that in today's age of immodesty, a God-fearing Jew must teach himself to limit his range of vision whenever he needs to walk in the street.

the Midianite women, who had already enticed the Jews to commit sins of immorality and idol worship (*Bamidbar* 25:2; see *Rashi*), should be annihilated.

The second proof is found in *Parashas Balak*. When Bilaam set out toward Balak, who desired that Bilaam place his curse upon the Jewish nation, Hashem sent an angel with an unsheathed sword to block his path. The donkey upon which Bilaam rode was able to see the angel, while Bilaam could not. The angel blocked the donkey's path three times. The first time, the donkey veered off the path and Bilaam hit it. The second time, the angel stood in a narrow walkway and when the frightened donkey moved toward the side, Bilaam's foot was squeezed against a fence. Again, he hit the donkey. When the angel then presented himself in an even narrower path in which there was no place to turn, the donkey settled down on the ground, only to be hit a third time by an angry Bilaam. It was then that the great miracle occurred whereby the donkey spoke, rebuking Bilaam for embarking on his journey, a rebuke to which he was unable to respond (see *Bamidbar Rabbah* 20:14). Finally, Hashem permitted Bilaam to see the angel. The angel asked him (22:32), "Why did you hit your donkey these three times . . .?" Bilaam replied (22:34), "I have sinned, for I did not know that you were standing opposite me on the road . . ."

Asks *Sefer Chassidim*: What was the angel demanding of Bilaam? Is it a sin for a rider to hit his donkey in order to steer it back on the road, let alone when it is pressing his foot against a fence?! Also, what did Bilaam mean when he responded, "I have sinned . . ."? His not having seen the angel is precisely why he had *not* sinned, since he had no idea as to why his donkey was behaving so erratically.

Sefer Chassidim explains Bilaam's sin as follows: He should have considered that the donkey's wayward behavior was a Heavenly signal that God was upset with him for his wrongful intentions in going to meet Balak. For although he had told Balak's emissaries, ". . . I cannot transgress the word of Hashem . . ." (22:18), Bilaam was hoping to oblige Balak and place his curse upon the Jewish nation; it was for this reason that the angel was sent to block his path. Thus, Bilaam correctly admitted: חָטָאתִי, "*I have sinned.*"

A person who permits himself to coast merrily along the path of life, never reflecting upon his personal life or events of note, is guilty of sinful behavior. It is a Jew's obligation to *think*, to be ever mindful of the lessons and Heavenly messages that can be derived from a given happening.

One must approach his Torah studies in a similar manner. No matter how many times one has studied a given *pasuk* or teaching of *Chazal*, he must ponder it anew each time he comes across it and draw out the lessons hidden in its words.

Yet another great lesson can be derived from the episode of Bilaam and his donkey, as we shall explain.

✺§ Human Dignity

In his words to Bilaam (22:32), the angel alluded to his having killed the donkey. *Rashi* elaborates:

> I [i.e., the angel] killed her, so that people should not say, "This is the donkey that brought about Bilaam's downfall through her rebuke . . ." For the Omnipresent has consideration for human dignity.

This same idea is found in the *mishnah* (*Sanhedrin* 7:4) regarding the Torah requirement that the animal also be killed (*Vayikra* 20:15) in a case where someone is punished by death for bestiality. Asks the *mishnah*:

> If the person sinned, what sin did the animal commit? . . . So that the animal should not pass in the street and people will say, "This is the animal on account of which that person was stoned."

In the *mishnah*, we are dealing with someone who intentionally committed an abominable act after having been warned by two witnesses that he would be punished by death were he to commit it. Yet the Torah concerned itself with the dignity of such a man.

Even more astounding is the case of Bilaam. He had been warned by Hashem, "Do not curse the nation, for it is blessed" (22:12). Despite this warning, Bilaam set out with Balak's emissaries, his heart 'one with theirs' (see *Rashi* to v. 21). One would think that concern for כְּבוֹד הַבְּרִיּוֹת, *human dignity*, does not apply to a *rasha* (wicked person) of this sort.

Consider also the following: Keeping Bilaam's donkey alive would have resulted in a great *kiddush Hashem* (sanctification of Hashem's Name). People would have pointed to the donkey and remembered that it been granted a miraculous ability to speak in order to rebuke one who sought to transgress his Creator's will. The donkey's having spoken was one of the great wonders of creation (see *Avos* 5:8); a classic illustration of Hashem's Omnipotence and His limitless ability to deal with those who disobey Him.

All this was overlooked for the sake of Bilaam's honor. Even a great *kiddush Hashem* did not justify dishonoring a thoroughly evil individual. How careful must one be with regard to the honor of his fellow! Regardless of our opinion of our neighbor, he deserves our respect and consideration.

Further insight regarding a Jew's obligation toward his fellow can be gleaned from a *mishnah* in *Bava Kama* (3:8) which states that if two men who are fighting wound one another, then the one who caused more damage must pay the full excess. *Rosh* (§13) explains that the *mishnah* deals with a case in which the two men began fighting simultaneously; only then are they both obligated to pay for the damage they each inflicted. However, should one provoke the other by striking first, the latter may respond in self-defense, *but only to the extent required to defend himself!* Should he inflict any more damage than necessary, then he is obligated to pay for that damage.

In the case of the *mishnah*, the two men are not engaged in childish pranks. Hatred has turned into physical assault — and even then one must exercise caution in not responding more than is necessary. Otherwise, he will be held accountable for his actions. Can a person be expected to make such judgments at a time when he is furious over the attack against him? If the *halachah* requires this of us, then obviously it *is* possible to maintain one's composure even under such circumstances. Moreover — not only is it possible, it is an obligation. Such are the demands which the Torah places upon a Jew in his dealings with his fellow.

⇜§ Divergent Paths

כָּל מִי שֶׁיֵּשׁ בְּיָדוֹ שְׁלֹשָׁה דְבָרִים הַלָּלוּ, הוּא מִתַּלְמִידָיו שֶׁל
אַבְרָהָם אָבִינוּ; וּשְׁלֹשָׁה דְבָרִים אֲחֵרִים, הוּא מִתַּלְמִידָיו שֶׁל
בִּלְעָם הָרָשָׁע. עַיִן טוֹבָה, וְרוּחַ נְמוּכָה, וְנֶפֶשׁ שְׁפָלָה, תַּלְמִידָיו שֶׁל

אַבְרָהָם אָבִינוּ. עַיִן רָעָה, וְרוּחַ גְּבוֹהָה, וְנֶפֶשׁ רְחָבָה, תַּלְמִידָיו שֶׁל בִּלְעָם הָרָשָׁע.

Whoever has the following three traits is a disciple of our forefather Avraham; and [whoever has] three different traits is a disciple of the wicked Bilaam. Those who have a good eye, a humble spirit, and a meek soul are among the disciples of our forefather Avraham. Those who have an evil eye, an arrogant spirit, and a greedy soul are among the disciples of the wicked Bilaam (Avos 5:22).

In his commentary, *Rabbeinu Yonah* questions the lengthy wording of this *mishnah*. It would seem that the author could have said simply: *Whoever has a good eye ... is a disciple of Avraham. Whoever has a bad eye ... is a disciple of the wicked Bilaam.*

We may suggest that the *mishnah's* opening sentence is conveying the constant need for הִתְבּוֹנְנוּת, *reflection*, for that is the key to attaining Avraham's traits. The *mishnah* is, in effect, saying to us: Decide for yourself which path you wish to follow, that of Avraham or that of Bilaam. The road to becoming a disciple of Avraham requires reflection, in contrast to the way of Bilaam who gave no thought to satisfying the Divine will. Once a person realizes the necessity for such הִתְבּוֹנְנוּת, he can then learn the various attributes he must acquire to be counted among Avraham's disciples.

In explaining Bilaam's trait of נֶפֶשׁ רְחָבָה, *a greedy soul*, *Rashi* (in his commentary to *Avos*) cites Bilaam's words to Balak's original emissaries: "Even if Balak will give me his house full of silver and gold, I cannot transgress the word of Hashem" (24:13). It has been noted that Bilaam could have said, "If Balak will give me all the money in the world" (as in *Avos* 6:9). His choice of words indicates that his desire for enormous sums of money was not rooted purely in a craving for wealth. Bilaam's arrogance caused him to lust after the wealth of *others*, so that his rise in stature would be coupled with their fall. Thus Bilaam epitomized selfishness and lack of regard for his fellow man.

Through proper הִתְבּוֹנְנוּת, one learns a way of life that gains him the status of a disciple of Avraham *Avinu*. May we merit to achieve that lofty status.

The Greatness of Yehoshua

וַיֹּאמֶר ה׳ אֶל מֹשֶׁה, קַח לְךָ אֶת יְהוֹשֻׁעַ בֶּן נוּן, אִישׁ אֲשֶׁר רוּחַ בּוֹ.
Hashem told Moshe: "Take Yehoshua the son of Nun, a man of spirit" (27:18).

◄§ The Guardian of the Tree

Yehoshua bin [son of] Nun was chosen to succeed Moshe *Rabbeinu* as leader of the Jewish nation and transmitter of Torah, though there were others whose stature initially surpassed his own. In *Parashas Shelach*, *Ramban* (13:4) writes that the מְרַגְּלִים, *Spies*, are listed in order of greatness, and Yehoshua is listed fifth. Moreover, *Baal HaTurim* (ibid. v. 3) finds an allusion to the Spies' being שָׂרֵי חֲמִשִּׁים, *commanders of fifty*, placing them lower in rank than the שָׂרֵי מֵאוֹת, *commanders of hundreds* and שָׂרֵי אֲלָפִים, *commanders of thousands* (see *Sh'mos* 18:21).

Midrash Rabbah tells of the qualities that deemed Yehoshua worthy of his awesome role:

> The Holy One said to Moshe: "Yehoshua has served you exceedingly and honored you exceedingly; he would arise early and remain late in your study hall; he would arrange the benches and spread out the mats. Since he served you with all his ability, it is fitting that he serve Israel, for he should not forfeit the reward due

him. Designate Yehoshua the son of Nun [as your successor], to fulfill that which is written (Mishlei 27:18), 'He who guards the fig tree shall eat its fruit' '' (Bamidbar Rabbah 21:14).

The *Midrash* delves further into the words נֹצֵר תְּאֵנָה יֹאכַל פִּרְיָהּ, "He who guards the fig tree shall eat its fruit." In the case of other species in *Eretz Yisrael*, all the fruits on an individual tree become ready for picking at roughly the same time; a farmer can harvest the crop of that tree and put it out of mind until the next year. Figs, however, ripen at different intervals even on the same tree. Each fig must be examined and picked separately. The study of Torah, too, requires careful attention to each aspect of the *Halachah*, and it requires the patience to ponder and delve into each point. A proper understanding of the laws and their nuances and corollaries will not come all at once; as one's perception ripens, his comprehension deepens, and even what he once thought he knew takes on new dimensions and reveals new meanings and applications.

Yehoshua attached himself to his teacher, Moshe *Rabbeinu*, unremittingly for forty years, never leaving his side, never letting a word of the teacher escape the ear of the disciple. Yehoshua understood that the fruits of Torah ripen at different times, so he was always ready to pluck them lest he miss even one fruitful teaching through inattentiveness or absence. *He who guards the fig tree shall eat its fruit.*

⋙ Total Dedication

The degree of Yehoshua's faithfulness to his teacher can be seen from his having accompanied Moshe to Mount Sinai after the giving of the Torah, when Moshe ascended to the heavens to receive the first *Luchos* (Tablets):

וַיָּקָם מֹשֶׁה וִיהוֹשֻׁעַ מְשָׁרְתוֹ, וַיַּעַל מֹשֶׁה אֶל הַר הָאֱלֹקִים.
And Moshe arose, along with his attendant Yehoshua, and Moshe ascended the mountain of God (Sh'mos 24:13).

Rashi comments:

> *It seems to me that the student was escorting the teacher until the boundary at the mountain, past which he [Yehoshua] was not permitted to continue. From there Moshe ascended alone upon the mountain of God. Yehoshua set up his tent and remained there the entire forty days, for we find that when Moshe descended (ibid. 32:17), "And Yehoshua heard the noise of the people in their tumult" — we see that Yehoshua was not with them.*

Yehoshua remained at the foot of the mountain alone for forty days so that he could be with Moshe the very moment that he would descend the mountain. Yehoshua did not want to miss the opportunity to be with his teacher the few minutes it would take Moshe to return from the mountain to where the Jews were encamped, lest he be deprived of even a single lofty teaching!

Why did Yehoshua not remain in the camp until the thirty-ninth day, since he knew that Moshe would not return until the fortieth day? The answer to this is that Yehoshua wanted to avoid the possibility of some unusual occurrence preventing him from returning to welcome Moshe. Therefore, he remained at the foot of the mountain all forty days. His prudence paid off, for on the thirty-ninth day the Jews worshiped the Golden Calf. It is quite possible that amid the tumult of that tragic episode, Yehoshua might have been prevented from going out to greet the leader who the people believed was no longer alive (see *Sh'mos* 32:1).

Yehoshua's faithfulness received Heavenly endorsement, for as the *Gemara* (*Yoma* 76a) relates, the מָן, *manna*, fell at the mountain for Yehoshua throughout his forty-day sojourn there.

⊷§ Perseverance and Prayer

In *Parashas Ki Sisa* (33:7), the Torah refers to an individual who went to Moshe's tent seeking the Divine word as a מְבַקֵּשׁ ה', *one who seeks [the word of] Hashem*. Yehoshua was the classic מְבַקֵּשׁ, unrelenting in his clinging to his teacher and in his diligent guarding of the fruit of Torah, as he toiled to attain an understanding of Torah in all its depth and breadth. Because he was such a מְבַקֵּשׁ he was privileged to succeed Moshe and to transmit Torah to the next generation.

The *Gemara* relates:

> The Sages taught: "Twelve things were asked of R' Yehoshua ben Chananiah by the people of Alexandria [one of them being]: 'What shall a person do to become wise?' He replied, 'Let him persevere in study and minimize his business affairs.' They countered, 'Many have done so and have not been successful.' 'Then they should seek mercy from He to Whom wisdom belongs, as it is written, "For Hashem grants wisdom; and from His mouth, knowledge and understanding"' [Mishlei 2:6] . . . What is the conclusion? That one without the other does not suffice" (*Niddah 70b*).

It is impossible for anyone to fathom his own inherent potential for greatness. Who would have thought when Yehoshua was still young that he would one day become the leader of the Nation of Hashem? It is within the ability of every *ben Torah* to emulate Yehoshua in attaining a level of Torah knowledge and overall greatness that far surpasses his apparent capabilities and appears to be out of reach. Perseverance in study is the key. Included in this is *ameilus*, persistent diligent toil, and the utilizing of every moment — even a minute here or there! — to its fullest advantage. A good barometer of how dedicated one is to his learning is whether or not he begins his study sessions on time.

The *Gemara* cited above mentions *tefillah* as the other crucial ingredient for acquiring Torah wisdom. Note that the terminology used was not יִתְפַּלְּלוּ, *they should pray*, but rather, יְבַקְשׁוּ רַחֲמִים, *they should seek mercy*.[1] Simple prayer is not enough. One must beseech

---

1. *Maharsha* (*Niddah 69b*) cites the teaching that at the time of conception, an angel announces whether a given child will grow up to be wise or foolish, implying that this is a matter of fate. Says *Maharsha*: "However, they said here, 'What shall a man do to become wise?' — to change the decree that he will not be wise. They answered, 'Let him persevere. . .' — for through effort and great toil coupled with the Heavenly assistance earned through *tefillah*, in addition to other merits, one can alter the decree . . . Similarly, regarding matters of livelihood and [having] children [which *Chazal* say are determined by fate], one can alter the decree through personal effort and *siyata dishmaya* [Heavenly assistance]."

the Heavens in the way of a true מְבַקֵּשׁ, to whom Torah is life itself. In the words of *Rambam:*

> וְחַיֵּי בַּעֲלֵי הַחָכְמָה וּמְבַקְשֶׁיהָ בְּלֹא תַּלְמוּד תּוֹרָה כְּמִיתָה חֲשׁוּבִין.
> *The life of the masters of wisdom and its seekers without Torah is considered like death (Hilchos Rotze'ach 7:1).*

❧ ❧ ❧

The *Gemara* (*Bava Basra* 75a) relates that after Yehoshua succeeded Moshe, the elders of the generation said:

> פְּנֵי מֹשֶׁה כִּפְנֵי חַמָּה, פְּנֵי יְהוֹשֻׁעַ כִּפְנֵי לְבָנָה. אוֹי לָהּ לְאוֹתָהּ בּוּשָׁה, אוֹי לָהּ לְאוֹתָהּ כְּלִימָה!
> *The face of Moshe was like the face of the sun, the face of Yehoshua is like the face of the moon. Woe for this shame, woe for this humiliation!*

Most commentators understand these words in the way of *Rashbam* (ibid.): "In such a brief time, the glory of [Israel's leadership] became so diminished! — for though Yehoshua was a prophet and leader like Moshe, he could not attain Moshe's glory."

The Chofetz Chaim, however, understood the elders' words in an entirely different sense. True, Yehoshua's luster paled beside the brilliance of Moshe. But they now realized that he was at least a moon, a reflection of Moshe's brilliance, and had outshone them all to become the nation's leader — though initially many others had seemed more worthy of this role. Yehoshua had surpassed everyone because he was the greatest מְבַקֵּשׁ of all. If only they had striven and struggled as he did! *"Woe for this shame, woe for this humiliation!"*

May we merit to follow in Yehoshua's ways and may our love for Torah be intense and everlasting.

Constant Vigilance

וּמִקְנֶה רַב הָיָה לִבְנֵי רְאוּבֵן וְלִבְנֵי גָד עָצוּם מְאֹד, וַיִּרְאוּ אֶת אֶרֶץ יַעְזֵר וְאֶת אֶרֶץ גִּלְעָד וְהִנֵּה הַמָּקוֹם מְקוֹם מִקְנֶה.

And a multitude of cattle belonged to the sons of Reuven and the sons of Gad, mighty in measure; and they saw the land of Yaazer and the land of Gilad and lo! The region was one well suited for herds (32:1).

◄§ Suspicions

As *Klal Yisrael's* forty-year sojourn in the wilderness drew to a close, the tribes of Reuven and Gad put forth a request to Moshe *Rabbeinu*. Rather than receive a portion in the land of Canaan, which the nation would begin conquering soon after Moshe's death, they preferred to remain in the fertile land of Sichon and Og in Trans-Jordan which had already been conquered. They asked of Moshe: אַל תַּעֲבִרֵנוּ אֶת הַיַּרְדֵּן, "Do not make us cross the Jordan" (v. 5).

Moshe replied in the strongest possible manner:

> *Shall your brethren go to war while you remain here? And why should you turn the hearts of your brothers away from desiring to cross into the Land that Hashem has given them?*
>
> *This is what your fathers did, when I sent them from Kadeish Barnei'a to see the Land. They went up until*

the valley of Eshkol and saw the Land; then they
turned away the hearts of the Children of Israel from
wanting to enter the land that Hashem had given them.
The wrath of Hashem raged on that day and He swore,
saying: "If the men from twenty years of age and
above who ascended from Egypt will see the Land
regarding which I swore to Avraham, Yitzchak, and
Yaakov; for they did not follow Hashem faithfully —
except for Calev son of Yephuneh the Kenizzi, and
Yehoshua son of Nun, for they did follow Me faith-
fully." The wrath of Hashem raged against Israel, and
He caused them to wander in the wilderness for forty
years, until the generation that did the evil in the eyes
of Hashem had expired.

And now, you have arisen in place of your fathers,
you band of sinful men, to add to the wrath of Hashem
toward Israel. For if you will turn away from Him, then
He will again leave them in the wilderness — and you
will have destroyed this entire nation (vs. 6-15).

Ramban is of the opinion that Moshe actually suspected these
tribes of not wanting to cross the Jordan out of fear of the mighty
Canaanites, the same fear which the Spies had expressed after
returning from scouting out the land (see *Bamidbar* ch.13). This also
seems to be the interpretation of *Targum Onkelos*, which translates
תַּרְבּוּת אֲנָשִׁים חַטָּאִים (v. 14) as תַּלְמִידֵי גֻבְרַיָּא חַיָּבַיָּא, *[you] disciples of*
guilty men.[1] Moshe therefore chastised them for their lack of faith
and warned that their attitude would result in Hashem's wrath being
aroused toward the nation once again.

The essence of the tribes' response to this was, to quote *Ramban*:

Heaven forfend that we should be fearful of them;
rather, we shall cross over armed for war and will be
swift, and in front of the nation, to fight against the
enemies of Hashem, for they are our bread.[2]

As proof of their sincerity, the tribes of Reuven and Gad promised
to remain with the rest of the nation in Canaan until the seven years

---

1. For alternate interpretations, see, for example, *Ohr HaChaim* and *Malbim*.

2. An expression borrowed from *Bamidbar* 14:9, where Yehoshua and Calev declared
that with Hashem's help, the nation would devour the Canaanites as easily as one
consumes his food.

of apportioning the land had passed, though Moshe had only stipulated that they remain there for the seven years of conquering (see *Rashi* to v. 24).

Ramban's interpretation serves as the basis for an important principle. *Chazal* state: הַחוֹשֵׁד בִּכְשֵׁרִים לוֹקֶה בְּגוּפוֹ, "One who suspects innocent people will be punished physically" (*Yoma* 19b). From this *parashah* we see that the above principle does not apply when one is responsible for the spiritual welfare of others. To the contrary, one who is responsible for others is *required* to scrutinize their behavior and air his suspicions when the possibility of wrongdoing exists. When Moshe heard the request of the tribes of Reuven and Gad, especially when they specifically requested, "Do not make us cross the Jordan," he felt it proper to accuse them of the worst, though he knew full well that they might have intended otherwise. His accusation demanded an explanation on their part, which, as *Ramban* explained, made clear their innocence. In forcing such an explanation, Moshe was merely fulfilling his obligation as leader and teacher of his people.

One might wonder, though, how it could have been possible for anyone in that generation to have repeated the Spies' grave errors. The *Midrash* (introduction to *Eichah Rabbah*, §33) relates that each year in the wilderness, on the eighth day of Av, all those against whom death had been decreed as a result of the Spies' slander would dig graves for themselves. On the night of the Ninth of Av, the anniversary of the night of weeping that followed the Spies' slanderous report,[3] the men would lie down in their graves. The next morning, Moshe would announce, "Stand up and separate the dead from the living!" and those who had survived would arise from their graves. This scene repeated itself until the last year in the wilderness, by which time all those included in the decree had already died.[4]

---

3. It was the episode of the Spies that transformed the Ninth of Av (*Tishah b'Av*) and the weeks preceding it into a time of potential sadness and misfortune. As the *Gemara* relates (*Ta'anis* 28b), "R' Yochanan said that this day [of the Spies' return] was *Tishah b'Av* eve. HaKadosh Baruch Hu said, 'You wept in vain. I will establish it for you as a time of weeping for all generations.' "

Both the first and second *Battei Mikdash* were destroyed on *Tishah b'Av*.

4. The *Midrash* continues that in that last year, when no one died on the Ninth of Av, the people thought that they had perhaps erred in their calculation of the new month, and they continued to lie down in their graves on each successive night. On the fifteenth of Av, they saw the full moon and realized that the Ninth of Av had surely passed and that those who were still alive were not included in the decree. It was then that the fifteenth of Av became a day of great rejoicing.

Thus, the Jews in the wilderness had a painful, frightening reminder each year the damage wrought by the Spies' sinful words. How, then, could anyone have dared to act as their 'disciples'?

That these tribes were suspected of this by Moshe illustrates man's tendency to become swept up by a momentary tumult to a point where he all but forgets what was once as clear as day. Moshe *Rabbeinu* understood well this weakness in man's personality: that unless he maintains a constant vigilance, the *yetzer hara*, evil inclination, can ensnare him at any time by befuddling his thoughts and presenting arguments that are both appealing and convincing.

True, the tribes of Reuven and Gad had previously given no indication of wayward attitude or behavior. True, also, they had witnessed the yearly grave ritual and deaths on the Ninth of Av. Nevertheless, this did not preclude their somehow becoming fearful of entering the Land and planning therefore to remain behind, contrary to Hashem's will. It was therefore Moshe's obligation to voice his concerns and demand an explanation.

⋑ Be Alert

In *Parashas Vayeitzei*, when Hashem revealed Himself in a dream to Yaakov, He said, "I am Hashem, God of Avraham your father, and God of Yitzchak" (*Bereishis* 28:13). *Rashi* there (citing *Tanchuma*) notes that Yitzchak was still alive at that time, and that, with this exception, God does not associate His Name with the living. This is in keeping with the principle הֵן בִּקְדֹשָׁיו לֹא יַאֲמִין, "He puts not trust even in His holy ones" (*Iyov* 15:15), meaning that since even the righteous have the potential to succumb to temptation while they are still alive, Hashem does not allow His Name to be associated with them in a permanent manner. *Rashi* explains that in Yitzchak's case כָּהוּ עֵינָיו וְכָלוּא בַבַּיִת, *his eyes were dimmed and he was confined to his house*. Therefore, the *yetzer hara* had departed from him and there was no chance that he would sin. Note that blindness alone would not have been sufficient for Hashem to associate His Name with Yitzchak. The additional factor of Yitzchak's having been housebound was necessary to guarantee that this Patriarch could not possibly sin.

The righteous are themselves forever alert to the potential

enticements of their own inclinations. Thus, when Avraham intervened in the War of the Kings (*Bereishis* ch. 14) and achieved a miraculous victory, he invoked an oath against his accepting any possessions from the king of Sodom. A simple declaration to this effect was not enough for Avraham, because a *tzaddik* adjures his *yetzer hara* in order to avoid any possibility of sin (*Sifri*, cited by *Ramban* to *Bereishis* 14:22).[5]

Only those who strive to better themselves spiritually can perceive the constant dangers which their natural inclinations present. However, those who live an earthly existence, and accord their spiritual pursuits a secondary status, actively place themselves in situations that are spiritually destructive, with nary a worry at all.

Such was the case with Lot, the nephew of Avraham. It is a mistake to view Lot as a lowly fellow with not the slightest interest in spiritual achievement. That Lot accompanied Avraham on his journey from Charan (*Bereishis* 12:5) without having received any prophecy or Divine promise, as Avraham had, is sufficient proof that he did have spiritual aspirations.[6] However, he failed when he fell victim to a craving for materialism. "So Lot raised up his eyes and saw the entire plain of the Jordan, that it was well watered everywhere — before Hashem destroyed Sodom and Amorah — like the garden of Hashem, like the land of Egypt, going toward Zoar. So Lot chose for himself the whole plain of the Jordan ..." (ibid. 13:10-11). Lot's desire for 'the good life' clouded his vision, preventing him from recognizing the truth of how wrong it was to live among the corrupt, perverse Sodomites. Quite possibly, Lot deluded himself into thinking that rather than be affected by his evil surroundings, *he* would exert a positive influence on the natives. This was not to be.

After Lot settled in Sodom, Hashem spoke to Avraham. The Torah makes a point of mentioning that this prophecy occurred "after Lot departed from him [Avraham]" (ibid. v. 14). *Rashi* comments, "This is mentioned because as long as the wicked one [Lot] was in his [Avraham's] company, the word of God departed from him." Even before he had actually moved to Sodom, Lot was already deserving of the title רָשָׁע, *wicked one*. He had been faced with a test when Avraham suggested that the two of them part. In choosing to live in

---

5. See discourse to *Parashas Lech Lecha*.
6. *Zohar* states that Lot attached himself to Avraham to learn from his ways.

Sodom, Lot demonstrated an inability to see past his desires and confront his *yetzer hara* in the way of Avraham. It was this attitude that determined his fate and earned him the title רָשָׁע.

❧ ❧ ❧

With regard to the אָשָׁם תָּלוּי, the guilt-offering brought when one is in doubt as to whether or not he has committed a sin that obligates him to bring a חַטָּאת, *guilt offering*, the Torah states: אָשָׁם הוּא אָשֹׁם, אָשֹׁם לַה׳, "It is a guilt offering, he has become guilty before Hashem" (*Vayikra* 5:19). *Sforno* explains these words as follows: Since the person is not sure if he sinned, he might feel apprehensive that the offering is unnecessary, and hence improper, for one is not allowed to offer unconsecrated animals (חולין) in the Temple courtyard. The Torah therefore states that, to the contrary, he *is* guilty and is required to seek forgiveness for his carelessness in allowing the possibility of sin to have occurred.

To act without contemplating the ramifications of one's deeds is in itself a sin. A Jew must train himself to be ever alert to the spiritual tests that he faces daily.

⊷§ The Test of Battle

Related to the above discussion is another episode found in *Parashas Matos*. After Hashem commanded that the Jews wage war against Midian, Moshe addressed the people:

> וַיְדַבֵּר מֹשֶׁה אֶל הָעָם לֵאמֹר: הֵחָלְצוּ מֵאִתְּכֶם אֲנָשִׁים לַצָּבָא, וְיִהְיוּ עַל מִדְיָן לָתֵת נִקְמַת ה׳ בְּמִדְיָן.
>
> Moshe spoke to the people, saying: "Arm from among you men for the military, that they may go upon Midian to bring the retribution of Hashem in Midian" (31:3).

Rashi comments that the word אֲנָשִׁים, *men*, denotes צַדִּיקִים, *men of righteousness*. These were the kind of men chosen to wage Hashem's war against the evil Midianites. After relating Israel's successes in battle, the Torah (v. 11) states that the soldiers brought all the spoils to Moshe. *Rashi* comments, "This teaches that they were honorable and righteous and were not suspected of robbery to send forth their hands to take from the booty without permission." This seems superfluous, since the Torah already informed us that those chosen for battle were *tzaddikim*.

Participating in battle is a great test of character, for war can bring out the very worst in an individual. Note the moral decline which nations experience following their involvement in war. If this is true of the general populace, how much more so with regard to those who are on the battlefield. As he prepares for battle, a soldier must quell any feeling of faintheartedness and gird his strength to attack the enemy. By war's end, many who were once considered gentle and compassionate often have become callous and uncaring — and their other character traits are affected as well.[7]

The men who fought against Midian were, indeed, righteous — until that point. But what effect did the war have on them? Had they maintained a constant awareness that their shedding Midianite blood was solely in fulfillment of Hashem's will that those who had lured Israel to sin be punished? — or had they had allowed themselves to be overwhelmed by the brutality of war, sinking spiritually with each blow that they dealt the enemy?

By not partaking of the spoils they proved their true worth. Had their righteousness been corrupted, they would surely have rationalized that they were entitled to at least some of the spoils that had been captured. That they did not proved that they were still worthy of being called *tzaddikim*.

At times when spiritual dangers are particularly great, personal vigilance is that much more vital. Summer is surely one such time. Daily schedules are lighter and people find themselves with plenty of free time. How will this time be spent? Daily Talmudic study sessions are a must, as is the study of *mussar*, if one seriously seeks to

---

7. *Parashas Re'eh* (*Devarim* ch.13) relates the laws of עִיר הַנִּדַּחַת, a town whose (Jewish) inhabitants have been found guilty of idolatry. The town is burnt to the ground and its inhabitants are put to death. At the conclusion of these laws, the Torah states (ibid. v. 18), "... and He will grant you mercy and show you compassion." *Ohr HaChaim* explains this apparent redundancy as follows: In the natural way of things, the act of decimating an entire town and its inhabitants should cause those involved to be left with a tendency toward cruelty. Therefore, Hashem promises that those who carry out such destruction solely to fulfill His command will be granted a measure of compassion that will neutralize the harmful effects of their actions. (See discourse to *Parashas Ki Savo*.)

withstand the spiritual dangers of the season. Particular caution must be exercised when one finds it necessary to leave his lodging and make his way to a given destination. We are not like Yitzchak *Avinu* whose situation made it impossible for him to fall prey to the dangers of the street! We *can* see, and if we are forced to walk among today's society, let us first contemplate our obligation that we not *follow our hearts and our eyes* (see *Bamidbar* 15:39). One who is unconcerned in this regard will undoubtedly be affected and is risking a spiritual fall in the way of Lot, ר״ל.

May we merit to be counted among the righteous, both before and after the moment of trial.

דברים

Devarim

Shabbos Chazon

◄§ Sources of Destruction

On this Shabbos, we read the *haftarah* of *Chazon Yeshayahu*, The Vision of Yeshayahu, in which Yeshayahu prophesies regarding Israel's sinfulness in the period prior to the First Destruction. As the Shabbos preceding the fast of *Tishah b'Av*, it is a time to reflect upon the factors that led to the destruction of both Temples and subsequent exiles.

Chazal state:

> *Why was the first Mikdash destroyed? Because during its period there were three sins: idolatry, immorality, and bloodshed ... But [regarding the period of] the second Mikdash — we know that they studied Torah, performed the mitzvos, and did kind deeds — why was it destroyed? Because there was baseless hatred among them. This teaches us that baseless hatred is equivalent to the three sins of idolatry, immorality and bloodshed (Yoma 9b).*

The statement regarding the Second Destruction is particularly noteworthy. A generation that was benevolent and did kindness for one another was at the same time guilty of שִׂנְאַת חִנָּם, *baseless hatred*. Kindness and hatred can coexist. Take, for example, a man who performs kindness in abundance, involving himself in a host of noble endeavors. He is a picture of benevolence — until someone begins questioning the correctness of his approach in his benevolent work. Rather than appreciate the corrective criticism, the man is offended and concerned lest his own ideas and goals be impeded. Anger and resentment begin to surface, until the one who previously was a picture of kindness and compassion is venting hatred of his fellow Jew.

Another example is the person whose championship of *chesed* (benevolence) activity in his community earns him much glory and admiration. The day comes when someone else who is likewise capable in this area joins him in his efforts and shares the spotlight with him. The first man feels that his partner has stolen half the glory that is rightfully his, and he is deeply resentful of this. In both of the above examples, the *chesed* being performed is sorely lacking in motive and intent. One who performs kindness for others solely because it is Hashem's will that a Jew seek to help his fellow man could not possibly be guilty of such negative feelings.[1] Apparently, though, such was the case in the period prior to the Second Destruction.

ᴥ§ The Palace Is Proof

The above *Gemara* continues:

> R' Yochanan and R' Elazar both said : "With regard to the generation of the First Destruction, since their sins were revealed [i.e., they sinned openly], the end of their exile was likewise revealed; with regard to the Second Destruction, since their sins were not revealed [for their hatred was hidden in their hearts, while openly they feigned brotherly love (Maharsha)], the end of their exile was likewise hidden." Said R' Yochanan: "The fingernails [i.e., the ignorant] of the first were better than the stomachs [i.e., those of stature[2]] of the latter." Said Reish Lakish to him: "To the contrary, the latter are superior, for although there is שִׁעְבּוּד מַלְכִיּוֹת

---

1. See *Chazon Ish — Emunah U'Vitachon*, ch. 3; see also the discourse to *Parashas Sh'mos* in this volume.

2. See *Maharsha*.

*(subjugation to the nations), they toil in Torah study.''
R' Yochanan responded: "The palace [i.e., the Beis
HaMikdash] is proof, for it was returned to the former
but not to the latter.''*

The first exile lasted but seventy years, and its end was foretold by
the prophet Yirmiyahu. The present exile is nearly two thousand
years old, and its end remains hidden. This is proof that the cause of
the second exile is more destructive than that of the first. In unity
there is strength, while the divisiveness and strife brought about by
שִׂנְאַת חִנָּם causes the Jewish people to forfeit its claim to Divine
protection. This alone, however, is not enough to make שִׂנְאַת חִנָּם
worse than the three cardinal sins. What makes שִׂנְאַת חִנָּם so severe is
that it can lead to transgression of the entire Torah. When one deems
it permissible to foster hatred towards his fellow, what begins as
enmity can blossom into full-scale rage. Rage does not permit a
person to think rationally and causes one to lose control of himself in
other ways as well. Someone who is not in control of himself is liable
to transgress the most serious sins.[3]

Chazal state: "Any generation in which the *Beis HaMikdash* is not
rebuilt is considered as if it had destroyed it" (*Yerushalmi Yoma* 1:1).
The meaning of this statement is simple. If a given generation has not
merited the Redemption, then it has obviously not rectified the causes
that resulted in the Destruction. Thus, even if by the grace of God the
Mikdash were to be rebuilt in that generation, it would inevitably be
destroyed once again.

A *Beis HaMikdash* cannot endure in a generation which has not
rectified the sin of שִׂנְאַת חִנָּם. Each generation that fails to rectify this
sin is considered as having destroyed the place where Hashem's
Presence comes to dwell. If we truly desire to merit *Mashiach's*
arrival and the building of the third *Beis HaMikdash*, then we must
rid ourselves of ill feelings toward our fellow Jew.

---

3. This explains why *Chazal* compare becoming angry to idol worship (see *Shabbos*
105b).

✑§ The Cure

A prime method of uprooting this devastating trait is by striving to fulfill the *mitzvah* of וְאָהַבְתָּ לְרֵעֲךָ כָּמוֹךָ, to love one's fellow Jew as oneself (*Vayikra* 19:18). *Ramban* (ibid.) understands this commandment as instructing us to desire only good for our neighbor in all facets of his existence, just as we desire only good for ourselves, be it with regard to material needs and acquisitions, honor, or attainment of wisdom. Moreover, there should be no limit to the good that we desire for others. *Ramban* adds that developing such an attitude means that one rid himself of any jealousy toward his fellow. Fulfilling this *mitzvah*, which R' Akiva called, "a great rule in the Torah" (*Rashi* ibid.), is surely within our reach. As an example, *Ramban* cites the love of David and Yehonasan. Though David was ascending the throne which would have otherwise been Yehonasan's, Yehonasan removed all envy from his heart, to the extent that he said to David, "You shall rule over Israel" (*I Shmuel* 23:17). It is because of this that the prophet writes (ibid. 20:17): אֲהֵבוֹ אַהֲבַת נַפְשׁוֹ, *he loved him as his soul.*

One who lives up to these words of *Ramban*, rejoicing in his neighbor's successes even when they surpass his own, will surely be found guiltless with regard to שִׂנְאַת חִנָּם.

Related to this discussion is the *mitzvah* of לֹא תוֹנוּ, to refrain from causing hurt to another Jew through the spoken word. Surely one who seeks to improve his relations with others will avoid transgressing this prohibition. In seeking to fulfill *mitzvos bein adam lachaveiro* (*mitzvos* between man and his fellow), it is imperative that we study ethical works which discuss these obligations. If we will incorporate their teachings within ourselves and deal with each other in a manner that is pleasing to Hashem, then surely we will merit witnessing the rebuilding of Hashem's dwelling on this earth.

❀   ❀   ❀

Kinus on the morning of *Tishah b'Av* should be recited slowly and with proper intent. "Better a little with proper intent than a lot without proper intent" (*Orach Chaim* 1:4). The remainder of the day should likewise be spent doing that which is considered אֲבֵלוֹת, *mourning.*

Chazal taught that whoever mourns over Jerusalem will merit to see it in a state of joy (*Taanis* 130b). *Yesod V'Shoresh HaAvodah* (§9) writes that from the injunction against studying Torah on *Tishah b'Av*[4], we see how important it is that one not divert his attention on this day from mourning over the Destruction. To spend the afternoon of *Tishah b'Av* engaged in light conversation or involved in other activities that will 'make the time pass quickly' is counter-productive. From the beginning of the fast until its very end, one should not cease from pondering the Destruction, its causes, the sufferings that our people have endured as a result of it, and, most important, the means by which we can arouse the Heavenly attribute of mercy so that this long and bitter exile will finally come to an end. Those who conduct themselves in this manner are the true mourners of Jerusalem, and they will surely merit to see it restored to its former glory.

---

4. *Orach Chaim* 654:1. The reason for this is that Torah study gladdens the heart. The *halachah* permits only the study of that which is in some way related to the fast.

Striving for Perfection

וּמִי גוֹי גָּדוֹל אֲשֶׁר לוֹ חֻקִּים וּמִשְׁפָּטִים צַדִּיקִם, כְּכֹל הַתּוֹרָה הַזֹּאת
אֲשֶׁר אָנֹכִי נֹתֵן לִפְנֵיכֶם הַיּוֹם.

And what nation is so great that it has such righteous statutes and laws, like this entire Torah that I am presenting before you today? (4:8).

A good character is the primary requisite to fulfilling the 613 mitzvos (R' Chaim Vital, Sha'arei Kedushah 2:2).

The person who strives for perfection must be ever mindful of his midos and he should evaluate his actions and carefully examine his character traits every day (Shemoneh Perakim L'HaRambam, ch. 4).

◆§ Bava ben Buta

In speaking of character refinement, two incidents cited in the *Gemara* come to mind. The first happened with the *Tanna* (Mishnaic sage) Bava ben Buta:

A native Babylonian once ascended to Eretz Yisrael, where he married a certain woman. [It happened once that] he told her [in his native tongue], "Cook for me two טַלְפֵי, animal's feet." [Being unfamiliar with his language, she interpreted his words differently, so] she cooked for him two lentils. He was angry with her. The next day ... he said, "Go fetch me two בוצִינֵי, *melons." She went and brought him two candles. [Frustrated,] he told her, "Go and break them* עַל רֵישָׁא דְּבָבָא, *at the top of the doorway." At that time, Bava ben Buta was sitting by a gate adjudicating court cases. The woman went and broke the candles on his head [for she had understood* עַל רֵישָׁא דְּבָבָא *to mean 'over the head of Bava.'] Bava said to her, "What is this that you have done?" She explained, "This is what my husband commanded." He responded, "You have fulfilled your husband's desire. May the Omnipresent bring forth from you two sons like Bava ben Buta" (Nedarim 66b).[1]*

Whenever one studies an incident recorded by *Chazal*, he should ask himself, "How would I have acted in such a situation?" It is through such reflection that one comes to appreciate the greatness of our Sages and how distant our ways are from theirs. The result of this should be a conscious effort to go in their ways through character refinement and an improvement in one's relationship with his fellow man.

There is little doubt that few of us, if any, would have reacted in the way of Bava ben Buta. How many of us would maintain our composure and refrain from screaming at a woman who smashes candles upon our heads? Yet Bava ben Buta reacted by blessing her! Bear in mind that the woman appeared before Bava suddenly; he had no advance warning of her arrival. Without faltering for an instant he reacted as he did. Whence did he derive the superlative qualities that resulted in such incredible behavior?

The Torah requires the bringing of a חַטָּאת sacrifice for unintentional transgression of a sin of which the intentional violation incurs כָּרֵת, *spiritual excision*. When one is in doubt as to whether or not he has transgressed such a sin, he is required to bring an אָשָׁם תָּלוּי, *a guilt-offering of doubt*.

---

1. This statement does not contradict the profound humility which every Torah leader epitomizes. To quote the Chazon Ish, "Humility means that one realizes his true worth ... but he must not seek honor or glory because of it, for this is his purpose in life. 'If you have studied much Torah, do not take credit for yourself, because that is what you were created to do' " (*Avos* 2:9).

The *Mishnah (Kreisus* 6:3) relates:

> R' Eliezer says: "A person may offer an אָשָׁם תָּלוּי on
> any day or time that he desires [even if there is nothing
> to suggest possible transgression[2]]. This is called אָשָׁם
> חֲסִידִים, guilt-offering of the pious." It is said of Bava
> ben Buta that he offered an אָשָׁם תָּלוּי every day, except
> for the day following Yom Kippur [for the day of Yom
> Kippur would have atoned for any sin (Rav)]. He
> [Bava] said, "[I swear by] this Dwelling Place [i.e., the
> Beis HaMikdash] that if they would let me, I would
> bring [an offering even on the day following Yom
> Kippur[3]]; however, they have told me, 'Wait until you
> encounter a situation of doubt.'"

The above reveals much about Bava ben Buta. People often
question the behavior of their neighbors while they find their own
attitudes and actions very much in order. Thus they do not strive to
improve themselves, for they see no need for improvement.
Obviously, this was not the way of Bava ben Buta, who questioned
himself even when there was no hint that his behavior was in any
way wanting! Bava ben Buta was forever pondering his ways, forever
searching for any possibility of sin, forever striving to improve.

When one works *consistently* to improve a particular *midah*,
character trait, he ingrains within himself a way of thinking that is in
consonance with Torah, and this approach eventually becomes
second nature to him. Bava ben Buta had mastered the trait of סַבְלָנוּת,
tolerance, to such a degree that he could react instantly to an
unwarranted disgrace by blessing his disgracer.

We can perfect our own trait of סַבְלָנוּת through the *mussar*
method of reviewing the pertinent teachings of *Chazal* until their
message becomes ingrained in our minds and hearts. The following
teaching is particularly relevant to the trait we are discussing:

תָּנוּ רַבָּנָן: הַנֶּעֱלָבִין וְאֵינָן עוֹלְבִין, שׁוֹמְעִין חֶרְפָּתָן וְאֵינָן מְשִׁיבִין,

---

2. *Rav* explains that in R' Eliezer's opinion, an אָשָׁם is a voluntary offering (קָרְבַּן
נְדָבָה) which can be brought at will, so long as there is any possibility of the need for
atonement. Since there is always the chance that one has inadvertently sinned, it is
therefore proper to bring such an offering at any time. This is not the accepted
opinion.

3. This was due to Bava ben Buta's concern that he seek atonement even in the most
remote possibility of sin. See *Tiferes Yisrael* ibid.

עוֹשִׂין מֵאַהֲבָה וּשְׂמֵחִין בְּיִסּוּרִין, עֲלֵיהֶן הַכָּתוּב אוֹמֵר, וְאֹהֲבָיו
כְּצֵאת הַשֶּׁמֶשׁ בִּגְבֻרָתוֹ.

The Rabbis taught: "Those who are disgraced and do not [respond with] disgrace, who hear their shame and do not respond, who do this [i.e., who demonstrate such tolerance] out of love [of Hashem] and are joyful in their affliction [i.e., their shame] — regarding them does Scripture state (Shoftim 5:31), 'And those who love Him are like the sun when it goes forth in all its strength' " (Shabbos 88b).[4]

One who studies the above teaching and reviews it consistently again and again will thereby instill within himself the attribute of סַבְלָנוּת, so that he will be prepared for the moment of trial in the way of Bava ben Buta.

⊰§ Mar Ukva

In a second incident, the subjects are the *Amora* (Talmudic sage) Mar Ukva and his righteous wife:

There was a poor man in Mar Ukva's neighborhood into whose door-socket Mar Ukva would place four zuz each day. One day, the poor man told himself: "I will go and see who it is that does this kindness for me." On that day, Mar Ukva tarried in the beis midrash. [His wife went out to meet him; thus when he went to deposit the four zuz] his wife accompanied him. As soon as the poor man observed the door hinge being moved by Mar Ukva, he went out after them. They ran away from him [so that their identities would remain hidden and he would not feel ashamed when encountering them]. They went up into an oven whose cinders had just been swept. The feet of Mar Ukva were getting

---

4. *Mussar HaNevi'im* explains that just as the sun can soften that which is hard, so do the righteous soften the hearts of their disparagers by exercising extreme tolerance when shame and insult is cast upon them. As is stated in *Avos D'R' Nosson* (ch. 23): "Who is considered the mightiest of mighty? One who can transform his enemy into a loyal friend."

burnt. His wife told him, "Take your feet and place them on top of mine [for her feet were not being burnt]." Mar Ukva felt dispirited [that he was not worthy of the miracle that his wife had merited]. She told him, "[It is because] I am found at home and the pleasure [which I give the poor] is near at hand." [She would give them food and drink which were ready to eat; Mar Ukva, on the other hand, gave the poor money with which they purchased their needs (Rashi).]

And what is all this? [i.e., why did Mar Ukva and his wife go to such lengths so that the poor man should not discover their identities?] For ... R' Yochanan taught in the name of R' Shimon bar Yochai: "Better that a person let himself be cast into a fiery furnace rather than shame his friend in public" (Kesubos 67b).

It is difficult to emulate the actions of Mar Ukva and his wife, to say the least. However, we can at least learn from them to be exceedingly careful not to cause shame to others. They, as in the case of Bava ben Buta, had surely instilled within themselves the necessary trait *well before the moment of trial arrived.* When the incident with the poor man occurred, they did not hesitate for a moment. Instinctively, they both knew what had to be done. *"Better that a person let himself be cast into a fiery furnace rather than shame his friend in public."* This dictum was deeply embedded in their souls and had instilled within them a heightened sensitivity for the dignity of their fellow man.

Note that in reference to this dictum, *Tosafos (Sotah 10b)* equates shaming another Jew in public with the three cardinal sins,[4] in that the requirement of יֵהָרֵג וְאַל יַעֲבֹר, *be killed rather than transgress,* applies. That it is not reckoned as a fourth cardinal sin, says *Tosafos,* is only because its prohibition is not explicit in the Torah.[5]

Every God-fearing Jew is totally removed from transgression of the three cardinal sins, yet not everyone is above shaming his fellow. As is evident from *Tosafos,* such should not be the case. That proper caution is often lacking in this area is primarily due to the *chinuch, training,* which parents give their children regarding the sin of

_____

4. Idolatry, immorality and murder.
5. The *Gemara (Arachin* 16b) derives this prohibition from *Vayikra* 19:17 (see *Rambam, Hilchos Dei'os* 6:8).

shaming others. From their youth, people do not ascribe to the terrible sin of הַלְבָּנַת פָּנִים, *shaming someone*, the stringency that is associated with idolatry, immorality, and murder — though they should![6] The laxity of one generation in this regard is conveyed to the next, so that both young and old commit this sin without contemplating the seriousness of their transgression — or whether they have transgressed at all.

We must instill within ourselves an awareness of the tragedy of causing others shame. We can begin by reviewing the story of Mar Ukva and his wife. Then we should review again and again the dictum which the *Gemara* cites at the close of that incident:

נוֹחַ לוֹ לְאָדָם שֶׁיַּפִּיל עַצְמוֹ לְתוֹךְ כִּבְשָׁן הָאֵשׁ וְאַל יַלְבִּין פְּנֵי חֲבֵירוֹ בְּרַבִּים.

Better that a person let himself be cast into a fiery furnace rather than shame his friend in public.

By following this approach, we will surely develop a heightened sense of concern that our actions and deeds not lead to another's shame, and we will transmit this concern to our children.

◄§ Shemiras HaLashon

The way children are raised is likewise the primary source for widespread laxity with regard to *shemiras halashon*, guarding one's tongue. We train our children to observe stringently the prohibitions against eating unkosher foods, but we do not convey

---

6. R' Baruch Ber Leibowitz (the Kaminetzer *Rosh Yeshivah*) was once present when a certain *rav* addressed a public gathering. During the *rav*'s speech, R' Baruch Ber urgently needed to exit the hall for a short while, yet he made no move to leave. Only after the *rav* had concluded his address did R' Baruch Ber rise from his seat at the front of the hall and go out. Later, he explained:

"Had I left the room in the middle of the *rav*'s speech, some may have taken this as a sign of my disapproval with something that had been said. Even had I returned to the room while the *rav* was still speaking, I could not have undone the few minutes of shame which the *rav* would have felt during my absence. Shaming a person is akin to killing him. I therefore accepted upon myself the requirement of יֵהָרֵג וְאַל יַעֲבֹר until the *rav* had concluded his address."

this sort of stringency to the numerous Torah prohibitions against forbidden speech.[7] How wonderful it would be if parents instilled in their children an awareness of the destructiveness and severity of speaking *lashon hara!* The laws of *shemiras halashon* should be learned in every home. Of course, the best way to teach is by example. If children see parents exercising proper caution with regard to forbidden speech, then they will learn to do the same.

How can we train ourselves with regard to the sin of forbidden speech? Again, the answer is through consistent study. This is the purpose of the daily study schedule of two *halachos* in *Sefer Chofetz Chaim* and one page of *Sefer Shemiras HaLashon.*[8] Through such study, we will gain a knowledge of these detailed laws, achieve an awareness with regard to the severity of their transgression, and will prepare ourselves to avoid such transgression when the moment of trial is suddenly upon us. One who studies the laws of *shemiras halashon* consistently will have the fortitude to leave the company of gossipers, or to at least turn a deaf ear to their words.

Any person who is familiar with the severity which our Sages attach to *lashon hara* should be spurred by that alone to dedicated study of these laws. One should also be aware of the great reward that awaits those who observe these laws. The Vilna *Gaon* cites a *Midrash:*

> *For every moment that one remains silent [in abstaining from speaking that which is forbidden] he merits to bask in a hidden radiance that is beyond the comprehension of any man or angel.*

Let us strive toward character perfection, in deed, speech, and thought.

---

7. See citation from *Sefer Chofetz Chaim* in a footnote to the *Parashas Vayishlach* discourse.
8. HaRav Segal is referring to a yearly calendar published in England through which Jews around the world maintain a daily study schedule of the laws of *shemiras halashon. Sefer Chofetz Chaim* and *Sefer Shemiras HaLashon* are both works of the Chofetz Chaim and are published in a single volume.

To Walk in His Ways

☙ A Seeming Contradiction

In *Sefer Ahavas Chesed*, the Chofetz Chaim resolves an apparent contradiction between three verses in this *parashah*, all of which speak of lofty levels of Divine service.

וְשָׁמַרְתָּ אֶת מִצְוֹת ה׳ אֱלֹקֶיךָ, לָלֶכֶת בִּדְרָכָיו וּלְיִרְאָה אֹתוֹ.

And you shall keep the commandments of Hashem your God; to go in His ways and to fear Him (8:6).

וְעַתָּה יִשְׂרָאֵל מָה ה׳ אֱלֹקֶיךָ שֹׁאֵל מֵעִמָּךְ, כִּי אִם לְיִרְאָה אֶת ה׳ אֱלֹקֶיךָ לָלֶכֶת בְּכָל דְּרָכָיו וּלְאַהֲבָה אֹתוֹ וְלַעֲבֹד אֶת ה׳ אֱלֹקֶיךָ בְּכָל לְבָבְךָ וּבְכָל נַפְשֶׁךָ.

And now, Israel, what does Hashem your God require of you, but to fear Hashem your God, to go in His ways and to love Him, and to serve Hashem your God with all your heart and all your soul (10:12).

כִּי אִם שָׁמֹר תִּשְׁמְרוּן אֶת כָּל הַמִּצְוָה הַזֹּאת אֲשֶׁר אָנֹכִי מְצַוֶּה אֶתְכֶם לַעֲשֹׂתָהּ, לְאַהֲבָה אֶת ה׳ אֱלֹקֵיכֶם לָלֶכֶת בְּכָל דְּרָכָיו וּלְדָבְקָה בוֹ.

For if you shall diligently guard this entire commandment that I command you to carry out; to love Hashem your God, to walk in all His ways, and to hold steadfast to Him (11:22).

In the first verse, הֲלִיכָה בִּדְרָכָיו, *walking in Hashem's ways*, precedes יִרְאָה, *awe of Hashem*, indicating that the former is a prerequisite for attaining the latter. However, in the second verse

יִרְאָה precedes הֲלִיכָה בִּדְרָכָיו, which in turn precedes אַהֲבָה, *love of Hashem*. Yet in the third verse, אַהֲבָה precedes הֲלִיכָה בִּדְרָכָיו, which is followed by the sublime quality of דְּבֵקוּת, *steadfast attachment to Hashem*.

The Chofetz Chaim explains as follows: One must first attain יִרְאָה before he can attain אַהֲבָה, and only after he attains אַהֲבָה can he strive for the deep and constant love that is manifest in דְּבֵקוּת.[1] The Torah is teaching us that all of this must be preceded by הֲלִיכָה בִּדְרָכָיו, emulation of Hashem's attributes of compassion and benevolence in our relationship with our fellow man. Only after one walks in Hashem's ways can he achieve true יִרְאָה. This is the intent of the first verse.

Now, one might be inclined to think that the acquisition of יִרְאָה demands a drastic change in the individual's manner of Divine service. Should not one who has attained awe of Hashem dedicate his days and nights to pondering His greatness and studying His Torah? As for caring for the needs of his fellow, that can be left for those who have not yet achieved a heightened perception of their Creator. The second verse teaches that this is incorrect. One who has attained יִרְאָה must also 'walk in His ways'; moreover, one who fails to emulate Hashem's goodness towards His creatures will never attain the next level of His service, אַהֲבָה. It is thus that in the second verse, הֲלִיכָה בִּדְרָכָיו is preceded by יִרְאָה and is followed by אַהֲבָה.

One who has attained אַהֲבָה is certainly removed from the mundane matters of this world. He is also one step away from דְּבֵקוּת, steadfast attachment to His Creator, the pinnacle of Divine service. One would think that the way to achieve a steadfast love for Hashem is by incessant pondering of His ways and statutes. Surely such spiritual strivings preclude and exonerate one from giving of himself for the sake of others. The third verse teaches us that this too is incorrect. The Chofetz Chaim notes that the verse states לָלֶכֶת, *to walk* [*in all His ways*], rather than וְלָלֶכֶת, *and to walk*. The absence of the conjugative ו indicates that הֲלִיכָה בִּדְרָכָיו is the way to attain the דְּבֵקוּת with which the verse continues. Moreover, the words בְּכָל דְּרָכָיו, *in all His ways*, which appear in both the second and third verses, indicate that one can only attain אַהֲבָה and דְּבֵקוּת if he emulates all of Hashem's Thirteen Attributes of Mercy.[2]

---

1. See *Ramban* to 11:22.

2. See *Sh'mos* 34:6-7.

∽§ A Twofold Process

Elsewhere in this *parashah*, we are exhorted: אַחֲרֵי ה' אֱלֹקֵיכֶם תֵּלֵכוּ, *After Hashem your God you shall walk* (13:5), to which our Sages comment:

> *Is it possible to walk after the Divine Presence? — Does it not say, ". . . for Hashem your God is a fire that consumes" (Devarim 4:24)? Rather, [this means] that one should emulate the attributes of HaKadosh Baruch Hu. Just as He clothes the naked[3] . . . so shall you clothe the naked; HaKadosh Baruch Hu visits the sick[4] . . . so shall you visit the sick (Sotah 14a).*

A similar teaching is derived from a homiletic understanding of זֶה קֵלִי וְאַנְוֵהוּ, *This is my God and I will glorify Him* (Sh'mos 15:2). In one interpretation, the word וְאַנְוֵהוּ, *and I will glorify Him*, is seen as a contraction of אֲנִי וְהוּא, *I and Him*, meaning that a Jew should glorify God by emulating His ways:

> *"And I will glorify Him" — emulate Him; just as He is gracious and merciful, so should you be gracious and merciful (Shabbos 133b).*

Ostensibly, these teachings seem to be imparting the identical message. In *Kochvei Ohr*, R' Itze'le Peterburger[5] explains that this is not so. He begins by citing the following verse:

טוֹב אֶרֶךְ אַפַּיִם מִגִּבּוֹר, וּמֹשֵׁל בְּרוּחוֹ מִלֹּכֵד עִיר
One who is slow to anger is superior to a warrior, and one who dominates his spirit [is superior] to a conqueror of a city (Mishlei 16:32).

R' Itze'le explains that אֶרֶךְ אַפַּיִם, *slow to anger*, represents the containment of one's evil inclination, while מֹשֵׁל בְּרוּחוֹ, *dominates his spirit*, represents the eradication of negative traits and inclinations

---

3. As He clothed Adam and Chavah (*Bereishis* 3:21).

4. As He visited Avraham after the latter was circumcised (*Bereishis* 18:1).

5. R' Yitzchak Blazer, known as 'Peterburger' because he served as *rav* of the Czarist capital of St. Petersburg (modern-day Leningrad). He was a prime disciple of R' Yisrael Salanter.

from one's soul. Together, these two qualities comprise the purpose of man's inner struggles: first one must successfully contain his negative desires, then he must strive to uproot them in totality, thereby changing his very nature.

So it is with regard to benevolence. Initially, one must perform acts of kindness and compassion even when he does not feel inclined toward such behavior. *"Just as He clothes the naked, so should you clothe the naked."* Having contained his natural inclination in this regard, one should then strive to become an individual whose nature *impels* him to assist his fellow man. *"Just as He is gracious and compassionate, so should you be gracious and compassionate."*

R' Itze'le's words complement the Chofetz Chaim's elucidation above. The ultimate הֲלִיכָה בִּדְרָכָיו is infusing within oneself the merciful attributes of Hashem. Only someone who has achieved this can attain the intense and constant attachment to Hashem (דְּבֵקוּת) that is the pinnacle of spiritual service. For דְּבֵקוּת is oneness with God, a oneness in which an individual's personal qualities are reflective of those of the One to Whom he holds steadfast.

∼§ Two Sides of a Coin

In *Ohr Yisrael* (§30), R' Yisrael Salanter writes:

> *The most difficult aspect of spiritual refinement is the perfection of midos (character traits). For an important rule regarding midos is that most positive midos are applicable only with regard to oneself; with regard to others, however, one is obligated to make use of the very opposite to the fullest degree. For example, to flee from honor is a precious quality. As the Sages have taught (Avos 4:28), a lust for honor can drive a person from this world. However, with regard to one's fellow the Sages have taught (ibid. 4:1), "Who is honored? He who honors others."*
>
> פְּרִישׁוּת, *abstention from permissible earthly pleasures, is an exalted quality for men of spiritual striving — but with regard to the benefits and pleasures of one's fellow, the obligation is clearly to make use of the converse of this trait. One must go out to the markets*

and thoroughfares of the city to seek to fulfill the needs of his fellow, and all the more so with regard to the needs of a community.

This is what the Sages intended in saying (Devarim Rabbah 11:4): "What is meant by אִישׁ הָאֱלֹקִים, man of God [with which the Torah describes Moshe Rabbeinu] (Devarim 31:1)? R' Avin said: 'He was partly אִישׁ (an earthly being) and partly אֱלֹקִים (a spiritual being).' " For Moshe Rabbeinu, while he was a man of God and was totally removed from all earthly desires, was nevertheless an earthly man with respect to [recognizing and fulfilling the needs of] Israel, who depended upon him.

So it is with most midos, especially with regard to humility, the greatest of all midos. One's obligation [regarding himself] is to make use of this trait to its very limits, as the Sages have said (Sotah 5a), "Not from it [i.e., pride], nor from even a portion of it." And as Rambam explains the mishnah (Avos 4:4), "Be exceedingly humble."[6] But Heaven forfend that one apply this trait with regard to his fellow, to degrade his status, God forbid.

R' Yisrael's last point is particularly noteworthy. Chazal speak of pursuit of honor most disparagingly, and warn, as R' Yisrael mentions, that it can drive a person from this world. One would be inclined to think that it is proper to scorn those who needlessly seek glory for themselves, for perhaps this will cause them to recognize the folly of their ways. R' Yisrael makes clear that this is not so.

In Mesilas Yesharim (ch. 19), we find:

One should strive to provide his neighbor with every satisfaction possible, whether with regard to honor or any other matter. It is a mitzvas chassidus (act of saintliness) to do for one's neighbor anything from which he will derive pleasure; and certainly one should not do anything that will cause his neighbor any sort of pain, regardless of the circumstance.

---

6. Rambam quotes the above-cited Gemara and a host of other Talmudic dictums in discussing the imperative of acquiring true humility.

Regarding a Jew's obligation to assist the needy, the Torah states: כִּי פָתֹחַ תִּפְתַּח אֶת יָדְךָ לוֹ . . . דֵּי מַחְסֹרוֹ אֲשֶׁר יֶחְסַר לוֹ, "For you shall surely open your hand for him . . . sufficient for his need which he lacks" (*Devarim* 15:8). To the words אֲשֶׁר יֶחְסַר לוֹ, *which he lacks*, our Sages (*Kesubos* 67b) comment that a poor man must be provided with a horse upon which to ride or a servant to run before him, should these be among his particular needs. As an illustration, the *Gemara* relates that Hillel the Elder hired a servant to run before the carriage of a formerly wealthy individual. When it happened that a servant could not be gotten, Hillel — leader of his generation — ran before the carriage. While such excess is certainly unnecessary even for the rich, this man had accustomed himself to it during his affluent days. To have been deprived of it in his poverty would have caused him great distress. It was thus that Hillel found it necessary to provide the man the meaningless honor that he needed.

The *Gemara* there also cites the case of Mar Ukva, who every year on *Erev Yom Kippur* sent a certain poor man four hundred *zuz*. One year, Mar Ukva sent the money with his son, who found the poor man indulging in vintage wine. The son came home and related his discovery, while commenting that it was obviously unnecessary for his father to continue providing the man with funds. Mar Ukva responded, "He is so particular [with regard to what he drinks]?" From then on, Mar Ukva doubled his yearly gift.

Being a true *ba'al chesed*, master of benevolence, requires careful contemplation and a sensitivity toward the needs of those around us. Moreover, when we seek to help others, our efforts should be guided by the way *Chazal* understood the Torah's commandments in this area. This may sometimes define our obligations in a manner that seems contrary to our own way of thinking. Nevertheless, this is the course that we must follow, a course that we may call 'Chesed shel Torah,' the Torah's brand of benevolence.[7] It is a course that clearly differentiates between our own needs and those of our fellow. It is by using this approach in our *chesed* endeavors that we will merit to be among those who walk in Hashem's ways.

---

7. See discourse to *Parashas Sh'mos.*

Trust in Hashem[1]

לְמַעַן תִּזְכֹּר אֶת יוֹם צֵאתְךָ מֵאֶרֶץ מִצְרַיִם כֹּל יְמֵי חַיֶּיךָ.
*That you may remember the day when you came out of
the land of Egypt all the days of your life (16:3).*

*The great wonders and signs are faithful testimonies
for belief in the Creator and in the entire Torah. In that
HaKadosh Baruch Hu does not perform a wonder or
sign in every generation before the eyes of every wicked
man or non-believer, He therefore commanded us to
forever make a remembrance and sign of that which
our eyes beheld, and record the matter for our children
and their children ... until the last of generations; and
to write it on the doorposts of houses on mezuzos and
mention it with our lips every morning and evening ...
in that it is written:* לְמַעַן תִּזְכֹּר אֶת יוֹם צֵאתְךָ מֵאֶרֶץ מִצְרַיִם
כֹּל יְמֵי חַיֶּיךָ. *... as well as many other mitzvos which are
a remembrance of the Exodus from Egypt.*

*... And from the great and well-known miracles, one
comes to recognize the hidden miracles, which are the
foundation of the entire Torah. For a man has no share
in the Torah of Moshe Rabbeinu until he believes that
all our happenings and occurrences are miraculous —
there is nothing natural in them at all (Ramban to
Sh'mos 13:16).*

---

1. This discourse complements 'Tangible Faith' (*Parashas Vayeira*).

◆§ Emunah and Bitachon

The above words of *Ramban* are the basis of true *emunah*, faith. *Bitachon*, trust, is the practical application of *emunah*. To cite the words of *Ramban* in *HaEmunah V'HaBitachon* (Ch. 1):

> Emunah and bitachon are two matters of which the latter is dependent on the former, while the former is not dependent on the latter. For emunah precedes bitachon and is ingrained in a believer's heart even when bitachon is not present . . . However, [the presence of] bitachon is indicative of emunah, for it [bitachon] cannot precede it [emunah] and cannot exist without it. Anyone who is a בּוֹטֵחַ (one who trusts) must be a מַאֲמִין (one with faith), but not every מַאֲמִין is a בּוֹטֵחַ. Emunah is like the tree and bitachon the fruit; the fruit is proof of the tree whence it grew, while the existence of a tree is not in itself proof of fruit. Since a מַאֲמִין is not necessarily a בּוֹטֵחַ, while a בּוֹטֵחַ must be a מַאֲמִין, Scripture therefore cautions us with regard to bitachon more than with regard to emunah.

It is not enough for a person to *say* that he has faith. A person must *feel* that the Creator is aware of and involved in his daily affairs and he must conduct his affairs accordingly. A true *bote'ach*, one who trusts, knows that it is Hashem and not his *hishtadlus*, effort, that is the real Source of his every need. Moreover, a true *bote'ach* lives a life of tranquility, for he knows with certainty that all is from Hashem and all is for the good. True *bitachon* means true tranquility.

◆§ Epitome of Trust

In discussing *bitachon*, the following *Midrash* regarding Yosef HaTzaddik is particularly noteworthy:

> ,,אַשְׁרֵי הַגֶּבֶר אֲשֶׁר שָׂם ה׳ מִבְטַחוֹ״ — זֶה יוֹסֵף. ,,וְלֹא פָנָה אֶל רְהָבִים״ — עַל יְדֵי שֶׁאָמַר לְשַׂר הַמַּשְׁקִים ,,זְכַרְתַּנִי . . . וְהִזְכַּרְתַּנִי״ נִיתוֹסַף לוֹ שְׁתֵּי שָׁנִים.

"Praises to the man who made Hashem his trust" —
this refers to Yosef, "and turned not to the arrogant"
(Tehillim 40:5) — because he said to the chamberlain of
the cupbearers, "Remember me . . . and mention me [to
Pharaoh]' (Bereishis 40:14), two years were added to
his [prison term] (Bereishis Rabbah 89:3).

Ostensibly, this *Midrash* seems paradoxical. First, it praises Yosef
as a man who trusts in Hashem. Then, it criticizes him for having
placed his trust in the "arrogant" rather than in the One Above. The
reference here is to the incident in which Yosef interpreted the
dreams of two chamberlains with whom he was languishing in
prison. After having foretold the eventual release of the chamberlain
of the cupbearers, Yosef asked that upon being released, the
chamberlain mention him before Pharaoh. This did not happen.
"And the chamberlain of the cupbearers did not remember Yosef,
and he forgot him" (40:23). For making his request, Yosef was
punished from Above by having to remain in prison for an
additional two years.

It seems difficult to understand why Yosef was punished. While
bitachon in Hashem is a must, a Jew, in any given situation, should
engage in proper *hishtadlus* to attain his desired goal. It would seem
that Yosef's request was a proper and even required method of
hishtadlus.

The answer to this will resolve the above paradox. While every
God-fearing Jew surely possesses some degree of *bitachon*, this
all-important attribute can be acquired in varying degrees. The
degree of one's level of *bitachon* determines what sort of *hishtadlus* is
expected of him. The greater one's *bitachon*, the less he needs to be
mishtadel (expend effort). For the average person, asking the
cupbearer to mention his name before Pharaoh would have been the
obvious and expected thing to do. Yosef, however, was not the
average person. He was the classic *bote'ach*, which is why the
Midrash sees him as an embodiment of the words אַשְׁרֵי הַגֶּבֶר אֲשֶׁר שָׂם
ה' מִבְטַחוֹ. Because he had achieved this level of trust, Yosef was
expected to *not make any hishtadlus at all* to gain release from
prison. He was to rely completely on Hashem. His request of the
cupbearer was a momentary lapse in his lofty level of trust and,
consequently, he was punished.

One should note that a Jew is not to conduct himself in a

manner that is not commensurate with his actual level of *bitachon*. Take, for example, the person who has decided to follow the approach expected of Yosef *HaTzaddik*, namely, not to be *mishtadel* at all — yet he sits at home beset with worry over what the future holds in store! This is not *bitachon*; such a person *must* engage in some sort of *hishtadlus*.[2]

However, as *Chovos HaLevavos (Sha'ar HaBitachon)* writes, *every* Jew should engage in *hishtadlus* that is of relatively light nature, as opposed to one that will rob him of his peace of mind or is dangerous. To engage in such *hishtadlus* is to lack basic *bitachon*. טוֹב ה׳ לַכֹּל, וְרַחֲמָיו עַל כָּל מַעֲשָׂיו, *Hashem is good to all; His mercies are on all His works.* To consider oneself a *ba'al bitachon* is to believe firmly that in every occurrence *hashgachas Hashem* (Divine providence) is manifest and that, ultimately, all is for the good. This is not to say that all that transpires is to our liking. We often cannot perceive the goodness in a given occurrence. Still, we must realize that Hashem's decrees emanate from a vantage point that embraces not only the present but extends from creation to the End of Days. Only He can know what is in our best interest (see *Sha'ar HaBitachon*, ch. 1).

◆§ In the World of Business

The *Rosh*, in his *Orchos Chaim* (ch. 1), writes that one should trust in Hashem "with his whole heart." Complete trust in Hashem as

---

2. A classic *bote'ach* of recent times was R' Yosef Chaim Sonnenfeld, legendary *Rav* of Jerusalem early in this century. During the years when he served as *Rav*, R' Yosef Chaim refused the many gifts of money offered him. He placed his full trust in the One Above as the provider of his very minimal needs. More than once, when his financial situation became intolerable, R' Yosef Chaim went for a walk and found money in the street! This was the same person who, as a poor orphan in yeshivah, dreamt the winning number of the local lottery drawing, but refused to purchase a ticket with the few pennies he owned, for he felt that Hashem would want him to better spend the money on a 'sure' acquisition such as bread. When the lottery was drawn, he learned that, indeed, he had dreamt the winning number. He later said, "You must think that I was upset with my decision. Not at all!! I gave the whole incident not a second thought and occupied myself totally with my studies."

The Vilna *Gaon* is said to have remarked, "With perfect faith a person could cross the ocean on foot." When this remark was related to R' Yosef Chaim, he replied that it seemed quite plausible to him.

the Director of all our affairs is the key to a life of happiness and tranquility. This is especially true with regard to earning a livelihood. How often we see people contrive all sorts of ingenious plans for a successful venture, only to have their plans end in total failure. Even a 'sure' method of *hishtadlus* is doomed to fail, when such is the Divine will.

Conversely, no power in the world can deny someone that which Hashem has decreed as his. As *Chazal* (*Yoma* 38b) put it: *One does not touch even by a hairsbreadth that which has been preordained for his friend*. When one believes in this dictum with perfect faith, there is no room for jealousy between business competitors. Such jealousy is the product of resentment borne by a feeling that one's livelihood has been adversely affected by another's actions. This feeling is contradictory to the above Talmudic teaching. It cannot possibly exist in the heart of one whose *bitachon* is complete.

The level of *bitachon* one attains will have a pronounced effect on his behavior in business-related matters. As an example, let us imagine a *din Torah*, court case, between competitors. Reuven has apparently been guilty of *hasagas gevul*, encroachment into the business domain of Shimon. Shimon summons Reuven to *beis din*. Shimon's *bitachon* is unfortunately wanting. He becomes enraged during the court proceedings, openly venting his unbridled hatred of his opponent by hurling a cascade of insults and accusations at him. Reuven is not one to accept all this in silence and he responds in kind. How dreadful a scene!!

Now, let us imagine the same *din Torah*, only this time the plaintiff's *bitachon* is complete. Shimon begins the proceedings in this way: "Reuven, I love you with all my soul and I know that you cannot possibly deny me that which Heaven has bequeathed to me. Though I appear to have lost customers due to your encroachment, I believe firmly that, inevitably, I will earn whatever has been decreed for me. Why, then, have I summoned you to court? Though we must trust in Hashem, we are also required to engage in *hishtadlus* in pursuit of a livelihood. Since I believe that in opening your store you have been guilty of encroaching on my domain, I must summon you to court as an act of *hishtadlus*."

Chovos HaLevavos discusses the role of *hishtadlus* in light of the teaching that each man's earnings for the coming year are decreed on *Rosh Hashanah* (*Beitzah* 16b). On the one hand, the requirement that one be *mishtadel* demands that a storekeeper maintain a clean, neat

neat and properly stocked store; and that he talk with customers in a refined way so that they will want to do business with him. On the other hand, the storekeeper must believe that it is the word of Hashem and not *hishtadlus* that gains him his earnings. All his efforts will not bring him one additional cent more than has been decreed Above. Living by this principle is a great test of faith for anyone whose life is guided by Torah.[3]

◆§ Attaining It

The presence or lack of true *bitachon* makes all the difference in how a person faces up to the challenges of life. How does one acquire a greater measure of *bitachon?* A well-known piece in *Sefer HaChinuch* (§16) sheds light on the matter:

> . . . *Know that man is molded by his actions. His heart and thoughts are always drawn after the deeds with which he is occupied, whether for the bad or for the good.*
>
> *Even a thoroughly wicked man whose heart is forever preoccupied with evil thoughts — if he will arouse his spirit and place his effort and toil with constancy in Torah and mitzvos, even if not for the sake of Heaven, he will immediately become inclined toward good and through the power of his deeds his evil inclination will die. For the hearts of men are drawn after their deeds.*
>
> *And even a complete tzaddik whose heart is perfect and upright, desiring Torah and mitzvos — if he will constantly engage in negative actions, as for example, should the king forcibly appoint him to an evil*

---

3. In his *Ohr Yechezkel* (*Emunah* ch. 1), R' Yechezkel Levenstein explains that the need for *hishtadlus* stems from the curse which Adam received after eating of the Tree of Knowledge: בְּזֵעַת אַפֶּיךָ תֹּאכַל לֶחֶם, "By the sweat of your face you shall eat bread" (*Bereishis* 3:19), to which *Rashi* comments, "After you will toil for it exceedingly." That man's livelihood is attained in a manner which seems to point to the success or failure of his own efforts is nothing more than a test of faith. As *Ohr Yechezkel* puts it, "The man who is truly wise realizes that his efforts did not help him, and that all this is to fulfill the decree of בְּזֵעַת אַפֶּיךָ תֹּאכַל לֶחֶם."

vocation; if he will be constantly occupied with that vocation, then at some point in time he will turn away from the righteousness in his heart to become a thoroughly wicked person . . .

While the principle אָדָם נִפְעָל כְּפִי פְּעֻלּוֹתָיו, *man is molded by his actions*, does not seem relevant to the attaining of *bitachon*, *Sefer HaChinuch's* application of this principle is very relevant. Throughout his presentation, the author stresses that it is the *consistency* with which deeds are performed that has so pronounced an effect upon an individual. Incessant repetition of a given mode of behavior penetrates to the far reaches of the soul.

A Jew must forever seek to discover the Divine hand in his daily affairs and in that which transpires around him. Every act, every occurrence, should be analyzed in the light of *hashgachas Hashem*. The *hashgachah* is there. It is incumbent upon us to recognize it. When one accustoms himself to contemplating events in this way, the concept of *hashgachah* becomes firmly embedded in his mind and his *bitachon* is naturally strengthened.

It is through such incessant reflection that Yosef emerged from his years in Egypt spiritually intact. And it is through such an approach to life that we can survive *galus* in the way that Yosef did.

Responsibility and Restraint

וַאֲשֶׁר יָבֹא אֶת רֵעֵהוּ בַיַּעַר לַחְטֹב עֵצִים וְנִדְּחָה יָדוֹ בַגַּרְזֶן לִכְרֹת
הָעֵץ וְנָשַׁל הַבַּרְזֶל מִן הָעֵץ וּמָצָא אֶת רֵעֵהוּ וָמֵת, הוּא יָנוּס אֶל
אַחַת הֶעָרִים הָאֵלֶּה וָחָי.

*And whoever comes with his fellowman into the forest
to chop wood, and his hand swings the axe to chop the
tree, and the iron flies from the wood and finds his
fellowman and he dies, he shall flee to one of these cities
and live (19:5).*

❧ Insufficient Prayer

In this *parashah*, we learn the law of the רוֹצֵחַ בְּשׁוֹגֵג, *unintentional
murderer*, who, after committing this act, is required to flee to one
of six designated cities known as the עָרֵי מִקְלָט, *cities of refuge*. This
law is also found in *Parashas Masei (Bamidbar 35)*. There, the Torah
states that the murderer cannot leave the city until the death of the
Kohen Gadol (High Priest) who was serving in that capacity at the
time when the murderer was sentenced to exile. Should the murderer
leave the עִיר מִקְלָט at any time prior to the *Kohen Gadol's* death, then
he is liable to be killed by the גוֹאֵל הַדָּם, *avenger of the blood*, the
victim's closest kinsman.

The *Mishnah (Makos 2:7)* states that the mother of the *Kohen
Gadol* would supply the exiled murderers with food and drink so that

they would not pray that her son die, for they might otherwise have been tempted to do so since their gaining freedom was contingent on the *Kohen Gadol's* death. It would seem from this that had such prayers been offered, they may have been heeded. The reason for this, explains the *Gemara* (*Makos* 11b), is that the *Kohen Gadol* was somewhat at fault for the inadvertent death of the victim and the murderer's subsequent exile. For had the *Kohen Gadol* prayed with proper devotion for the welfare of the nation, such incidents would not have occurred. To illustrate this concept, the *Gemara* relates that the Talmudic sage R' Yehoshua ben Levi was visited regularly by Eliyahu *HaNavi*. However, when it happened that a man was devoured by a lion on the outskirts of R' Yehoshua's city, Eliyahu would not visit the sage for three days. R' Yehoshua was held at least partly responsible for what had occurred since his prayers should have prevented it.

The above is both astounding and insightful, for more than one reason. Let us understand what sort of fellow might pray for the *Kohen Gadol's* death. He has murdered inadvertently — but not blamelessly.[1] His sin requires atonement, which is why the Torah requires his exile. In exile, he is permitted to carry on a normal life, rather than be sentenced to any sort of forced labor. The עָרֵי מִקְלָט were cities of *Levi'im* who served in the *Beis HaMikdash* and taught Torah to the nation (see 33:10). Living amidst such holiness and purity presented those exiled with a perfect opportunity to engage in proper soul-searching and repent for having committed so tragic an act. Instead, this man is preoccupied with something else — to return home as quickly as possible. To this end, he is prepared to pray for the death of the one who performs the Temple service for the merit of the entire nation, the only one who is permitted to enter the *Kodesh HaKodashim*, where the *Shechinah* rests. It is somewhat astounding that prayers offered by so lowly a soul should carry any weight, especially when they were directed against the pure and saintly *Kohen Gadol*!

These prayers would have been effective, to the point that the *Kohen Gadol's* mother found it necessary to prevent their being offered, because laxity with regard to one's communal obligations is

---

1. A murderer is exiled only for a murder that was inadvertent but could have been avoided, had proper precautions been taken. There is no such punishment when the murderer is entirely blameless.

an extremely serious offense. Every Jew must concern himself with the needs of his brethren, their troubles and their trials, their wants and their hopes. The *Kohen Gadol's* position carried with it a heightened degree of responsibility, and this should have been manifest in the way he prayed. Furthermore, the *Kohen Gadol's* prayers for the community were particularly efficacious, for he bore the names of the twelve tribes upon his chest and performed the Divine service on their behalf. A lapse in this regard on the part of the *Kohen Gadol* was deemed so serious by Hashem that even a prayer offered by a self-centered sinner could have brought about the *Kohen Gadol's* demise.

✣ The Power of Restraint

Indeed, it now seems difficult to understand how the absence of the exile's prayers could have saved the *Kohen Gadol* from death! If his failure to pray sufficiently on behalf of his brethren deemed him deserving of such punishment, then retribution should have been exacted regardless of whether or not the exiles prayed that this occur. We can resolve this as follows: The exiles by nature wanted to pray that the *Kohen Gadol* should die; however, they restrained themselves from doing so because the *Kohen Gadol's* mother sustained them in their exile. Thus, it was the *Kohen Gadol's* mother who caused these lowly individuals to overcome the urgings of their evil inclination. This accomplishment was a great source of merit for the *Kohen Gadol*, so much so that it was enough to save him from death. Such is the power of כְּבִישַׁת הָרָצוֹן, *restraining one's natural desires!*[2]

We live in a time when the House of Yaakov endures intense trials and tribulations, both on a community and an individual level. Those of us who are fortunate to be living amidst relative tranquility dare not forget our less fortunate brethren. We dare not be found guilty of the charge against the *Kohen Gadol*, that he did not pray sufficiently on behalf of his fellow Jews. The ill and the destitute, the persecuted and those who live in fear of persecution must be uppermost in our minds when we *daven*. Pray for them we must, and our prayers *can*

---

2. *Ben Yehoyada* offers a very similar explanation.

accomplish. We must also seek to improve our conduct with one another, to restrain ourselves from doing that which might prove harmful to our fellow Jew. Such כְּבִישַׁת הָרָצוֹן will add potency to our prayers and will hopefully bring us to the end of all suffering with the coming of *Mashiach*, when peace and tranquility will reign.

The Power of Sin

זָכוֹר אֵת אֲשֶׁר עָשָׂה לְךָ עֲמָלֵק בַּדֶּרֶךְ בְּצֵאתְכֶם מִמִּצְרָיִם.

Remember what Amalek did to you on the way, as you departed from Egypt (25:17).

◄§ Roots of an Enemy

Only a few weeks after the Exodus from Egypt, the Jews were attacked by Amalek. The prayers of Moshe, the leadership in battle of Yehoshua, and the faith of the entire nation resulted in a great victory. It is clear from *Chazal* that Amalek's decision to attack was symptomatic of an incurable spiritual disease, that this nation is the embodiment of evil on earth and thus, the archenemy of our people. It is for this reason that we are commanded to obliterate Amalek (25:19) and that Hashem declared (*Sh'mos* 17:16) that neither His Name nor His throne are complete until Amalek is totally destroyed.

Incredible though it seems, we find that the evil perpetrated by Amalek can be traced to an error on the part of the Patriarchs. The *Gemara* (*Sanhedrin* 99b) relates:

> *Timna was a royal princess, as she was the sister of Lotan [Bereishis 36:22], an uncrowned prince. She desired to convert to Judaism. She went to Avraham, Yitzchak, and Yaakov, but they would not accept her.*

*So she went and became the concubine of Eliphaz,
Eisav's son, saying, "I would rather be a servant to one
of this people [i.e., the family of Avraham] than a
noblewoman of another nation." From her descended
Amalek, who afflicted Israel. Why? Because they [i.e.,
the Patriarchs] should not have rejected her.*

Avraham *Avinu* dedicated his life to bringing others "under the
wings of the Divine Presence." Certainly, if he would not accept
Timna, he must have had good reason for this. Yet, somehow he, as
well as Yitzchak and Yaakov, erred in his judgment.[1] The utter
wickedness which Amalek has directed toward Israel through the
ages is rooted in that rejection. Such is the power of a single sin,
specifically that which causes hurt to another.[2]

The following illustrations will demonstrate further the far-reaching effects that even one seemingly minor sin can have.

⋘ Yaakov's Fear

*Yaakov said: "God of my father Avraham and God of
my father Yitzchak; Hashem Who said to me, 'Return
to your land and to your relatives and I will do good*

---

1. *Ohr HaTzafun* (vol. 1, p. 201) explains that the Patriarchs' rejection of Timna was
undoubtedly because they perceived through Divine Inspiration the wickedness that
lay dormant within her. Nevertheless, they were faulted for denying her the
privilege of coming under the wings of the *Shechinah*, which she sincerely desired at
that time.

2. To the words, "And Yisro heard" (*Sh'mos* 18:1), *Rashi* comments: "What report
did he hear that prompted him to come [and join the Jewish nation in the
wilderness]? That of the splitting of the Sea and the war against Amalek."

The commentators wonder why the war against Amalek, which had the
appearance of a normal military confrontation, should have inspired Yisro (see
discourse to *Parashas Yisro*). *Yalkut Me'am Loez* offers the following explanation:
Yisro wondered how it was possible for Amalek to wage war against a nation of God
that had only recently merited the great miracle of the splitting of the Sea, a miracle
which caused all the heathen nations to quake with fear. He perceived that this war
must have been a form of Divine retribution inflicted upon *Klal Yisrael* for the
rejection of Timna by the Patriarchs. Yisro realized that the Jews would reach this
same conclusion, thus the moment was most opportune for him to seek acceptance as
a *ger*, convert. Surely he would not be rejected at such a time.

with you'; I have been diminished by all the kind-
ness and by all the truth that You have done Your
servant . . .
"And You have said, 'I will deal bountifully with
you and I will make your offspring like the sand of the
sea which is too numerous to count' " (Bereishis
32:9-12).

As Yaakov headed toward his encounter with a spiteful, blood-thirsty Eisav, he readied himself by organizing his camp for battle, preparing a tribute for Eisav and offering his *tefillos* to Hashem. In his *tefillah*, Yaakov invoked two earlier assurances of protection given him by Hashem (ibid. 28:13 and 31:3). Nevertheless, he was afraid: קָטֹנְתִּי מִכֹּל הַחֲסָדִים וּמִכָּל הָאֱמֶת אֲשֶׁר עָשִׂיתָ אֶת עַבְדֶּךָ, "I have been diminished by all the kindness and by all the truth that You have done Your servant." As *Rashi* (v.11) explains, Yaakov feared that with his sources of merit diminished by all that Hashem had already done for him, he might have forfeited the promises of protection due to sin. As *Ramban* (v. 13) makes clear, Yaakov feared not only for his family, but for himself as well. There would have been a Jewish nation in any event, for the promise that Hashem made to Avraham at the *Bris Bein HaBesarim* (Covenant Between the Parts) had to be fulfilled; but had Yaakov's life ended at that point, the very nature of *Klal Yisrael* would have been severely altered, for all that he was to bequeath to his children in the years to come would have been lost.

What sort of sin could have made Yaakov apprehensive? Numerous suggestions are offered by the commentators. *Ibn Ezra* says that it is the way of great people to view what we would term minor infractions as grievous misdeeds. Yaakov feared that he might have inadvertently sinned in thought, which could have caused Hashem to rescind His earlier assurances.

Such fear can be better understood in light of *Chovos HaLevavos'* statement (*Sha'ar HaBitachon*, ch. 4) that were a man's merits as many as the sand of the sea, they would not of themselves suffice to earn him even one of Hashem's blessings in this world — all the more so when man sins. The many blessings we receive can be attributed primarily to one source: וּלְךָ ה׳ חָסֶד, *And Yours, my Lord, is kindness* (*Tehillim* 62:13). Thus, while Yaakov was not certain that he had transgressed, he nevertheless found reason for fear.

ᵔᵛ The Sole Redeemer

As Moshe *Rabbeinu* was in the midst of his journey from Midian back to Egypt to begin the process that would lead to redemption, an angel of Hashem was sent to kill him for his having delayed the circumcision of his son Eliezer (*Sh'mos* 4:24). Moshe was saved when his wife Tziporah, realizing the cause of her husband's endangerment, grabbed a stone and circumcised her son.

Had Tziporah not acted, the ramifications would have, God forbid, been immeasurable. *Midrash Rabbah* (*Sh'mos* 3:3) relates that when Hashem first revealed Himself to Moshe and commanded him to return to Egypt, Moshe was told, "If you do not redeem them, no one will redeem them." The intent of the *Midrash* is that while the redemption was inevitable, only through Moshe's leadership could the nation raise itself from its lowly spiritual level in Egypt to the incredible heights of sanctity and prophecy that it later attained. A redemption without Moshe would have been a far cry from one with Moshe as leader. Yet this almost occurred, all because of a seemingly minor lapse on Moshe's part.

From the above illustrations, we see how potentially destructive even a single sin can be. It would do us well to ponder this point. There is something else, however, which must accompany such meditation. One must first be willing to recognize that he does, indeed, sin. Unfortunately, we often complacently see ourselves as pure and meritorious, while failing to take honest stock of our deeds in order to ascertain where we can improve. Such an attitude precludes any possibility of sincere *teshuvah*.

ᵔᵛ Taking a Lesson

In the days of Mordechai and Esther, *Klal Yisrael* was threatened with destruction at the hands of Haman, a descendant of Amalek. It was then, the *Midrash* relates, that the people were moved to *teshuvah* by taking a lesson from their forefather:

'Yaakov became very frightened and it distressed him'

(*Bereishis* 32:8). *R' Pinchas said in the name of R'*
Reuven: "Two people were given assurances by
HaKadosh Baruch Hu, yet they feared nonetheless.
*One was the chosen one of the Patriarchs (*הַבָּחִיר
שֶׁבָּאָבוֹת*), while the other was the chosen one of the*
*Prophets (*הַבָּחִיר שֶׁבַּנְּבִיאִים*). The chosen one of the*
Patriarchs is Yaakov, as it is written, 'For God chose
Yaakov as His own' (Tehillim 135:4). Hashem assured
him, 'Behold, I am with you' (Bereishis 28:15), yet in
the end, he was afraid, as it is written, 'And Yaakov
became very frightened' (ibid. 32:8). The chosen one of
the prophets is Moshe, as it is written, '... had not
Moshe, His chosen one ...' (Tehillim 106:23).
HaKadosh Baruch Hu told him, 'For I will be with you
...' (Sh'mos 3:12), yet later he was afraid, as it is
written, 'Hashem said to Moshe, "Do not fear him [i.e.,
Og the King of Bashan]' ' (Bamidbar 21:34). One says
'Do not fear' only to a person who is afraid.

"... Israel was fit to be annihilated in the days of
Haman; [this would, God forbid, have occurred] had
they not taken a lesson from their forefather Yaakov.
They said, 'If our forefather Yaakov, whom HaKadosh
Baruch Hu assured, "Behold, I am with you," was
nevertheless afraid, then certainly we [have reason to
fear]!' "

As *Matnos Kehunah* (ibid.) explains, *Klal Yisrael* could have found
reason for complacency when faced with Haman's decree. They had
their own sources of merit in addition to the assurances of.Hashem's
Providence in exile as stated clearly in the Torah (*Vayikra* 26:44).
Haman could plot all he wanted; they had nothing to fear! Their
attitude was, in fact, the very opposite. They took a lesson from
Yaakov that there are no assurances against the destructiveness of sin.
They looked into themselves and realized that their ways needed
mending. This is what saved them.

As *Mesilas Yesharim* (ch. 2) writes, the road to spiritual
achievement begins with *zehirus*, alertness, in all one's actions and
undertakings. One must forever contemplate his ways, discerning
which are correct and which are not, which require refinement and
which should be abandoned. One should become accustomed to

acting only after having first pondered what it is he is about to do. With proper contemplation, one will surely discover room for improvement.

May we merit that Hashem open our eyes to see the true worth of our deeds so that we will return to Him with a *teshuvah* that is complete.

The Imperative of Mussar Study — A Teshuvah Address to Men[1]

◈§ "Return, Return . . ."

יַכְּכָה ה' בְּשִׁגָּעוֹן וּבְעִוָּרוֹן, וּבְתִמְהוֹן לֵבָב.

Hashem will strike you with insanity and with blindness, and with numbness of heart (28:28).

Rashi (ibid.) defines תִמְהוֹן לֵבָב as אוֹטֶם הַלֵב, a spiritual numbness that brings a weakening of faith and prevents one from viewing life through the looking glass of Torah. Troubles befall a person and he wonders why, instead of recognizing the guiding hand of Providence. While אוֹטֶם הַלֵב is an outgrowth of sin, as in the context of this verse, it is a cause of further sin and a prime impediment to *teshuvah*. Thus do we say in the very last עַל חֵטְא of the *Yom Kippur viduy* (confession): וְעַל חֵטְא שֶׁחָטָאנוּ לְפָנֶיךָ בְּתִמְהוֹן לֵבָב, *And for the sin that we have sinned before You with numbness of heart.*[2]

There are times when such numbness is overcome, and one is awakened to *teshuvah*, but then Satan approaches from a new angle, insisting that the person has strayed too far, to a point of no return, ר"ל. This was the feeling of the generation that witnessed the First Destruction. As the prophet Yechezkel states:

---

1. Delivered at a gathering in London.
2. See *Michtav Me'Eliyahu*, vol. II, p. 96.

וְאַתָּה בֶן אָדָם, אֱמֹר אֶל בֵּית יִשְׂרָאֵל: כֵּן אֲמַרְתֶּם לֵאמֹר, כִּי פְשָׁעֵינוּ וְחַטֹּאתֵינוּ עָלֵינוּ, וּבָם אֲנַחְנוּ נְמַקִּים, וְאֵיךְ נִחְיֶה.

Now you, Ben Adam, say to the family of Israel: "Thus have you said, saying, 'For our sins and iniquities are upon us, and through them we pine away — so how can we live?' " (Yechezkel 33:10).

As explained in *Kochvei Ohr* (ch. 30), the reality of the destruction shocked the people into an awareness of the enormity of their guilt. Having caused the *Shechinah*, Divine Presence, to depart from their midst, they could not conceive of a mercy great enough to pardon their sins. Hashem, however, responded:

אֱמֹר אֲלֵיהֶם, חַי אָנִי נְאֻם ה' אֱלֹקִים, אִם אֶחְפֹּץ בְּמוֹת הָרָשָׁע כִּי אִם בְּשׁוּב רָשָׁע מִדַּרְכּוֹ וְחָיָה, שׁוּבוּ שׁוּבוּ מִדַּרְכֵיכֶם הָרָעִים וְלָמָּה תָמוּתוּ בֵּית יִשְׂרָאֵל.

Say to them: "As I live," vows Hashem Elokim, "I do not desire the death of the wicked one, but the wicked one's return from his way that he will live. Return, return from your evil ways; why should you die, O family of Israel?" (ibid. v.11).

Hashem desires that we return to Him through sincere *teshuvah*. He awaits our initial step, then He guides us along the path to complete return.

In his *Chochmah U'Mussar* (II §355), R' Simchah Zissel Ziv[3] adduces proof that one receives infinite reward for the mere act of *trying* to come closer to Hashem. In *Parashas Re'eh*, the Torah records the law concerning the מֵסִית, *instigator*, who attempts to influence others to idol worship. The Torah commands that he be stoned to death, ". . . for he sought to draw you away from Hashem your God . . ." (13:11). Though the instigator was unsuccessful, he is killed for merely attempting to draw another Jew away from belief in Hashem.

We know that the measure of Divine reward for a good deed is five hundred times greater than the measure of Divine retribution for a sin (*Tosefta Sotah* 4:1). It follows, says R' Simchah Zissel, that infinite reward awaits one who merely attempts to better his ways.

Those who study *mussar* do so for the purpose of drawing closer to Hashem through refinement of their *midos*, character traits, and

---

3. Known as the *Alter* of Kelm, and a prime disciple of R' Yisrael Salanter.

increased zealousness in *mitzvah* performance. When a person sits down and opens a *Sha'arei Teshuvah*, *Mesilas Yesharim*, or other *mussar* work, he has already endeared himself to his Creator and has earned himself immeasurable reward. The same applies to one who makes the effort to attend a lecture dedicated to *hisorerus*, spiritual awakening.

৵§ A Single Hisorerus

A student of *mussar* pursues perfection of character, control over his natural inclinations, and purification of his motives and values. Sincere *mussar* study means that one studies a pertinent work with the goal of changing oneself. With the help of Hashem, *mussar* study can totally transform a person. The transformation may be subtle at first, perhaps even focusing on a single *mitzvah*. One might, for example, come upon a passage that speaks ominously of dishonesty in monetary dealings. The student pauses for a moment and contemplates his personal standing in this regard. He knows that his own business integrity is unacceptable by Torah standards, and he resolves to improve. From that small awakening can come an awakening that will eventually embrace his entire personality and service of Hashem to a point that he will become a totally changed person.

Never underestimate the power of a single moment of spiritual awakening. A classic illustration is the story of Nevuzaradan, the Babylonian general who conquered Jerusalem at the time of the First Destruction. The *Gemara* (*Sanhedrin* 96b) relates that when Nevuzaradan entered the *Beis HaMikdash*, he found blood seething on the floor. Forced to explain this phenomenon, the Jews confessed that this was the blood of Zechariah, the *Kohen* and prophet who had been slain by his own people for foretelling the impending destruction. Upon hearing this, Nevuzaradan said, "I will appease him [i.e., Zechariah]." On that spot, he ordered the slaughter of scholars, school children, and finally, young *Kohanim* — more than ninety-four thousand in all. But Zechariah's blood continued to seethe, until Nevuzaradan exclaimed, "Zechariah, Zechariah! I have destroyed the flower of them. Do you wish me to massacre them all?" Then the blood rested.

Thoughts of repentance came to Nevuzaradan's mind: "If the Jews, who killed but one man, have been so severely punished, what will be my fate?" He left and ultimately converted to Judaism.

Ponder this. Nevuzaradan was a bloodthirsty gentile and had slaughtered tens of thousands of people. Regarding those who carry out the death penalty against the עִיר הַנִּדַּחַת, an entire town that has been found guilty of idolatry, the Torah writes, "And He will grant you compassion and be merciful toward you" (Devarim 13:18). Ohr HaChaim explains this apparent redundancy as follows: It is natural that the act of killing should have a decidedly detrimental effect on a person's character. Cruel behavior breeds a cruel nature. This should certainly be true in the case of those who execute the laws of עִיר הַנִּדַּחַת, where an entire city of people and livestock is annihilated. Therefore, Hashem found it necessary to assure those who carry out this punishment that though their actions should naturally infuse them with cruelty, they will be granted compassion from Above to counteract any harmful effects.

Can we imagine, then, how cruel and ruthless a man was Nevuzaradan, when in that one scene alone he was responsible for such mass-scale slaughter?

Consider also: Babylon had long waited for the conquest of Jerusalem and the destruction of the Beis HaMikdash. Had Nevuzaradan led his armies on a triumphant return home, he no doubt would have been given a hero's welcome. Yet Nevuzaradan, murderer and conqueror, decided instead to convert to the very faith of those whom he had killed and conquered! The source of this turnabout was a single moment of reflection, a single moment of yiras ha'onesh, fear of retribution. Nevuzaradan had seen Zechariah's blood seethe and he had seen it stop seething. He realized that the Jews had been held accountable for their murder of Zechariah, and it suddenly dawned on him that he would be held responsible for all those that he had killed. The truth of that realization penetrated his ruthless, vile nature and caused him to ignore whatever honor was awaiting him back home. Fear of retribution led him to sincere remorse and, ultimately, to embrace the teachings of the true God. Can there be a greater transformation?

Such is the power of hisorerus.

∽§ The Way to Change

When a person departs this world, he comes before the Heavenly Court for a final reckoning. When confronted with the record of his misdeeds, he may offer a variety of excuses, including the argument that his innate nature impelled him to behave in the way that he did. This and similar claims will be countered with a single response: Had the person studied *mussar*, he could have transformed himself totally, so that the tests which he failed could have been easily passed. To this argument, there is no response.[4]

Changing oneself is not easy. A person cannot expect to change himself completely overnight, for it simply cannot be done. We tend to think that when standing in *shul* on *Yom Kippur* and beating our chests as we recite '*Al Chet*,' that we have been transformed anew. Proof that this is not so is the manner in which we recite *Maariv* immediately following *Neilah* — in a haste, like always! The *shofar* blast is sounded, and already we revert to our old habits.

Nevertheless, there is no reason for despair. One *can* change himself, but the change must be gradual. R' Chaim Volozhiner (*Ruach Chaim* 1:13) illustrates this with a parable:

> *A person cannot ascend to the top rung of a ladder without first placing his foot on the bottom rung. It is therefore not considered an infraction on the part of a servant if when commanded by his master to ascend a ladder, he begins by stepping on the bottom rung. However, if the servant refuses to move from his place and ascend upward, but instead goes back and forth on the bottom rung, then he is rebelling against his master.*

All Hashem asks of us is that we take the first sincere step towards change. Then, we will be worthy of the assurance that "One who seeks to purify himself is granted Heavenly assistance" (*Shabbos* 104a).

---

4. In *Mishnah Berurah* (1:12), the Chofetz Chaim writes: "One must set aside a specific time each day to study *mussar* works, be it a small or large amount of time. The greater one is than his fellow, the greater, too, is his evil inclination [*Succah* 52a], and the antidote for the evil inclination is the reproof found in the teachings of *Chazal*."

Each of us must take a work of *mussar* in hand, one that is most suited for his own particular needs. *Sha'arei Teshuvah, Chovos HaLevavos, Mesilas Yesharim, Reishis Chochmah, Pele Yoetz, Sefer Chofetz Chaim,*[5] or any other such work — what is crucial is that one set aside a fixed time each day for *mussar* study.

The manner of study is likewise crucial. In *Pirkei Avos,* we often find the maxims of the Sages preceded by the phrase, הוּא הָיָה אוֹמֵר, *He [i.e., the Sage] used to say.* Similarly, in *Gemara* we find a Sage's proverb introduced by, מַרְגְּלָא בְּפוּמָא דְרַבִּי מֵאִיר, *R' Meir was in the habit of saying,* or the like. The intent is that the Sage was forever repeating a given teaching that he considered to be of prime significance. As *Rabbeinu Yonah* writes in *Sefer HaYirah:*

> Make fluent upon your lips words of *yiras shamayim,* such as, "Be bold as a leopard . . . to carry out the will of your Father in Heaven" (*Avos* 5:23); "The sum of the matter when all has been considered: Fear God and keep His commandments, for that is man's whole duty" (*Koheles* 12:13); "And now, O Israel, what does Hashem, your God, ask of you? — only that you fear Hashem . . ." (*Devarim* 10:12); "Be exceedingly humble" (*Avos* 4:4); and similar sayings. Make them fluent upon your lips, for then you will not stumble.

Such was the way of all the Sages of the *Mishnah* and *Gemara*, as well as those of succeeding generations. When they came upon a verse such as תּוֹעֲבַת ה' שִׂפְתֵי שָׁקֶר, "Lips of falsehood are loathsome to Hashem" (*Mishlei* 12:22), or an ethical teaching such as "One who becomes angry is akin to having worshiped idols" (*Zohar, Parashas Bereishis*), which is fundamental to man's purpose in this world, they repeated it to themselves hundreds of times, without propounding any new insights. They did this simply to allow the teaching to penetrate deep into their minds and souls, so that they could live by its words in a very real sense. This is essential to effective *mussar* study, for *mussar* study by definition must leave a pronounced impression on the student.[6]

---

5. HaRav Segal commented that one who studies the Chofetz Chaim's many works will find that they cover the full range of Torah *hashkafah* (outlook) that is needed to go through life.

6. For further elaboration, see discourse to *Parashas Chayei Sarah.*

✅ The Call of the Shofar

Elul is upon us and the Day of Judgment is approaching. It is incumbent upon us to heed the call of the *shofar*, to realize that we are soon to stand in judgment — and to conduct ourselves accordingly. Let us ask ourselves: How would we feel were we summoned to trial on this world, with a sizable fine as possible punishment? In all probability, we would be nervous and apprehensive. Were the possibility of imprisonment to exist, we would become frantic, and would surely seek every possible means for vindication. If a possible death sentence loomed before us, there is little doubt that we would spend many a sleepless night worrying over our fate.

Yet, preparation for *Rosh Hashanah* often involves little more than the sending of '*leshanah tovah*' cards and the wish for a good year to one another. The new year arrives and we have given nary a thought to the awesome words of the '*U'nesaneh Tokef*' prayer:

> Let us now relate the power of this day's holiness, for it is awesome and frightening ... It is true that You alone are the One Who judges, proves, knows, and bears witness; Who writes and seals; Who remembers all that is forgotten ...
>
> On Rosh Hashanah it will be inscribed and on Yom Kippur will be sealed how many will pass from the earth and how many will be created; who will live and who will die; who will die at his predestined time and who before his time; who will enjoy tranquility and who will suffer; who will be impoverished and who will be enriched ...
>
> But repentance, prayer and charity remove the evil of the decree!

In *Ohr Yisrael* (§14), R' Yisrael Salanter speaks of the varying ways in which Jews approach these days:

> In days past, as I recall, every man was seized with dread by the voice which proclaimed the sanctification of the month of Elul. This trembling bore fruit in drawing one close to the service of Hashem, each man

according to his worth. However, it was not as one might be inclined to think, that the man who all year was distant from His service now became wrapped in dread and fear of the impending judgment, from whose punishments, ל"ר, only repentance and good deeds can serve as a shield. Rather, it was the very opposite. A change for the better [during these days] was seen much more in the man who all year long treaded a path of holiness according to his worth[7] than it was in the man who, according to his own worth, walked all year in darkness, with nary a ray of light.

The reasons for this difference are both natural and spiritual. It is natural for man's behavior to be dictated by habit, whether for good or for bad. The spiritual reason is likewise simple enough, for when man sins, he draws upon himself a spirit of impurity which sullies his spirit and confuses his thinking. In the words of our Sages, "A man does not sin unless accompanied by a spirit of folly" (Sotah 3a).

It is thus not difficult to understand why we approach the month of Elul the way we do. "Sin dulls the heart of man" (*Yoma* 39a). Our sins have erected barriers between ourselves and Heaven, and we fail to perceive the tremendous opportunity for drawing close to Hashem during these days. Our spiritual senses have been dulled and we do not quake with fear at the thought that our ways will soon be scrutinized by the One before Whose throne nothing is forgotten.

Mateh Ephraim writes that it is proper to have one's *tefillin* and *mezuzos* inspected during these days. What is most important, however, is that one inspect *himself*, looking inwards to see where he stands with regard to anger, falsehood, *lashon hara*, earthly passion, and other such traits. To this end, there is no alternative to the study of *mussar*.[8]

הַחֲזֵק בַּמּוּסָר אַל תֶּרֶף, נִצְרֶהָ כִּי הִיא חַיֶּיךָ, "Cling tightly to *mussar*, do

---

7. HaRav Segal commented that R' Yisrael's disciples would relate how they could perceive a difference in their *rebbi's tefillas Mussaf* on *Shabbos Mevarchim Elul*.
8. HaRav Segal added that, during these days, one should also study works that will infuse him with a proper appreciation of *tefillah*. To this end, he urged the study of *Yesod V'Shoresh HaAvodah* and similar works, along with the study of the laws of *tefillah* in *Tur* and *Shulchan Aruch*.

not loosen your grip! Guard it, for it is your life" (*Mishlei* 4:13). *Mussar* study is crucial — for us and for our families. In the words of R' Yisrael:

> The subject of mussar is unlike any other. Whereas the obligation to study other subjects [in Torah] does not encompass all Jewish souls — women are exempt from the obligation to study Torah[9] — ... such is not the case with this subject. The obligation to study mussar encompasses everyone — no one is exempt (Ohr Yisrael §3).

While the teachings of R' Yisrael require no proof, their correctness here is obvious. Every Jew is obligated to fulfill the *mitzvah* of אֶת ה׳ אֱלֹקֶיךָ תִּירָא, "You shall fear Hashem your God" (*Devarim* 10:20). This *mitzvah* can be fulfilled properly only through the study of *mussar*.

It is proper for every man to study *mussar* with his wife. There is nothing shameful about this. Who among us is greater than the great *Rav* of Jerusalem, R' Yosef Chaim Sonnenfeld[10], who studied with his *rebbetzin* each day for one half hour? Obviously, this is not a 'modern' concept.

Baruch Hashem, there is to be found today a plethora of English works on ethical themes, including many that deal with the subject of *shemiras halashon*. Today, there are many households where even children are careful regarding these all-important laws. I myself have been asked questions by women regarding the laws of *shemiras halashon*. One cannot begin to fathom the degree of sanctity that permeates a home in which caution is exercised in matters of speech — including speaking the truth and in a refined manner.

Rabbeinu Yonah writes in *Sefer HaYirah*: "From the onset of Elul until the close of *Yom Kippur*, one should feel awe and dread from fear of the [impending] judgment." May we merit to experience this feeling, so that we may enter *Rosh Hashanah* with proper readiness. May we merit to strengthen ourselves in all areas of our service of Hashem, and thereby be inscribed and sealed בְּסֵפֶר חַיִּים טוֹבִים, גְּאֻלָּה וִישׁוּעָה, "in the book of good life, redemption and salvation."

---

9. Women are, of course, required to be knowledgeable in the *halachos* that pertain to their own daily lives.

10. b. 1848 — d. 1932.

Preparing for the Day of Judgment — A Teshuvah Address to Women[1]

כִּי הַמִּצְוָה הַזֹּאת אֲשֶׁר אָנֹכִי מְצַוְּךָ הַיּוֹם, לֹא נִפְלֵאת הִוא מִמְּךָ
וְלֹא רְחֹקָה הִוא. לֹא בַשָּׁמַיִם הִוא, לֵאמֹר מִי יַעֲלֶה לָנוּ הַשָּׁמַיְמָה
וְיִקָּחֶהָ לָנוּ וְיַשְׁמִעֵנוּ אֹתָהּ וְנַעֲשֶׂנָּה . . . כִּי קָרוֹב אֵלֶיךָ הַדָּבָר מְאֹד,
בְּפִיךָ וּבִלְבָבְךָ לַעֲשֹׂתוֹ.

For this mitzvah which I am commanding you today is not hidden from you, nor is it distant. It is not in the heavens, so that one will say, "Who will ascend to the heavens and get it for us and inform us regarding it, so that we may do it?" . . . For the matter is exceedingly close to you; it is within your mouths and hearts to do it (30:11-14).

'This mitzvah' refers to teshuvah (Ramban, ibid.).

⚜ The Meaning of 'Teshuvah'

I am reminded tonight of the Chofetz Chaim, who in the last years of his life journeyed to Vilna on an important mission. He was

---

1. Delivered in English to a gathering of women in London.

then in his nineties and, as there was no railway station in Radin, was forced to make part of the trip by horse and wagon. He was so weak that he traveled lying down. That he felt it necessary to undergo such personal sacrifice is proof of the urgency which he accorded his mission.

The Chofetz Chaim went to Vilna to address a gathering of women on the subject of *taharas hamishpachah*, family purity. The gathering was held in the Great *Shul* of Vilna, the women seated downstairs in the men's section as you are seated here tonight. Tonight, we shall endeavor to touch on a number of topics; with Hashem's help, we will try to say what the Chofetz Chaim might have said.

The prophet Yeshayahu stated: דִּרְשׁוּ ה׳ בְּהִמָּצְאוֹ, קְרָאֻהוּ בִּהְיוֹתוֹ קָרוֹב, "Seek out Hashem when He is accessible, call upon Him when He is near" (*Yeshayahu* 55:6). Our Sages (*Rosh Hashanah* 18a) tell us that this refers to the *Aseres Yemei Teshuvah*, Ten Days of Repentance, which commence with *Rosh Hashanah* and conclude with *Yom Kippur*. Rambam (*Hilchos Teshuvah* 2:6) writes: "While *teshuvah* and penitential prayer avail at all times, they avail even more during the ten days from *Rosh Hashanah* to *Yom Kippur* and are accepted immediately, as it is written: ... דִּרְשׁוּ ה׳ בְּהִמָּצְאוֹ"

What is *teshuvah*? I have noticed that the common translation of the word '*teshuvah*' is 'repentance.' This is incorrect, for repentance, meaning remorse, is only one aspect of the *teshuvah* process. A more precise translation of '*teshuvah*' is 'return,' a return to Hashem, as it is written: שׁוּבָה יִשְׂרָאֵל עַד ה׳ אֱלֹקֶיךָ, כִּי כָשַׁלְתָּ בַּעֲוֹנֶךָ, "Return, O Israel, up to Hashem your God, for you have stumbled due to your sins" (*Hoshea* 14:2). How does one return to Hashem? The prophet Yirmiyahu tells us:

נַחְפְּשָׂה דְרָכֵינוּ וְנַחְקֹרָה וְנָשׁוּבָה עַד ה׳.
Let us search and examine our ways and return to Hashem (*Eichah* 3:40).

Teshuvah cannot be accomplished with mere pounding on the heart and recitation of *viduy* (confession). As Yirmiyahu stated, it is imperative that we examine our ways to see whether or not they are in complete accordance with Torah. If we find that our ways are indeed wanting, then we must regret our behavior (חֲרָטָה) and resolve in our mind that we will never again repeat our iniquities — and live up to our resolution (עֲזִיבַת הַחֵטְא). And we must speak to Hashem, saying: "*Ribono shel Olam*, I have done such and such. I realize that this was wrong, and I will seriously strive to improve my ways." This is *teshuvah*.[2] The days from *Rosh Hashanah* to *Yom Kippur* are most opportune for this sort of soul-searching.

Let us now discuss certain specific areas of *mitzvah* observance.

◆§ Shabbos and Family Purity

Shabbos. One must ask oneself: Do I keep Shabbos properly? To answer that, "Yes, I don't carry on Shabbos, nor do I turn on lights or transgress other well-known prohibited acts," is insufficient. The laws of Shabbos are detailed and often complex. There are many observant individuals who have but a limited knowledge in certain fundamental areas of the laws of Shabbos, and there are others who unfortunately do not ascribe sufficient importance to certain aspects of Shabbos observance.

During these days of introspection, one should ask: Is my observance of Shabbos as it ought to be? Is my knowledge of *hilchos Shabbos* adequate? Have I perhaps unwittingly been guilty of *chillul Shabbos*, desecration of Shabbos?

It is of utmost importance that women attend lectures discussing the laws of Shabbos. Also, there is today, ב"ה, an abundance of English literature pertaining to these laws. One who begins the new year with a firm resolve to improve her observance of Shabbos, and acts upon that resolution, is a true *ba'alas teshuvah*.

Taharas HaMishpachah. As we enter the new year and seek to merit a favorable judgment, a woman must ask herself whether or not she is well versed in these all-important laws. I have heard that in this subject, too, there are some who are stringent regarding certain requirements and lax with regard to others. We are not *ba'alim* (masters) over the *Shulchan Aruch*! We dare not make our own rules in deciding whether a given practice is right or wrong. True, the observance of certain areas of these laws may prove difficult — at first. However, as time goes on and one observes the *halachos*

---

2. *Sha'arei Teshuvah* (section I) lists twenty components of *teshuvah*, but חֲרָטָה, remorse, and עֲזִיבַת הַחֵטְא, *giving up the sin for the future*, are absolutely essential. The commentators agree that *viduy* falls under the category of חֲרָטָה. In fact, *viduy* is the only aspect of *teshuvah* which is specifically ordained by the Torah (see *Rambam, Hilchos Teshuvah* 1:1).

correctly, it becomes a way of life and is really not all that difficult. In any event, strict adherence to *Halachah* is not a matter of choice.

◄§ Sincere Confession

At the opening of the *viduy* we say אָשַׁמְנוּ, *we have become guilty.* Included in this confession is אָכַלְתִּי מַאֲכָלוֹת אֲסוּרוֹת, *I have eaten forbidden foods* (see *Chayei Adam* 143). Unfortunately, we are often lax regarding what sort of foods we bring into our homes. That the word 'kosher' appears on a wrapper is not sufficient; one should not eat something without knowing whose *kashrus* certification the item carries and whether or not that certification can be relied upon. *Kashrus* standards must be maintained outside the home as well. Social etiquette is no excuse for eating something whose *kashrus* is questionable. When visiting friends or relatives whose standards in this area may be wanting, one should politely refrain from eating. One must be equally vigilant when vacationing. One should never stay at a resort or hotel without first ascertaining definitively that its kitchen is run in strict accordance with *Halachah*.

When saying אָשַׁמְנוּ, one should ponder whether or not he or she has been lax in this area — and resolve to be careful in the future.

In that same section of the *viduy*, we say גָּזַלְנוּ, *we have robbed.* One must ponder: Do I truly deal honestly in my monetary affairs? Is my 'word' a word? Have I perhaps been guilty of *chillul Hashem*, desecration of Hashem's Name, through improper business behavior? In fact, the sin of robbery can take on many forms. If someone purchases groceries or meat on credit and does not pay his bill, that is also robbery.

Time does not allow for us to discuss each of the confessions recited during these days. In general, one should enter *Yom Kippur* with an understanding of the *viduy* and honestly ask oneself where he or she has sinned in a given category and how one can improve — for improve we must.

Hashem does not expect us to become *tzaddikim* and *tzidkonios* overnight. What He does expect of us is that we seriously ponder our conduct and that we sincerely strive to better ourselves in the varied areas of *mitzvah* observance. This is *teshuvah*.

◆§ Realizing Our Purpose

In the *viduy* of the *selichos* prayers, we say: אָשַׁמְנוּ מִכָּל עָם. This does not mean *we have sinned more than any other nation*. The correct translation is: *We have sinned from all the nations*, meaning that our sins are a result of our being influenced by the gentile world. Unfortunately, we often forget a truth that is explicit in the Torah: "I am Hashem, your God, Who has separated you from the nations" (*Vayikra* 20:24). We dare not learn from the ways of the gentiles, whose goal in life is diametrically opposed to our own. A gentile lives for this world, a Jew for the World to Come. As the *mishnah* states:

רַבִּי יַעֲקֹב אוֹמֵר: הָעוֹלָם הַזֶּה דּוֹמֶה לִפְרוֹזְדוֹר בִּפְנֵי הָעוֹלָם הַבָּא,
הַתְקֵן עַצְמְךָ בַּפְּרוֹזְדוֹר, כְּדֵי שֶׁתִּכָּנֵס לַטְרַקְלִין.

R' Yaakov said: "This world is like a lobby before the World to Come; prepare yourself in the lobby so that you may enter the banquet hall" (*Avos 4:21*).

Our purpose in life is to fulfill the will of Hashem and thereby merit a portion in the World to Come. It is a tragedy when secular influences gain entrance into observant homes, and life's true purpose becomes forgotten.

All of us are well aware that the idea of having large families is foreign and even scorned in secular society. To our shame, this way of thinking has had some degree of influence in our circles. Here, too, one must remember that all aspects of Jewish living are governed by the *Shulchan Aruch*. No one would dream of using a meat utensil into which fell a hot dairy spoon without first consulting a halachic authority. The same should apply to all areas of Jewish living.

Let us not forget how much our Matriarchs, Sarah, Rivkah, Rachel, and Leah, yearned to have children. It is because their *tefillos* were answered that we are here today, a part of the great nation of Hashem. Let us not forget the sacrifices of our own mothers and grandmothers who gave up everything in order to raise their families in the way of Torah. They understood their role as the builders of *Klal Yisrael* and willingly endured great hardships to realize this goal.

All of us are remnants of the great *churban*, destruction, of half a century ago. In what merit were our parents spared so that we could be born? We cannot know the answer to this, for those who died were surely as great as those who survived. Only Hashem can know why we were deemed worthy to live until this day. It is the holy duty of every Jewish woman to share in the rebuilding of the Jewish people, and to see this as her primary purpose in life. How many childless women wish that they could have the opportunity to have large families! And one can never know which of her children will be the one to become a leader of his people. Perhaps it was primarily to bring that particular child into the world that one was placed on this earth. It is a great source of merit for a mother and father when their child grows to become a מְזַכֶּה אֶת הָרַבִּים, *one who brings merit to the multitudes.*

↢ On Fashion and Furnishings

Another area of secular influence is manner of dress. There are those who feel a need to be in step with the latest fashions. I have heard that there are mothers who even dress their little girls in fashion! Let us think for a moment: Who are the designers of these fashions and what guidelines do they use in originating their designs? The designers are secularists and, more often than not, are immoral. Their goal is to design a style that will attract the attention of men. In other words, these styles are a direct contradiction to the attribute of *tznius,* modesty, that is the hallmark of Jewish daughters. This is not to say that a Jewish woman cannot dress nicely. Certainly she can, but she must do it with *tznius.*

There is yet another point to consider. Dressing in style is expensive, as is decorating one's home in elaborate style. A woman who places excessive emphasis on dress and interior decorating also places undue pressure on her husband to provide the money for her expensive desires. This is a contradiction to a woman's duty to ensure that her husband dedicate himself to the study of Torah to the best of his ability. Moreover, it is precisely these sort of pressures that can lead to a man's engaging in dishonest business practices. When one's budget is beyond his means, a feeling of desperation can set in, and this can drive a person to acquire through deception that which he simply cannot earn honestly. A Jewish wife must view life from a loftier perspective than her gentile neighbors. In this way, she will be a true עֵזֶר, *helpmate,* to her husband, and together they will bring the *Shechinah* into their home.

∾§ A Home of Kedushah

It is the mother who is primarily responsible for creating a home atmosphere that is *kadosh* and *tahor*, holy and pure. The kind of literature that is permitted to enter a home has a pronounced effect on the *kedushah* of that home. Today, there is, ב"ה, an abundance of Jewish literature for both young and old. There is no excuse for bringing into a home secular literature of questionable content. Secular magazines which years ago were considered acceptable even in certain Torah homes are today filled with material that is clearly forbidden to read. Bringing such literature into a Jewish home is inexcusable.

There is no need to elaborate on the dangers of television. It is obvious that television can destroy anyone spiritually and should not be allowed into one's home.

With regard to these negative influences, I would like to relate the following story:

In Poland there was a *rav* who was very close to the Chofetz Chaim. One day, a stranger came to this *rav*'s town selling *sefarim*. He entered the town's main *shul* and displayed his *sefarim* on a table for people to see. The *rav* came over and began examining the volumes' contents — and was shocked to discover statements which were pure *apikorsus,* heresy! Without asking any questions, the *rav* collected all the *sefarim* and threw them into the *shul*'s furnace. The merchant exploded with anger. "Rabbi!" he said. "Those books were my livelihood! People appreciate my work and it sells very well." The *rav* replied, "Come back tomorrow and I will provide you with a job."

The next day, the merchant returned to the *rav* and was told, "I have heard that the old gentile who used to ring the church bells is now retiring. I will speak to the priest and recommend you for the position."

The merchant stared at the *rav* in disbelief. "Rabbi," he said, "are you serious? How can a Jew think of earning money in such a manner?" The *rav* replied, "If you will ring those bells, you will be summoning gentiles to their house of falsehood, but if you sell those books, then you will be summoning Jews to *your* house of falsehood!"

A mother and father are guardians designated by the *Ribono shel Olam* to care for the precious souls with whom they have been entrusted. A *Midrash* in *Shir HaShirim Rabbah* (1:4) beautifully depicts the uniqueness of Jewish children and how precious they are to Hashem. As God prepared to give the Torah at Sinai, He asked that Israel present Him with guarantors that they would faithfully observe the *mitzvos*.

"Sovereign of the universe," the nation answered, "our Patriarchs will be our guarantors."

Hashem was not satisfied.

"Then our prophets will be our guarantors," they suggested.

But Hashem was still not satisfied, and He challenged *Klal Yisrael* to bring better guarantors.

"Our children will be our guarantors!"

"They are indeed good guarantors," said Hashem. "For their sake I will give you the Torah."

Let us do our very best in fulfilling our awesome charge to raise children that are holy and pure.

ܝܐ Trust in Hashem

It is especially important in these trying times that we strengthen ourselves in matters of *emunah* and *bitachon*, faith and trust in Hashem. In his commentary to *Mishlei* (3:26), *Rabbeinu Yonah* writes:

> The meaning of bitachon is that one knows in his heart that all is through the hand of Heaven and that it is in God's power to deviate from the ways of nature. . .Even when someone is so deathly ill that according to the natural way of things there is no chance that he will survive, one should believe and trust that Hashem can save him. He [Hashem] can change the fortunes of man and no one can stop Him. Though travail seems near, salvation can be near as well.

There are couples who are told by doctors that they cannot have children. There are ill people for whom doctors say there is no hope, ר"ל. There are other vicissitudes which one may encounter at some point in life. It is regarding such situations that David *HaMelech* proclaimed: בִּטְחוּ בוֹ בְכָל עֵת, עָם; שִׁפְכוּ לְפָנָיו לְבַבְכֶם; אֱלֹקִים מַחֲסֶה לָנוּ סֶלָה, "Trust in Him at every moment, O nation! Pour out your hearts before Him; God is an eternal refuge for us" (*Tehillim* 62:9). Nothing is beyond Hashem's power. Infusing oneself with this belief is the key to a happy and tranquil life.[3]

On the eve of *Yom Kippur*, following *Kol Nidrei*, we recite the *Shehechiyanu* blessing, thanking Hashem for having permitted us to live to this day. While we recite this blessing at the commencement of every *yom tov*, it has particular significance on *Yom Kippur*. That we are alive on Yom Kippur is proof that on the previous *Yom Kippur*, Hashem sealed us in the Book of Life, and for this our gratitude should be boundless. We also thank Hashem for having permitted us to experience yet another *Yom Kippur* so that we can again benefit from the unique purifying powers of this awesome holy day and hopefully become complete *ba'alei teshuvah*.

People often wish one another, "Have an easy fast." While this wish is surely uttered with good intentions, one should be careful not to overlook the primary purpose of the day. Fasting is only one aspect of the unique *teshuvah* process of *Yom Kippur*. Moreover, it is counter-productive to overemphasize the discomforts of fasting. Rather than count the hours left until the fast ends, one should count the precious hours remaining to return to Hashem before the Gates of Mercy close.

May we all merit to be signed and sealed in the Book of Life, to return to Hashem with all our heart, and to follow a path of life that is in complete accordance with Torah and free of all secular influences. May we merit to have children who will be a pride and joy to Hashem and His Torah, and may we be granted long life to enjoy the *nachas* of seeing our children carry on the charge of the Chosen Nation.

---

3. See discourse to *Parashas Vayeira*.

Hakaras HaTov

⊷ Fundament of Divine Service

הֲלַה׳ תִּגְמְלוּ זֹאת, עַם נָבָל וְלֹא חָכָם; הֲלוֹא הוּא אָבִיךָ קָנֶךָ, הוּא
עָשְׂךָ וַיְכֹנְנֶךָ.

*Is it to Hashem that you do this? O vile and unwise
nation! Is He not your Father, your Master; has He not
created you and firmed you? (32:6).*

The term נָבָל generally refers to a group or individual whose
behavior is vile and shameful (see *Ramban* to *Vayikra* 19:2). Here,
both *Rashi* and *Ramban* understand the shamefulness as a lack of
hakaras hatov, gratitude, towards Hashem:

> *O vile nation — that has forgotten that which was done
> for it (Rashi).*
> *To my understanding, one who performs a kindness
> without any thought of recompense is called נָדִיב, while
> one who repays a kindness with wickedness is called
> נָבָל (Ramban).*

In the *haftarah* of Shabbos *Chazon*, the generation living prior to
the First Destruction is rebuked in harsh terms for this very sin:

> יָדַע שׁוֹר קֹנֵהוּ וַחֲמוֹר אֵבוּס בְּעָלָיו; יִשְׂרָאֵל לֹא יָדַע, עַמִּי לֹא
> הִתְבּוֹנָן. *The ox knows its owner, and the donkey its
> master's crib; but Israel does not know, my people do
> not understand (Yeshayahu 1:3).*

As *Radak* (ibid.) explains, an animal recognizes its owner through whose efforts its needs are provided. It is this natural recognition that impels the ox and donkey after a hard day's work to return to their owner's domain without being forced. At the time of the Destruction, *Klal Yisrael* was remiss in their recognition of all the good that Hashem had bestowed upon them, and as a result, they strayed from His path.

In his commentary to *Avos*, *Rabbeinu Yonah* writes that *hakaras hatov* is basic to proper service of Hashem. The *Mishnah* (*Avos* 1:3) there teaches that we should serve Hashem "like servants who serve their master not for the sake of receiving reward." Explains *Rabbeinu Yonah*: "A person should serve Hashem not in order to receive reward, but because of even one of the thousands and thousands of kindnesses that He has bestowed upon him, and because of the greatness of the Master, Who is fit to be served in this way."

In *Tomer Devorah*, R' Moshe Cordovero[1] awakens us to appreciate the depths of Hashem's kindness and to strive to emulate it. To better understand his point, consider how you would react if you had given someone a generous cash gift, only to see that person use the money to ruin *your* business! Imagine your rage, your resentment toward that person!

Says *Tomer Devorah:* Hashem is patient with His creations to a degree beyond human comprehension. Consider that at every moment of man's existence, he is dependent upon his Creator for the gift of life. It is man's obligation to utilize this gift in accordance with Hashem's will. When man sins, he is, in effect, taking this most precious gift and using it in defiance of its Giver. Yet, Hashem does not say, "If you choose to offend Me, then I must withdraw the power that I have granted you." Rather, He patiently bears insult and sustains life that is used *against* Him — in the hope that man will repent.

---

1. Known as *Ramak* (an acronym for משה קרדובר 'ר), he was one of the most profound and systematic teachers of the *Zohar*, as well as a leading figure among the great Kabbalists of sixteenth-century Tzefas (Safed). Even the *Arizal* refers to *Ramak* as his teacher and master.

An interpretation of the Thirteen Attributes of Mercy as enumerated by the prophet Michah (*Michah* 7:18-20) is the theme of *Ramak's* classic work, *Tomer Devorah*.

⊰ Priceless Gifts

Thrice daily in *Shemoneh Esrei* we express a general *hakaras hatov* to Hashem. "We shall thank you and relate Your praise — for our lives, which are committed to Your power, and for our souls that are entrusted to You; for Your miracles that are with us every day; and for Your wonders and favors in every season — evening, morning, and afternoon."

Often, we take the gifts of good health and life for granted and bemoan things that are trivial by comparison. For this and other reasons, it is good to visit a hospital from time to time. Aside from fulfilling the *mitzvah* of *bikur cholim*, visiting the sick, one will come in contact with people who were well only yesterday and are unfortunately ill today, ר״ל. This will serve as a vivid reminder to be forever grateful for the gifts of good health and life.

⊰ Between Man and His Fellow

Hakaras hatov is surely not limited to our relationship with Hashem. Inter-personal gratitude is fundamental in the relationship between man and his fellow. This is pointedly illustrated in the Torah's command (*Devarim* 23:8) that we not reject entirely those of Egyptian lineage who convert to the Jewish faith. Whereas female descendants of Avraham, Yitzchok and Yaakov may never marry male converts from the nations of Amon and Moav, it is permissible to marry the third- generation descendant of an Egyptian convert.

> Do not reject an Egyptian (convert) — entirely, even though they cast your male (infants) into the river. And what is the reason for this? Because they were your hosts in your time of need (Rashi ibid.).

True, the Egyptians enslaved our ancestors, persecuted them, and murdered some of them. Nevertheless, as Jews we are expected to recognize whatever good has been done for us, other considerations notwithstanding. The fact is that Yaakov's family descended to Egypt to escape the hunger in Canaan. In Egypt, the natives — under Yosef's direction — permitted Yaakov and his family to live in peace, with ample sustenance, and allowed them to serve their God undisturbed until the last of the *shevatim* (tribal ancestors) had died. For this we must be grateful.

According to *Ramban*, a lack of *hakaras hatov* is at the root of the prohibition regarding marriage to converts of Amon and Moav.

> An Amonite or Moavite shall not enter into the congregation of Hashem ... because they did not meet you with bread and water on the way when you came forth out of Egypt (Devarim 23:4-5).

> It seems to me that Scripture distances these two brothers because they were recipients of kindness from Avraham, who rescued their father and mother[2] from sword and captivity, and in whose [i.e., Avraham's] merit Hashem removed them from the overturning [of Sodom]. Thus, they were obligated to do kindness for Israel, but instead were wicked toward them ... (Ramban).

Ramban's comment provides us with the insight that the obligation of *hakaras hatov* is in no way limited to the actual beneficiary and benefactor of the kindness performed. The Amonites' and Moavites' failure to provide Israel with provisions occurred many generations after Avraham had rescued Lot and his daughters. Those nations would never have come into being were it not for Avraham. Thus, they were obligated to show gratitude to Avraham's descendants and were faulted for their lack of recognition in this regard. A people which lacks the attribute of *hakaras hatov* is not fit to enter the Congregation of Hashem.

---

2. These two nations bore the names of their respective ancestors, who were born from the union of Lot with each of his two surviving daughters (see *Bereishis* ch. 19).

✍ Parents, Teachers, and Friends

In explaining the *mitzvah* to honor one's parents, *Sefer HaChinuch* writes:

> Among the roots of this mitzvah is that it is fitting for man to recognize and bestow kindness upon one who has done him a kindness, and he should not be vile in not granting such recognition and being ungrateful — for this is an exceedingly revolting and wicked trait in the eyes of God and men. One must take to heart the fact that his father and mother are the causes of his being on this world. It is therefore truly fitting that he grant them every honor and benefit that he can, for they brought him into this world and toiled many toils for him in his youth.

A lack of proper *kibud av v'eim* usually stems from one's taking his parents' efforts for granted. Inasmuch as a father and mother provide their child with his or her every need from the moment of birth and will make every sacrifice for the child's material and spiritual welfare, the child tends to think that these efforts are due him and are to be expected. As *Sefer HaChinuch* makes perfectly clear, this attitude is not the Torah way. A lack of *kibud av v'eim* means that one is lacking in the vital trait of *hakaras hatov*.

We often take for granted, as well, others who are close to us. Let us ask ourselves honestly — Do we feel proper gratitude toward our friends for the good they do for us? True friendship alone warrants boundless feelings of gratitude, while a lack of *hakaras hatov* toward one's friends will inevitably affect his relationship toward Hashem. As *Chazal* (*Sh'mos Rabbah* 1:10) put it, "Whoever denies the good done for him by a friend will in the end deny the good of the Omnipresent."

We have made mention of the *hakaras hatov* that one should feel toward his parents. Eternal gratitude should likewise be felt toward one's spiritual parents, namely those who have taught him Torah. Again, we refer to a dictum of our Sages: "Whoever teaches the son of his friend Torah is considered as if he bore him" (*Sanhedrin* 19b). The obligation for such gratitude can be extended to the great

Rishonim and Acharonim, whose written works illuminate both the Written and Oral Law. Do we feel proper gratitude toward Rashi, without whose commentaries one could not begin to understand Chumash or Talmud Bavli? Imagine how much easier it would be to study Talmud Yerushalmi had Rashi authored a commentary to that body of Torah Sheba'al Peh!

Do we feel a debt of gratitude to the compiler of Mesoras HaShas, who cites the source for every citation found in Talmud, in addition to citing the source for the halachah that is derived from each Gemara, as found in Rambam and Shulchan Aruch? We can go on and on, for the list of those to whom we owe eternal gratitude is endless.

In explaining the mitzvah of kibud av v'eim, Sefer HaChinuch concludes:

> When one will have set this trait [i.e., hakaras hatov] firmly in his soul, he will then come to recognize the goodness of God, Blessed is He, Who is the source of his existence and that of all his ancestors until Adam; and Who brought him into this world and provided him with all his needs all his days, endowed him with a complete anatomy of wholesome limbs, and placed inside of him a soul that is intelligent and understanding. For without this soul with which God has graced him, man would be like a horse or mule, devoid of all wisdom.
>
> One should therefore realize to what great extent he should be meticulous in his service of Hashem.

Hakaras hatov is the primary means for returning to Hashem with a teshuvah sheleimah, a complete repentance. It is this trait that can inspire us to please Hashem by dedicating our God-given abilities and resources to His service. As Rashi comments with regard to sacrificial offerings:

אִשֶּׁה רֵיחַ נִיחוֹחַ לַה' — A fire-offering, a satisfying aroma to Hashem: "For I have spoken and My will has been done."

Let us therefore strengthen ourselves during this season of teshuvah to achieve a heightened level of hakaras hatov — to those people from whom we and our ancestors have benefited and to Hashem, the Source of all good.

The Torah Study of Children[1]

תּוֹרָה צִוָּה לָנוּ מֹשֶׁה, מוֹרָשָׁה קְהִלַּת יַעֲקֹב.
Moshe prescribed the Torah to us, an eternal heritage for the congregation of Yaakov (33:4).

For all generations will the sons of Yaakov inherit it and study it, for it will not become forgotten from the mouths of his descendants (Ramban).

◆§ Unsullied by Sin

I n *Masechta Shabbos* (119b), we find:

Reish Lakish said in the name of R' Yehudah Nesiah, "The world is sustained only in the merit of the breath [of Torah study] of school children."

Said R' Papa to Abaye: "And what is with yours and mine [i.e., their Torah study]?"

Abaye replied, "There is no comparison between breath that is tainted by sin and breath that is free of sin."

It is impossible for us to fathom the spiritual greatness of Abaye and R' Papa, who were among the foremost sages of the Talmud. When Abaye spoke of "breath tainted by sin," he referred to any

1. Delivered at a dinner on behalf of Yeshivah Beis Dovid of Monsey, N.Y.

possible utterance that might have been considered sinful according to the awesome level of Divine service that we associate with the Talmudic sages.

From here, says the Chofetz Chaim, we see the devastating effect that forbidden speech can have on one's Torah study. Abaye declared that any possible verbal infraction on the part of himself or his colleagues automatically lowered the quality of their study. Man has been granted one mouth and one tongue. The same mouth and tongue that are used for mundane conversation are used to perform the greatest *mitzvah* of all, the study of Torah. To the degree that one's mundane conversations are sprinkled with comments of *lashon hara* or falsehood, or with words that bring shame or hurt to others, to that degree has the purity of his Torah study been blemished.

We know that in preparation for Torah study, it is proper to arouse in oneself a sense of Heavenly fear and to take note of the fact that when studying Torah, one attaches himself to his Creator, as it were (*Nefesh HaChaim* 4:6). Also, we know that Torah is to be studied *lishmah*, for its own sake, and that the study of Torah *lishmah* can raise a person to the most sublime spiritual heights (see *Avos* 6:1). Now, these concepts are surely beyond young school children who learn *Aleph-Beis* or *Chumash*. Yet, it is their untainted study that sustains this world. How precious is the pure and holy study of our *tinokos shel beis rabban!*

⋙ A Question

A question, however, remains. The above dialogue between Abaye and R' Papa is commonly known. Thus, people are well aware that when they give financial support to a yeshivah they are helping to maintain the world's existence, literally. Can we begin to fathom the great *z'chus* of having a share in such a *mitzvah*? Why, then, is it necessary for yeshivos to host lavish affairs in order to induce their guests to support their institutions? Should not a mere announcement suffice? Should not people be rushing forward to share in the furtherance of the Torah study of *tinokos shel beis rabban?!*

I recall that during the Arab-Israeli wars, world-wide fund-raising was coordinated without the necessity of a single dinner being held. Announcements were made in every Jewish community and millions of dollars poured forth. Surely that cause merited such a universal response — but so does the Torah study of our youth!

The following *Midrash*[2] sheds light on the matter:

> *"And they shall take for Me an offering [... And let them make for Me a Mishkan (Sanctuary) so that I may dwell among them]" (Sh'mos 25:2,8): The One regarding Whom it is written, "Hashem's is the earth and its fullness" (Tehillim 24:1); "His is the sea and He perfected it" (ibid. 95:5); "Behold, unto Hashem are the Heavens" (Devarim 10:14) — He requires [the offerings of] flesh and blood? Rather, He yearned to rest His Presence amidst Israel in the way of a father who yearns for his children. Thus it is written:* וְיִקְחוּ לִי תְּרוּמָה, *"Take 'for My sake' an offering." From this we can deduce: If to build a Mishkan, which is an honor and atonement for Israel, Hashem said* דַּבֵּר אֶל בְּנֵי יִשְׂרָאֵל, *"Speak to the Children of Israel" — an expression of conciliation in the way of* דַּבְּרוּ עַל לֵב יְרוּשָׁלַיִם, *"Comfort the heart of Jerusalem" (Yeshayahu 40:2), then what [sort of retribution] awaits the nations of the world who oppress Israel and deprive them of their possessions! (Yalkut Shimoni, Terumah §25).*

This *Midrash* is perplexing. Hashem, as it were, was conciliatory in His request that *Bnei Yisrael* contribute to the building of the *Mishkan*. If conciliation was necessary, then Hashem obviously perceived a reluctance on the part of the people to contribute. Now, it is perhaps comprehensible that a person might be reluctant to surrender his personal earnings for even a lofty cause, since this money comes to him through much sweat and toil. However, this was not the case with the Jews in the Wilderness. Most of their riches had been amassed upon leaving Egypt when they took with them the precious possessions of their former overlords (*Sh'mos* 12:36). Later, the Jews more than doubled their wealth with treasures which they found at the splitting of the Sea. It was plainly clear that whatever they had acquired was God given, with little or no effort on their part. How, then, could they have been at all reluctant to contribute these treasures toward the building of a dwelling place for the *Shechinah*?

---

2. This *Midrash* is also discussed in the discourse to *Parashas Terumah*.

The answer to this is rooted in the inexorable struggle between the body and the soul. The soul yearns for the spiritual, while the body craves the physical. Man's intellect would easily direct him to use his possessions for spiritual pursuits, would it not be for the body's urgings that one utilize his possessions to satisfy his earthly desires. These earthly cravings were present in the Wilderness as well. While the people knew perfectly well that their possessions were God given, there nevertheless existed the possibility that they would not want to contribute generously toward the building of the *Mishkan*. Thus did Hashem find it necessary to express Himself in a manner of conciliation.

This seems to explain the necessity for yeshivos to engage in such costly fund-raising affairs. While one's heart is well aware of the principal role which the Torah study of children occupies in Creation, his earthly cravings blur his vision. The sumptuous meal that is customarily served at these gatherings brings satisfaction to one's corporeal being, leaving the intellect free — hopefully — to perceive and respond to the message of the hour: *"The world is sustained only in the merit of the breath [of Torah study] of school children!"*

ⰶ The Leaders of Tomorrow

We live in very difficult times. To our misfortune, so many of our *gedolim* who illuminated the world with their Torah and fear of Heaven have been taken from us. It is incumbent upon every *ben Torah* to do his share to fill this great void. The new generation must strengthen itself in Torah study and service of Hashem and perceive in the fullest sense the truth of David *HaMelech's* declaration: אַשְׁרֵי יוֹשְׁבֵי בֵיתֶךָ, "Praiseworthy are those who dwell in Your house!"

It is likewise the obligation of every father and mother to do whatever possible to help their sons realize their potential as *bnei Torah*.

In the world of medicine, there are general practitioners and there are specialists. The general practitioners have an overall knowledge of medicine as it relates to the complete human anatomy, but generally speaking, they lack the expertise of the specialist to whom serious problems are referred. In today's day and age, the specialist's role is crucial.

In the world of Torah, there are also the general practitioners, who amass a significant amount of knowledge but who lack the expertise that qualifies them as truly great *talmidei chachamim*. Every parent should strive to have his child become a 'specialist' in all areas of Torah, a genuine *gadol*, great in his knowledge and comprehension of Torah, and equally outstanding in *midos* and fear of Heaven — for only in this way can greatness in Torah be attained. A particular obligation rests upon those parents who have been blessed with a child of exceptional ability.

Without *gedolim* we are lost. It is our responsibility to mold the leaders of the next generation.

◂§ R' Meshulam's P'sak

In striving to guide our sons along the path of Torah scholarship, it is important that we recognize the key ingredient for success in Torah study. *Ameilus*, diligent toil in the study of Torah, is the primary tool through which one acquires knowledge of Torah, is united with it, and becomes elevated through it. The importance of *ameilus* is illustrated in the following anecdote, which was related to me by R' Sholom Schwadron, *shlita*, who heard it from R' Aharon Kotler, of blessed memory:

R' Meshulam Igra,[3] *rav* of the city of Tismenitz, Galicia, was a genius among Torah geniuses. The *Chasam Sofer* said of him that his two hands were like two Torah scrolls. Among his disciples were the illustrious authors of *Nesivos HaMishpat* and *Ketzos HaChoshen*. It happened once that two men who were visiting Tismenitz appeared before R' Meshulam to request that he decide their monetary dispute. The complexity of the case forced R' Meshulam to ask the litigants to return the next day when he would render his *p'sak* (ruling). However, the men were anxious to return home, so they left without receiving a *p'sak* and agreed between themselves to bring the case before the *rav* of their city.

---

3. 1749-1802. He wrote *Igra Ramah* and *Sh'eilos U'Teshuvos Rabbeinu Meshulam Igra* (both published posthumously).

Their *rav*, while a *talmid chacham*, in no way approached the stature of R' Meshulam Igra. Yet the *rav* seemed to have little trouble deciding the case. After hearing the presentation of both sides, the *rav* excused himself and left the room, only to return minutes later with a scholarly *p'sak* that satisfied both parties.

Some time later, the travels of these two men brought them back to Tismenitz. They felt it only proper to visit the *rav* and apologize for having left so abruptly without waiting to hear his decision. During their visit, the men asked if R' Meshulam would relate to them what indeed he had decided regarding their case. R' Meshulam stated his *p'sak* and the two men could not help but smile to one another. They explained that their own *rav*, a virtual unknown, had arrived at the identical decision in a matter of minutes!

Upon hearing this, R' Meshulam, who was as humble as he as wise, said, "Only someone of incredible genius could have rendered this decision so quickly. It is obvious that your *rav*, though he is unknown, is a scholar of towering stature. I must honor him with a visit!" R' Meshulam was soon on his way.

When the *rav* heard that the great R' Meshulam Igra had come to see him, he became filled with fear over what might have prompted the visit. When they were alone, R' Meshulam related the chain of events and expressed his awe and amazement that such a *p'sak* could have been rendered so quickly. The *rav* then explained:

"I will tell you the truth. The complexity of that case was beyond me; I was at a loss as to where to even begin. Realizing that I was not capable of deciding the matter, I became fearful that as a result, my reputation among the townspeople would be severely damaged. I therefore excused myself to the litigants and went off to another room to pray. Tearfully, I beseeched the *Ribono shel Olam* to somehow grant me the ability to decide the matter. No sooner had I offered my *tefillah* than I suddenly had an idea to open a certain *sefer*. I opened it and immediately came upon this exact case and the author's ruling. Hardly believing what had happened, I quickly returned to the litigants and informed them of 'my *p'sak*.' "

R' Meshulam was unimpressed. He said, "Crying? We can also cry. The proper way, however, is through *ameilus ba'Torah*."

The point of the above anecdote is to underscore the role of *ameilus*; it is not, however, to negate the role of *tefillah* in successful Torah study. *Tefillah* must *complement* one's toil in study, rather than be used as a substitute, as was the case in the story above.[4]

₪§ Torah and Tefillah

The following incident illustrates the relationship between Torah and *tefillah* and also depicts true *cheishek*, yearning, to succeed in Torah study. R' Shimon Shkop, the famed Grodno *Rosh Yeshivah*, related that during his days as a student in the Volozhiner Yeshivah, he once found himself straining and struggling to plumb the depths of a comment of *Rashbam* in *Masechta Bava Basra*. It was late at night when he finally approached his *rebbi*, the *Netziv*,[5] for help. The *Netziv* told him:

"My son, many times have I visited the grave of R' Chaim Volozhiner to tearfully pray that the meaning of these words of *Rashbam* become revealed to me."

It is common for people to pray at the graves of *tzaddikim* when a dear one is seriously ill, ל״ר, or because of some other dire circumstance. However, we are not accustomed to hearing of people praying at the graves of *tzaddkim* that a Talmudic comment of a *Rishon* become clear to them. And who in fact offered such prayers? The *Netziv*, whose incredible breadth and depth of knowledge is plainly revealed in his many *sefarim*! The *Netziv*'s thirst for Torah was so intense that his being unable to fully comprehend a single comment of *Rashbam* was to him a calamity. Therefore he wept and prayed at R' Chaim Volozhiner's grave.

The *Netziv*'s prayers were undoubtedly preceded by diligent, intense study to understand *Rashbam*'s words. In fact, the *Netziv*'s diligence was legendary. It is told that every year on *Motza'ei Yom Kippur*, the *Netziv* was the first to be learning in the *beis midrash* after having broken his fast. One year, someone else decided that *he* was going to earn this distinction. As soon as the fast had ended, the

---

4. The Chazon Ish wrote: "Torah study and *tefillah* are bound to one another. Toil in study brings to illuminating *tefillah*, while *tefillah* aids one in his learning. *Tefillah* without feeling distances one from true study, while indolent study impedes one's *tefillah*" (*Kovetz Igros* §2).

5. R' Naftali Zvi Yehudah Berlin. He headed the Volozhiner Yeshivah for some forty years until its closing in 1892.

man rushed home, recited *havdalah* and grabbed a bite, then dashed back to the *beis midrash* — only to find the *Netziv* already there! The man later learned that the *Netziv* always stored some food in the *beis midrash* building on *Erev Yom Kippur* so that he would lose as little time as possible after the fast. Such was the *Netziv's* desire to learn.

Rabbeinu Yonah writes in *Sha'arei Teshuvah* (II:9):

> ... It is written, *"A righteous man will flourish like a date palm, like a cedar in Lebanon he will grow tall. Planted in the house of Hashem, in the courtyards of our God they will flourish"* (Tehillim 92:13-14). For the *tzaddikim* are 'planted' in the house of Hashem from their youth and mature in the houses of study from their young manhood, much like a flourishing date palm and a cedar that grows tall in Lebanon. Similarly did our Sages say (Midrash, Tehillim 92:14): " 'Planted in the house of Hashem' — these are the young children," in accordance with the verse, *"For our sons are like saplings, nurtured from their youth"* (Tehillim 144:12).

From their early youth, our children must be imbued with a true love for Torah and *mitzvos* and a yearning to grow great in Torah knowledge and fear of Hashem. It is for us to implant within our young saplings a desire to become the Torah leaders of tomorrow.

May all those who share in the support of our *yeshivos* be repaid in kind with children and grandchildren who are great in Torah and *yiras shamayim*. And may we soon merit the coming of *Mashiach*, speedily and in our days.